THE FIRST
THATCHER
GOVERNMENT
1979 - 1983

THE FIRST THATCHER GOVERNMENT 1979-1983

Contemporary Conservatism and Economic Change

MARTIN HOLMES

Lecturer in Politics
Lady Margaret Hall, Oxford

Routledge
Taylor & Francis Group

LONDON AND NEW YORK

First published 1985 by Westview Press, Inc.

Published 2019 by Routledge
52 Vanderbilt Avenue, New York, NY 10017
2 Park Square, Milton Park, Abingdon, Oxon OX14 4RN

Routledge is an imprint of the Taylor & Francis Group, an informa business

LCN 85-50406

ISBN 13: 978-0-367-29216-4 (hbk)
ISBN 13: 978-0-367-30762-2 (pbk)

Contents

Acknowledgements

Many people have greatly assisted me in the writing of this book, not least the many Cabinet ministers, junior ministers, civil servants, CBI representatives, MPs and Conservative party officials who gave their time to be interviewed.

Three people however deserve a special mention. First, my thanks are due to Julie Luzny, my research assistant, whose help was invaluable in the early stages of research. Her good nature and sense of humour when faced with near impossible demands in limited time was invaluable. Second, I am much indebted to Gillian Peele who read the manuscript with care and made numerous helpful suggestions and recommendations. Third, much gratitude is due to Jackie Brentnall for her skilled typing and secretarial assistance.

I would also like to thank the Principal and Fellows of Lady Margaret Hall, Oxford for providing a College atmosphere conducive to scholarship and appreciative of research.

Needless to say, any errors in the following pages are my responsibility alone.

Martin Holmes
Lady Margaret Hall, Oxford
November 1984

Introduction

This book has two aims: first, to analyse the change in economic policy formation between 1979 and 1983 and the way in which policy sources were translated into reality, and second, to analyse how the first Thatcher government has changed the nature of contemporary Conservatism. These two themes overlap so consistently that they are dealt with simultaneously. Economic policy and political ideology have always been closely linked in modern British politics and the Thatcher government proved no exception. In the following chapters, therefore, the stress is laid on how Mrs Thatcher's political aspirations affected the economic policy machine and how, in turn, the effects of these policies affected the presentation of Conservatism both within the party itself and, ultimately, to the electorate.

Thus, Chapter 1 deals with the government's objectives and how they were affected by the economic legacy, both short and long term, as well as considering the herculean political task Mrs Thatcher undertook in radically altering the nature of postwar Conservative thinking. Chapter 2 examines the first six months of office and how the expectations of government were prepared. In Part II, Chapters 3 to 8 deal with the great issues as they were perceived by the government, analysing how effectively the government succeeded both in its own terms and in the wider context. Alternative remedies are suggested in the handling of unemployment policy, public spending cuts and industrial aid programmes in particular. Although dealing as it does with controversial political topics, this account has not shirked from either suggesting improvements as alternatives where government policy did not succeed or from validating those policies which succeeded, in some cases beyond the expectations of the government. The political scientist should treat evidence with great respect and does a disservice by dodging the controversies of politics for the sake of a quiet life. Political scientists cannot condemn politicians for evading difficult decisions if the political scientists themselves shirk from conclusions soundly based on original research. This study does not claim that there are no lessons to be learned from the evidence of policy priorities between 1979 and 1983. Those who believe that scholarship should be little more than a recording of facts will be disappointed by this account. But those who believe that objectivity and neutrality are not synonymous and who value controversy and debate, should at least find food for thought in the following pages. Arguably, objective evidence and conclusions make for better scholarship| and public debate than any contrived neutralism or policy ambivalence.

One feature of this account is that although the problems the government faced were familiar—inflation, unemployment, trade union law, and so on—the policies adopted to remedy them were unconventional and, in some cases, untried. Policy experimentation in turn led to the Conservative party experimenting with ideas and images it had previously discarded as 'politically impossible'. The economic policies of R.A. Butler and Reggie Maudling were transformed into the policy prescriptions of Sir Geoffrey Howe and Norman Tebbit. No such fundamental change could leave the Conservative party unscathed. Indeed, the change in policy reinforced, and was consequently reinforced by, a new generation of Conservatives. At the apex of this process is Margaret Thatcher. Her style of Conservatism, as much as her style of premiership, is central to the account and analysis that follow. In Part III the concluding thoughts on this process are drawn together.

Readers familiar with my previous works, *Political Pressure and Economic Policy: British Government 1970–74*, and *The| Labour Government 1974–79: Political Aims and Economic Reality* will recognise the recurrent themes of trade union power, the role of the Treasury, the lobbying of the CBI, the extent of prime ministerial, as opposed to Cabinet, government, and the gap between economic policy intentions and actual performance. But this book also intends to go deeper—and is, indeed, forced to go deeper—into the ideological recesses of the party in power. The Heath government and the Wilson/Callaghan government were in many ways typical of their era; the Thatcher government in attempting to change so much was not. The great revolution in post-war British political life in the end has not come from the left. The Bennite solutions are still light-years away from the mainstream of British policy formation. It is from the right, Mrs Thatcher's radical right, that the revolution in thinking has come. This revolution has affected two areas of national life in particular: the Conservative party and the economic policy machine. The origin and development of this revolution, and its consequent effects within these two areas, are the subject of this work.

PART I

The Thatcher Government and the Conservative Context

1 The Government's Objectives

In one material respect the contrast between now and the pre-war years is markedly unfavourable. The last budgets which showed no inflationary trend were those of the late 50s, when Mr Selwyn Lloyd and Mr Heathcoat-Amory were Chancellors of the Exchequer. Ever since then, although some years have been better than others, we have signally failed to stabilize the value of money. The result has been that it has become more and more difficult for the individual or for a business to plan ahead with any confidence and the national purpose and performance has faltered.

Lord Home of the Hersel 1978

LEGACY OF POST-WAR CONSERVATISM

Few governments that come to power espousing radical political change find they are able to cast off entirely their past policies and image. The Conservative government that began its term on 4 May 1979 was no exception. However, led by Margaret Thatcher, it was determined not to repeat the mistakes of previous Conservative governments—notably those of the 1970–74 Heath government—and was equally resolute in the presentation of its Conservatism as a radical departure from the pre-Thatcher age. The 5.2 per cent national swing which projected Mrs Thatcher into Downing Street with an overall parliamentary majority of forty-three heralded large changes in policy direction, not only away from the outgoing Callaghan administration but also from the post-war consensus—the Butskellite, Conservative middle way so favoured by Mrs Thatcher's immediate party leader predecessors.

Of all the major policy changes of the first Thatcher administration, which this book analyses, the change in the nature of the Conservative party itself is one of the most

7

striking. Such a judgement is made with hindsight to be sure. Indeed, from the standpoint of May 1979 there were many in the Conservative party—and elsewhere in British politics—who expected that Mrs Thatcher's administration would be sidetracked into pragmatic U-turns as soon as the realities of government made themselves apparent. It is arguable that, despite well-publicised policy changes between February 1975, when Mrs Thatcher became leader, and May 1979 the new Prime Minister still presided over a government made up of stalwarts of the former Heath leadership. Moreover, the pace of change between 1975 and 1979 on specific policy commitments belied the initial difficulty the Thatcher leadership faced in maintaining party unity as well as in overhauling policy stances, some of which (e.g. incomes policy) stretched back to the late 1950s. As Lord Thorneycroft later recalled:[2]

During the 1975–79 period Mrs Thatcher sought to form the outlines of policy and the key changes were to get a grip of the finances, a return to free collective bargaining but only with tough union legislation after the abuses of the last 10 years. She didn't make any sensational changes in the Shadow Cabinet and she had to hold the party together in a period when she couldn't have any power to do anything anyway.

What was clear in May 1979 was not the inviolate strength of the Thatcher leadership, nor its ability to resist U-turns, but its intentions to redefine in government much that the Conservative party should be seeking to achieve. Essentially, the approach to office—declared in the 1977 policy document *The Right Approach* and the 1979 General Election campaign—was based on the critique of post-war Conservatism advanced by Sir Keith Joseph in the 1974–75 period when the Heath leadership was under challenge from the right. Joseph, Thatcher, John Biffen, John Nott and others on the economic right of the party had argued that the Conservative party had not reversed the advance of socialism but had merely halted it temporarily whilst in office. The 'socialist ratchet' critique saw middle-way Butskellite Conservatism as participating in a process in which Britain at successive stages descended into an East-European-style economy and society, where political freedom along with economic free enterprise would ultimately fall into dissolution.

Nor were previous Conservative governments viewed as entirely passive in this process. The pursuit of Keynesian economics, vainly aiming for full employment, was identified with the Heath government's massive increase in state spending, strict controls on prices, dividends, rents, profits and incomes and increasing government interference in industry. According to the Thatcher leadership, a return to free enterprise, sound money and the rolling back of the state was required. Fitting into the critique was the then new doctrine of monetarism advocated by Professors Hayek and Friedman, a doctrine which was naturally attractive to those disillusioned with the economic failures—and, for the Conservatives, electoral failures—of Keynesian political economy. To the Thatcher leadership the economic changes envisaged in Conservative policy were similarly matched by political changes to reverse the trend of the 1960s and the Heath leadership whereby between 1964 and 1974 Labour had won four out of five general elections. Thus, to restore the Conservatives' role, as they saw it, as the natural party of government was part of Heath's legacy to Thatcher.[3] The election result on 4 May 1979 meant that this task, at least, was well under way.[4]

In short, attention was focused on the new Thatcher government both in terms of its actual performance in trying to halt Britain's economic decline and in terms of the attempt to radically change the nature of Conservatism, not only for Conservatives themselves but also for the mass of essentially apolitical electors who would have to endorse Thatcher's performance at the polls. Arguably, the task of overturning Conservative post-war Keynesian middle-way orthodoxy was a long-term one. As the new party leader in 1975, Mrs Thatcher lacked the authority for an instant purge of the Heath supporters whom she wished to carry with her rather than alienate. Nevertheless, the ideological ferment of the 1975–79 period polarised opinion in Parliament and the party leadership in an inescapable way. Many on the left of the party openly repudiated 'monetarism' and re-affirmed their support for Heath-style policies. Mr Heath's extremely frosty personal relations with the new leader—constantly highlighted by the Press—added to the ideological conflict.[5] Discussions about the nature of 'true' Conservatism were never in short supply. As one Cabinet minister recalled, 'an enormous amount of rethinking of ideas—and restating of old truths—occurred in opposition. It was surprising how many academics in 1979 came out in support of the Conservatives. Mrs Thatcher liked the intellectual discussion—ideas are what interest her—that was developing from opposition to office'.[6]

Mrs Thatcher's attack on the Heath legacy, and the overall post-war leadership, even though moving by stealth before May 1979, represented another stage in the evolution of the Conservative party.[7] The Thatcher revolution within the party was not the first. The party of the 'squirearchy', the gentry, the Church of England, the industrial interest, the Empire, appeasement, Churchillian defiance, had become after 1945 the party of Keynesian consensus in order to suit a modern mass democracy unwilling to tolerate unemployment and social deprivation. At first in the 1950s the middle-way approach seemed to work. Labour was in disarray, and with public spending largely under control, the excesses of Keynesian demand management were avoided. Everyone seemed capable of living with 'creeping' inflation. The Joseph-Thatcher critique, while less convincing on the subject of an East-European-style socialist ratchet, was accurate in pinpointing Keynesian economics as a long-term source of Conservative decline. The Conservatives were suffering more from the Keynesian ratchet than the socialist ratchet. Evidence from the post-war period as a whole shows that at each notch of the Keynesian ratchet Labour, not the Conservatives, benefited in electoral terms and that traditional Conservative voters found themselves disillusioned with a Conservative approach to inflation, taxation and public expenditure which was scarcely different from that of the (ruling) Labour party. Ironically, and significantly, the Conservatives' only electoral success in the Wilson era came in 1970 when they offered a distinctly right-wing approach. Ian Gilmour is justified in arguing that there was not a sharp move to the left between 1951 and 1974, but he is less convincing in his denial that Conservative governments themselves moved steadily left. The leftward movement of the Heath government in its last two years of office was a culmination of the leftward-leaning 'hybrid Keynesianism', as

Gilmour describes it, not an exemplification of the middle way.[8]

Central to Thatcher's attack on the post-war Conservative legacy was the issue of inflation. Mrs Thatcher was mindful that it was the Heath government that had lost control of inflation and that middle-class voters with savings were more likely to prefer a sound money policy than an expansionary 'reflationary' one. Inflation control was a major tenet in the Thatcher reform of economic policy, and the failed and discredited statutory incomes policy of the Heath period was jettisoned. Monetary controls and public spending discipline were regarded as prerequisites for the control of inflation rather than artificial, bureaucratic restraints such as pay norms, targets and relativities commissions.[9] Relations with the unions were another legacy specifically from the Heath period, with its bitter memories of two defeats at the hands of the miners, the second of which led to the ill-fated February 1974 election debacle. Here the Thatcher approach showed all the signs of pragmatism, which according to the Conservative left was absent from the monetarist right-wing approach. A Heath-style comprehensive Industrial Relations Act was ruled out. Free collective bargaining—denied to the unions under the four stages of compulsory incomes policy under the Wilson/Callaghan government—was not regarded as economically damaging. Moreover, Shadow Employment Secretary Jim Prior was known to favour a softly, softly line over legislation to reform abuses in trade union law; Mrs Thatcher made no effort to remove him from such a crucial portfolio until 1981, two years after the election of her government. In the end it was the unions themselves who came to the Conservatives' aid by their highly unpopular industrial action of the 1978–79 Winter of Discontent, which helped to electorally undermine the Callaghan government and to validate Conservative arguments about specific reform of trade union law.[10] Nevertheless, in May 1979 the key question for many Conservatives was whether the new Thatcher government could escape from the legacy of confrontation inherited from the Heath period. Indeed, one of the most common misunderstandings of the Thatcher policy changes were that because they were 'right wing' or 'monetarist' they would inevitably lead to industrial conflict with Britain's allegedly all-powerful trade union movement.

Much of Thatcher's legacy from previous leaderships was philosophical in terms of the social obligations of Conservative governments. Consequently, the ideological polarisation that occurred between 1975 and 1979 took the form of restating the *objectives* of Conservatism as much as the policy means to carry them out. One former Conservative minister recalled that 'the policies evolving inside the party since 1964 were widely believed to have been adopted by Heath in the late 1960s. But Heath's lurch into statutory incomes policy reversed assumptions. Mrs Thatcher personally was on the side of what Heath didn't do and when she became leader in 1975 it was as the antithesis to Heath'.[11] When Mrs Thatcher came to office in 1979 the emphasis had switched away from accepting welfarism as a policy objective and towards individual self-reliance and thrift. The private sector was stressed as beneficial and the public sector subject to scrutiny as to the desirability of its component parts. The notion that the size of the public sector depended not on political decisions to expand it but on the private sector's ability to sustain it,[12] had gained ground in the late 1970s and the Thatcher leadership was attracted to such an analysis. Similarly, although the Thatcher approach to the Health Service and the social welfare system was to maintain state provision, this was—in theory at least—regarded as less significant than before as a hallmark of Conservative rule. It was only later on in 1982 that the problem with 'demand led' welfare spending occasioned an actual policy reappraisal of the state's detailed financial commitments.

As with the thinking about the social services, Opposition deliberations before 1979 on public spending and taxation also usually related to a broader philosophical approach as to what Conservative governments should try to do rather than to policy panaceas. (It can be argued that this is a sensible way to conduct policy reappraisals in Opposition.) Again, the legacy of high public spending under Heath was central to the Thatcher critique and emphasis was placed on the reduction of public spending both as an aim in itself and also to facilitate the tax cuts which had strongly featured in the Conservatives' 1979 election campaigning.

In summary, Mrs Thatcher, on entering Downing Street on 4

May 1979, did have a radical approach to economic policy compared to that of post-war Conservatism; she was determined not to be caught out by U-turns and she was prepared to shift contemporary Conservatism away from Keynesian Butskellism, as much as the 1950s One Nation Group had been determined to shift Conservatism away from its 1930s connotations. However, her position to achieve such changes was not initially impregnable. The senior personnel of the Heath leadership had essentially survived intact. The Conservative left wing was predicting, and hoping for, a more pragmatic policy to emerge. The general expectations that her government, unlike most post-war governments, would stick to its economic policy guns were low.

LEGACY OF THE POST-WAR ECONOMY

Like all governments in recent British politics, the Thatcher government inherited many problems from the previous administration. In Conservative election propaganda, the 1974–79 Labour government had bequeathed an appalling economic situation; the truth was that the Wilson/Callaghan government's record was a mixed one[13] and that many of the problems passed down to Mrs Thatcher stretched back over several governments. Arguably, the whole legacy of Keynesian post-war political economy was an underlying cause of many of the immediate economic and industrial difficulties which were obvious in May 1979. As Sir Walter Salomon has put it, with his own historical perspective:

My own experience in pre-war Germany enabled me in later years to see clearly the fallacies of post-war Keynesian policy which pretended to cure the unemployment resulting from inefficient production by 'creating' money through budget deficits (so-called 'borrowing requirements') that were all the more dangerous for giving a temporary illusion of prosperity. The fatal appeal of Keynes' theory was that it presented politicians with a respectable excuse for their natural tendency to overspend. Budget deficits seemed to offer a way of obtaining something for nothing so that the electorate could be offered more 'free' services than they were required to pay for in taxes.[14]

The long-term problems to confront Mrs Thatcher were more severe than the short-term legacy from the Callaghan years. The Thatcher critique had aimed to identify and then rectify the poor economic and industrial performance of the British post-war experience, and central to the analysis were a number of seemingly perpetual and intractable problems. Industrial relations and strikes was one; the strike record of British industry, while not at the top of the international league table, was lamentable. Too often trade unions had struck first rather than as a last resort and had regarded strikes as a legitimate weapon not only to pressure individual employers but also to intimidate governments and the general public. The 1978–79 Winter of Discontent had graphically illustrated the strike problem only months before Mrs Thatcher took power. The 'Who governs Britain?' question of the February 1974 election was to many—not only on the right of British politics—central to the inability of government to control Britain's economic destiny. Not surprisingly, the fact that the biggest display of trade union powers and disruption since the 1926 general strike had helped to destroy a Labour government, concentrated the minds of incoming Conservative ministers. The question (usually posed in the language of corporatist incomes policy) of whether or not the Thatcher government could 'work with' the unions was repeatedly asked as the new government took up the reins of office.

A second long-term economic legacy, also with a specific legacy from the 1974–79 Labour government, was the problem of inflation. One Cabinet minister recalled that 'I believed low inflation was possible. In Opposition we knew about Hayek and Friedman and how excessive government spending caused excessive government borrowing causing high interest rates. But I was confident that if we kept to the course we could succeed'.[15] The 'creeping' inflation of the 1950s had long since developed an acceleration of its own with successive reflationary bouts of public spending aimed at reducing unemployment. Savings were destroyed scarcely before they had begun to grow. Inflation had touched 30 per cent in 1975, eroding international competitiveness, creating long-term instability, obliterating profits, engendering uncertainty for investment and ultimately jeopardising jobs. However, while the Callaghan government, embracing a monetarist approach at the IMF's behest in 1976, had reduced the rate of inflation to 8 per cent by 1978, the actual rate the Conservatives inherited was rising rapidly.[16] Denis Healey's ill-judged 1978 expansionary budget had refuelled the economy's inflationary impetus; in addition, the wage surge during the Winter of Discontent had rekindled inflationary expectations. Even more damaging for the new government was the existence of the Clegg public sector comparability study set up by Callaghan to extricate his government from the strike wave which had engulfed him.[17] Having committed itself to respecting the Clegg awards during the 1979 election campaign, the Thatcher government faced an immediate dilemma of breaking a political pledge—for perfectly sound economic reasons—and so bringing upon itself the consequent political condemnation. But perhaps the most depressing inheritance was that of the incomes policy mentality to the curbing of inflation. For the whole of the period of Keynesian post-war orthodoxy, incomes policy was regarded, contrary to any evidence, as essential to restricting the inflationary 'spiral'. Norms, targets, pay pauses, relativities commissions, special cases, sanctions against employers, flat rates, percentage rates, freezes, secret agreements at Downing Street, beer and sandwiches, NEDC negotiations—all had been tried with lamentable results. Even though Mrs Thatcher had, in Opposition, ruled out the incomes policy route, there were many who thought in May 1979 that it would only be a matter of time before the corporatist language of incomes policy would be back. To eschew it would require a revolution in attitudes, one many regarded as long overdue.

As well as strikes and inflation, taxation was another legacy with both a short-term and long-term perspective. In the short term the unpopularity of the Labour government's tax increases between 1974 and 1979 had contributed not insignificantly to the Conservatives' election victory. The prospect of lower taxation had appealed to workers who only a Labour government had brought into the tax net and who felt, for the first time, overtaxed on average or below-average wages. The Conservatives' particular success among the affluent worker social group in 1979 has often been cited, rightly, as evidence for the electoral preference for lower taxation rather than higher public spending. In the long term Thatcher's inheritance was one of an increase in tax and social security contributions from 5 per cent of income in the 1950s to between 25 and 30 per cent in the late 1970s. Moreover, ideologically inspired rates of taxation on high earners were regarded as eroding incentives and preventing a spirit of entrepreneurship, which was regarded as essential to any serious economic recovery.

Allied to the taxation position was the legacy of public expenditure. Whilst it was true that it was the Heath government that had lost control of public spending and that the Callaghan government had imposed—for a Labour government especially—severe spending cuts and a 'cash limits' regime,ᵥ the Thatcher government inherited rising public spending and over-optimistic growth assumptions. Irrespective of much seemingly entrenched waste in public spending generally, the legacy passed down from Labour was further exacerbated by larger than expected state industry deficits and by the public sector pay bill, vastly augmented if the Clegg Commission was not to be repudiated. Suspicions during the election campaign that Labour's public expenditure arithmetic did not add up were confirmed, and with the financial year only two months old a fresh budget and spending priorities had to be drawn up with considerable haste.

One aspect of the public spending jungle that caused particular concern was the performance of the nationalised industries and other state-subsidised industrial concerns. The familiar pattern was again present: long-term fossilisation and inefficiency. The toleration by successive governments of poor management and industrial relations malpractices were compounded by the short-term policies of Labour from 1974 to 1979. The established nationalised industries were often incompetently run, providing an unsatisfactory service to the customer and existing on government grants and the so-called 'writing off' of debts. Profitability, always a difficult objective, had been made more unlikely by the Heath government's abandonment of financial targets and subsequent imposition of price restraint at the cost of massive increased subsidisation. In such circumstances it could be reasonably anticipated that morale in the nationalised sector would be low. The problems of the short-term inheritance of the Thatcher government were made more acute by the Callaghan government's jobs subsidy schemes and industrial strategy of 'saving' jobs irrespective of cost.[18] Similarly, a colossal grey area of industrial subsidisation in private industry had started to produce the same sort of dependence by the recipients as had occurred in the formally nationalised sector. In short, by the time Mrs Thatcher came to power the state industrial sector was in a chronic economic situation.

Unemployment, too, was regarded as a problem area of inheritance. Like all Oppositions the Conservatives had not resisted the temptation to attack the Labour government as unemployment rose between 1974 and 1979. During the 1979 election campaign the Conservatives repeatedly stressed Labour's failure to prevent unemployment rising. One Saatchi and Saatchi poster depicting a dole queue with the slogan 'Labour isn't working' exemplified the Conservatives' treatment of the issue. Yet the actual percentage rate was only 6 per cent on taking office, so the Thatcher government did not inherit a disastrous situation according to the statistics. However, the short-term figure was deceptive, for not only was a new oil shock about to hit the Western world following the Khomeini revolution's triumph in Iran but also the long-term trend was upwards, as it had been since the late 1950s. Customers, profitability and real growth create jobs not government induced reflations, and in the longer term international competitiveness was weak, profitability squeezed and growth negligible. Moreover, as Professor Minford has argued, the power of trade unions to price workers out of jobs had grown dramatically since the mid-1960s and was to manifest itself in particular in the late 1970s and early '80s.[19] In short, the Thatcher government inherited a long-term increase in unemployment based essentially on the many different areas of economic failure.

Given both the legacy of post-war Conservatism and the legacy of the post-war economy, the Thatcher government took office with a realistic appraisal of what needed to be done in the way of profound policy changes and, with hindsight, a will to stick with policies previously regarded as politically unacceptable. The objectives of government policy were to reduce inflation by setting targets for stable but declining monetary growth, cutting public expenditure with the intention of cutting taxation, reducing specific legal immunities which facilitated trade union abuses of power and reinvigorating the private, wealth-creating sector of the economy. Denationalisation rather than merely holding the tide of state control was central to dislocating the socialist ratchet effect, and similarly to be jettisoned were the incomes policy corporatism so essential to trade union power in policy decision-making and reflationary Keynesian policies aimed at reducing unemployment. The government thus came into power with its priorities laid out. One economic advisor recalled that 'policy was there by 1979. It almost didn't need to be made; at the very highest level there wasn't the need for more policy.'[20]

Not surprisingly, the government's approach became known simply as a 'monetarist' one. If by 'monetarism' one also means the whole package of encouraging the private sector, then the term is appropriate, though a better one would be 'political monetarism', to distinguish the government's broader approach from that of the 'technical' monetarist, whose policy approach is essentially only economic. The Thatcher government—and certainly not Mrs Thatcher herself—did not possess a single, simple monetarist shibboleth, as has wrongly been alleged; rather, the objective was to reduce inflation, encourage the private sector, reduce trade union power and abuses and ultimately to lower taxation.

THE FIRST BUDGET

Mrs Thatcher's Cabinet, formed largely though not exclusively from the Shadow Cabinet, strongly reflected the divisions over economic and industrial policy in the Conservative party as a whole. There was no attempt to exclude left-wingers or to suppress those who had expressed scepticism in opposition about the changes in policy direction. As *The Observer* rightly put it, Mrs Thatcher 'set a moderate seal on her government by appointing a balanced Cabinet'.[21] Indeed, it can be argued that Mrs Thatcher was generous to her potential critics by refusing to promote outspoken right-wing supporters to her Cabinet and in recalling Peter Walker, purged in Opposition, as Agriculture

Minister.

The new Chancellor, Sir Geoffrey Howe, and the Treasury Chief Secretary, the talented John Biffen, along with Industry Secretary Sir Keith Joseph, were the Prime Minister's natural allies on economic philosophy. Similarly, John Nott, the Trade Secretary, who had a deserved reputation for intellectual sharpness, gained from a long experience of economic and financial portfolios, was regarded as a Thatcherite along with the Energy Secretary, David Howell. However, at the outset the right-wingers were not regarded as the most politically heavy-weight members of the Cabinet. Nott, Howell and Biffen were sitting in the Cabinet for the first time and Joseph's Industry brief, while suitable to his interests and talents, was not as central to overall policy formation as it may at first have appeared. Howe, while a staunch supporter of Mrs Thatcher, had had a less than flattering reputation as the Shadow Chancellor since 1975. Less than a year before entering No. 11, rumours in the Conservative party had suggested he should have been moved sideways because of his unconvincing performance, and he never seemed to recover from Denis Healey's cruel jibe that an attack from Howe was like being savaged by a dead sheep. Howe's reputation, in short, was still to be built when he took office as Chancellor.

In contrast, the Cabinet left-wingers—or 'wets' as they were soon to be known—had greater Cabinet experience and between them important portfolios. Jim Prior, who was known not to favour a tough line with the trade unions, was Employment Secretary, Willie Whitelaw was Home Secretary, Lord Carrington was Foreign Secretary, Francis Pym was Defence Secretary, and the Tory left wing's most eloquent protagonist, Ian Gilmour, was Lord Privy Seal. Along with Peter Walker at Agriculture and Norman St John Stevas as Chancellor of the Duchy of Lancaster, the left wing was, in fact, in a majority in the first Thatcher Cabinet. Moreover, other members of the Cabinet, although not as explicitly associated with the Conservative left wing, could not be counted as 'monetarists'; for example, Michael Heseltine at Environment, Mark Carlisle at Education and Lord Hailsham, the Lord Chancellor. According to one former minister, 'she was very conscious of being a minister under Heath and came in with her

Heath past upon her being much more afraid than you think of ministers who disagree with her. It's one thing to sack ministers, it's another to prove them wrong'.[22] Lord Thorneycroft recalled that 'her first appointment was Lord Carrington from the aristocratic liberal wing of the party; Ian Gilmour was in the Cabinet and would talk round every lighted candle. She found herself with those who didn't fully sympathise with her with big departments behind them. Geoffrey Howe was fully behind her and was a suitable choice. He's an unemotional man who gets on with it when the battles are raging all around'.[23] A junior minister thought that 'the first two years were unhappy and uncomfortable in Cabinet. She was unwise not to have achieved a more cohesive Cabinet earlier'.[24]

At the junior ministerial level the Thatcherites were much better represented. Tom King, Nicholas Ridley, Leon Brittan, Norman Tebbit, Norman Fowler, Nigel Lawson, Peter Rees and Cecil Parkinson could all have considered themselves, without a lack of modesty, to be potential Cabinet material. But in May 1979 such allies of the Prime Minister's strategy were outside the Cabinet and many of those inside were, to put it mildly, apprehensive about the right wing, or political-monetarist approach. In an age of prime ministerial government, the initial Thatcher Cabinet deserves further comment. Unlike Edward Heath, who refused to promote to the Cabinet those who may have held strongly differing beliefs to his own,[25] Mrs Thatcher was fair to the point of generous to her potential opponents. It has been argued, usually by her political opponents, that later in her premiership she displayed the familiar characteristics of prime ministerial power in downgrading the importance of Cabinet; but it will not do to argue this in relation to her first Cabinet composition. This is not to argue that the wets were able to veto monetarist policy formation. Thatcher's biographers rightly noted that:

From the beginning, the Cabinet was divided. Although at first the divisions were concealed, it was clear to the interventionists that they were being excluded from formulating economic policy. They hoped that the force of circumstances would argue their case for them. Not only would the policy be seen not to work—it was based, they argued, on a fallacious cure-all theory which made no sense—but the political consequences of the misery that would be caused would force the Prime Minister to return to conventional methods. Thatcher was open about her hostility to her internal opponents. Borrowing public school slang, 'wets', she sharply divided in her mind those of her colleagues who were 'on my side' and those who were 'unreliable'. Her Parliamentary Private Secretary, Ian Gow, divided the Cabinet, and then the Party, between 'heroes' and 'reptiles'—a nomenclature snapped up by Denis Thatcher.[26]

The fact remains however that it was Mrs Thatcher herself who put the wets in the Cabinet. If purges of dissident ministers were to come later, it reflected as much prime ministerial initial generosity as the need to be a 'good butcher'.

The first major task of the new Cabinet on the economic policy side was to approve the Chancellor's swiftly prepared budget. The necessity for budgetary correction had been evident during the election campaign, and it was no surprise that a new administration, particularly a self-proclaimed reformist radical one, should have indicated its priorities early in its life. However, the run-up to the mid-June 1979 budget was made more difficult for the policy-makers by gloomy economic predictions and the difficult initial inheritance.

Mrs Thatcher cautiously ventured that measures to reduce inflation would take a considerable time. She told Scottish conservatives less than two weeks after taking office that 'we must approach our problems with realism and common sense. We face a great and continuing threat of inflation. The evil of inflation is still with us and we are a long way from restoring honest money. *The Treasury forecast when we took over was that inflation was on an upward trend*' (my emphasis).[27] The Queen's Speech also reflected anxieties and restated the 'priorities in economic policy to controlling inflation through the pursuit of firm monetary and fiscal policies'. It also went on to add that legislation would be introduced 'to amend the law on picketing and the closed shop and to provide for financial and for postal ballots'.

The priority in curbing inflation was accompanied by depressing figures. May's money-supply figures showed a 1.5 per cent jump during April with an annualised rate running well above the 8 to 12 per cent range set by Denis Healey in October

1978. May's inflation rate showed a rise to double-digit levels for the first time since December 1977, with the trend still upward. Gordon Richardson, the Governor of the Bank of England warned that the world economic environment could produce another recession, thus restricting the effectiveness of government policy initiatives. In a similarly pessimistic tone in the run-up to the June budget, the CBI envisaged a pay freeze, bankruptcies and a winter of confrontation over wages.[28] The trade unions, expectedly, warned the government. Len Murray talked of a controlled campaign of opposition with the possibility of industrial action to defend jobs and living standards. Moreover, a secret Treasury report, leaked to *The Observer*, predicted 20 per cent inflation in 1980 and two million unemployed.[29] The Cabinet, too, expressed reservations about public spending cuts in the run-up to the budget. As Wapshott and Brock have claimed:

At the meeting which informed the Cabinet of what was in store there were a number of groans. Although Cabinets do not always discuss the general direction of economic policy, this time the omission was more serious, because the policy to be followed was so radical and contentious. What is more, the Prime Minister knew how much hostility there was to it. The Cabinet opponents expressed their displeasure, but there was nothing to be done, except coded speeches, Cabinet leaks and as much delay as ministerial authority allowed them. The convention of Cabinet collective responsibility meant that they could not express that displeasure publicly.[30]

To such a pessimistic and gloomy background Sir Geoffrey Howe presented his first budget on 12 June 1979, representing the first major indication of the government's resolve in tackling both immediate and long-term economic and industrial problems.

The budget was a tough one, reflecting the semi-crisis build-up of the previous weeks. Income tax was cut from 33 to 30 per cent on the standard rate, with the top rate on earned income down from 83 to 60 per cent. A total of 1.3 million people were taken out of the tax net by the raising of tax thresholds, and pensions were increased to a cost of £2.7 billion in a full year. The tax cuts and pension increases were politically expedient and fulfilled promises made during the election campaign. High levels of personal taxation had become unpopular among virtually all socio-economic groups in the 1970s, destroying incentives and, arguably, fuelling the high wage claims which were seen as compensatory—a trade-off that had been recognised by Denis Healey.

As Sir Geoffrey put it in his budget speech:

Excessive rates of income tax bear a heavy responsibility for the lacklustre performance of the British economy. We need, therefore, to cut income tax at all levels. For the reasons I have already explained, I cannot do as much this year as I should have liked, and I cannot do as much as is needed. But although it is only a first instalment, there should be no doubt in anyone's mind that this Budget marks a turning point. It is universally recognised that the present top rate of 83 per cent on earned income is an absurdity. The rate of 98 per cent on investment income is even worse. Such rates bring in very little revenue.

... Everywhere one meets complaint and criticism that income tax erodes differentials, reduces the rewards of skilled workers and discourages effort, initiative and responsibility. This year I propose taking a first and significant step to deal with these complaints by reducing the rate from 33 per cent to 30 per cent. Our long-term aim should surely be to reduce the basic rate of income tax to no more than 25 per cent. Take-home pay will be substantially increased by these unprecedented cuts in income tax. This will more than make good the price effects of higher spending taxes. A further attempt to cover those price effects by higher pay-claims will be utterly self-defeating. The money will simply not be there to finance higher pay as well as lower income tax. Any attempt to have it both ways will simply end up by threatening jobs and putting firms out of business.[31]

However, the tax cuts totalling £4,540 million in a full year meant that other aspects of the budget brought harsher than expected medicine.

As a result VAT was increased from 8 to 15 per cent and petrol tax by 10p per gallon. The VAT increase was equivalent to a 3 per cent rise in the RPI, yielding £4,175 million in a full year. Prescription charges—as ever a politically emotive issue—were increased, dividend controls scrapped, the Rate Support Grant cut by £335 million, minimum lending rate increased from 2 to 14 per cent and exchange controls relaxed. In the key area of public expenditure, a total of £1,500 million was cut spread over a number of areas. Although this produced the greatest political outcry, the error, if anything, was on the generous side, given the imbalance in the public spending programme inherited from Labour. Moreover, the extent of the cuts had been deepened by Mrs Thatcher's insistance on making room for tax cuts. According to Wapshott and Brock, Mrs Thatcher rejected as insufficient Sir Geoffrey's initial spending cut of £500 million.[32] Nevertheless, the net effect was a welcome reduction in the PSBR from £9,250 million to £8,250 million and a reduced target range for M3 money supply from between 8 and 12 per cent to between 7 and 11 per cent, again correcting an unrealistic inheritance.

Few Chancellors in recent British politics receive praise for tough budgets at the time of their unveiling; usually any praise is with hindsight. Conversely, popular budgets are nearly always bad budgets, more often than not stoking inflation and postponing difficult choices. Sir Geoffrey Howe's June 1979 budget was no exception to this general rule. Even the successful reduction in income tax was immediately turned against him by the Opposition leader Jim Callaghan, who pushed back at him Sir Geoffrey's honest appraisal that 'every family in the land will have more money to pay their incoming bills'.[33] According to Mr Callaghan, the phrase would resound through the history books; with hindsight it resounds rather well, given the difficult circumstances of the time, particularly the need to control public spending and reduce an alarmingly high level of monetary growth. Thus, as Sir Geoffrey argued in his budget speech:

It is now clear that the public expenditure policies which we inherited would have made it quite impossible to meet his 8 to 12 per cent target without a further savage squeeze on the private sector, involving not just higher interest rates but a sharp increase in the total tax burden as well. Not for the first time, the levels of public spending and borrowing which he permitted were far too high to be compatible with his own monetary targets. The new target range to apply to the growth of sterling M3 in the 10 months to April 1980 will be an annual rate of 7 to 11 per cent. I will roll the target forward by six months in the autumn. I intend to improve the way in which the monetary target is achieved. We need to rely less on curbing the private sector, and put more emphasis on fiscal restraint and economy by the public sector.

That requires as a first step, a significant reduction in the public sector borrowing requirement from the figure of around £10 billions that it would otherwise have reached this year. The Bank of England will be rolling forward the supplementary special deposit scheme by three months on the existing basis. The Bank of England will increase its minimum lending rate by 2 per cent to 14 per cent. Changes in taxation and public expenditure which I am announcing today will be sufficient to reduce the PSBR to £8 billions in the current year, as compared with the out-turn of £9 billions for 1978–79. As a percentage of GDP that will represent a reduction from over 5 per cent last year to under 4 per cent in the current year. The public sector deficit will also fall from 4 to 3 per cent of GDP. I intend to continue along this path in the years ahead.[34]

As a statement on the changing nature of Conservative economic thinking, the budget was a primary example. It was also a realistic attempt to change and reverse the long-term pattern of Britain's economic decline—higher taxation, higher public spending, higher inflation and ultimately higher unemployment. It is difficult to agree with Denis Healey's assessment that Sir Geoffrey's first budget had thrown away five years painful work by the Labour government in bringing inflation down. Nearer the mark was John Biffen's comment that 'I do not deny for one moment that this is a severe package. The severity is made necessary by the situation we inherited'.[35] The Thatcher revolution in economic policy had cleared its first hurdle.

2 Policy Formation: The First Six Months

Tuesday, 17 March 1970

The first thing we had was a meeting of the PM's Housing MISC. This device of setting up hundreds of MISCS simply to deal with specific jobs, instead of sending awkward subjects to the standard Cabinet Committee, is one of the strange features of Harold's method of running things. I am not on many of these committees now because I am out of favour and too busy to be one of the Cabinet members who are put on them to add weight, but I do see how important they are for helping the Prime Minister to get his way. In the standing committees every important issue is appraised by a group of ministers who have been carefully balanced for the purpose and there is a rule that what is agreed there doesn't go to Cabinet, but now everything of real importance is pushed outside the normal channels and through special committees, specially packed, so the situation is very different and the Prime Minister can exert far more influence.

R.H.S. Crossman

THE KEY PERSONNEL

Prime ministerial control and dominance over economic policy formation and direction did not originate with Margaret Thatcher. In modern British politics since the mid 1960s all Prime Ministers have come to regard, with varying degrees of enthusiasm, economic aims as synonymous with political aims and, ultimately, with electoral strategy. Harold Wilson's handling of the 1967 devaluation, Edward Heath's U-turns, Jim Callaghan's acceptance of the IMF are all examples of prime ministerial power exercised at the expense of Cabinet government. The first Thatcher government was to continue this pattern, and indeed in many respects it was to surpass it. One official recalled that 'Mrs Thatcher is a terribly energetic and interfering person. By '79 her passionate interest was economics and she knew it would make or break her government. She put Geoffrey Howe under what to anyone else would have been strain'.[2]

The Prime Minister's essential difficulty was that, as already mentioned, she was in a minority in her own Cabinet on the vital economic strategy of political monetarism. As a result it soon became clear that the full Cabinet was not the forum for thrashing out economic policy differences, and in retaliation the Cabinet wets leaked to the press or made critical public speeches in coded language. As Hugo Young put it reviewing the government's first year in office:

At the centre of her strategy is an economic policy which she believes in passionately, but in which only a section of the Cabinet wholeheartedly concurs. Arguably, it is only the Treasury ministers, plus a few outsiders like Keith Joseph, John Nott and David Howell who even understand it in its theoretical perfection. The rest, of course, have no coherent alternative to it and this brings upon them the grim contempt of economic ministers who regard all sceptics as backsliders. It does not, however, prevent them from backsliding, at least by default. They feel in their bones that monetarism will not work. They are in a majority, which means that, under the surface, this Cabinet is more deeply and curiously split than any in recent times.[3]

As a result of this situation Mrs Thatcher came to rely on the Cabinet's economic committee—the E committee—in order to bypass the full Cabinet. Richard Crossman, that shrewdest observer of prime ministerial government, would not have been surprised by this procedure. The E committee would meet each Tuesday and contained only one wet, Jim Prior, thus building up resentment from those excluded from policy deliberations. Prior, unlike many other wets, was to survive in the Cabinet into the second Thatcher administration. One sympathetic portrait of him describes his position as follows:

In a Cabinet which is locked in to a monetarist hard line, impatient alike of trade union stubbornness and town hall obduracy, Jim Prior stands out like an antediluvian Tory: old-fashioned in his virtues and failings, and most unfashionably aware that it takes all sorts to make a nation.

Prior's manner and slightly indiscreet conversation suggests at best a lukewarm solidarity with the new Tory impatience with the innate conservatism of British society, the eagerness to rush it, streamlined and financially overhauled, into the Eighties. In the watchful and suspicious eyes of the Tory Right, he embodies the national caution towards change, a little too nostalgic for the corporatism of the post-war decade, too timid of trade union power, a potential exponent of U-turn politics.[4]

Prior, though a survivor, was definitely not one of the key personnel.

At least on the E committee, and as a spending minister, Prior's voice was heard by the monetarists. Moreover, only spending ministers were able to raise objections to expenditure cuts at full Cabinet meetings, thus effectively silencing such articulate wets as Sir Ian Gilmour and Norman St John Stevas who possessed no significant departmental budget fiefdoms. Institutional restraints on the wets, which previous Prime Ministers had developed over a number of years, were therefore considerable. Beloff and Peele have argued that 'the desirability of avoiding confrontation in full Cabinet acts as a powerful incentive to ministers and the Prime Minister to iron out inter-departmental, political and personal differences in committee. If a dispute is serious enough, of course, the most rigid convention will not contain it, but matters rarely reach that level of conflict'.[5] Experience of the first Thatcher administration has confirmed this view.

Nevertheless, despite the powers of prime ministerial government, the wets while losing the battles within the policy machine, conducted guerilla war within the parliamentary party and with selected leaks to such anti-Thatcher newspapers as *The Guardian* and *The Observer*. Ultimately, even the E committee met less frequently because of leaks.[6] Another Cabinet committee, Misc. 62, which became known as the Star Chamber, was created to try to settle the difference between the Treasury and spending ministers and was chaired by William Whitelaw. However, the Star Chamber was often unable to agree, and issues were thus referred back to full Cabinet which, while critical, was equally unable to derail the Thatcher strategy. The policy-making process was effectively centred on No. 10 and No. 11, not on the Cabinet. One Cabinet minister thought that 'Cabinet is a quango ... in political terms what really matters is the relationship between Prime Minister and

Chancellor. It's a relationship between rider and horse'.[7] As another senior Cabinet minister similarly recalled:

Mrs Thatcher likes to discuss matters in small groups and she doesn't use the full Cabinet as it has been used in the past. All Prime Ministers feel the need for more information and for outside views to be brought to them because they all feel the need for a Prime Minister's department. The Cabinet Secretary isn't the same as a permanent secretary. Tensions exist in all Cabinets and every PM has to disappoint someone. Macmillan was a great pragmatist but not Mrs Thatcher. She believes in her view of Conservatism. She leads from the front.[8]

Apart from the dissension of the Cabinet wets, the greatest obstacles to political monetarism were thought to come from the Civil Service. Mrs Thatcher shared the view of many monetarists that the senior Treasury knights were still wedded to the old Keynesian post-war orthodoxy. Furthermore, she shared the views of those—not only on the right of British politics—that the Civil Service itself was too pessimistic and inert, incapable of appreciating the need for radical solutions and reluctant to implement government policy. The loyalty of the senior personnel in Whitehall was to be a constant theme of her premiership, and the initial suspicion with which Mrs Thatcher took office was not diluted with time.

The Permanent Secretary to the Treasury, Sir Douglas Wass, and many of his senior officials, with the exception of Peter Middleton, who was to succeed him, were known to be extremely sceptical on the advisability of monetarist remedies, so conflict between the Treasury and No. 10 was inevitable. One economic adviser on the inside stated that 'I regarded inflation as the greatest evil in Christendom—and still do. Douglas Wass didn't take that view'.[9] According to one account:

During the pre-budget discussions, Mrs Thatcher became enraged with what she considered the dilatoriness of the Treasury in coming up with the required public expenditure cuts. It couldn't be done, said the mandarins. She promptly summoned all five Treasury ministers and all five Treasury knights to Downing Street. They came out shaking from what was an unprecedented joint dressing down. A week later the Treasury came up with £1,400 million in cuts.[10]

In October 1979, to enforce monetarist influence upon the Treasury Keynesians, Professor Terry Burns of the London Business School was appointed at the early age of thirty-five to be Sir Fred Atkinson's successor as Chief Economic Adviser to the Treasury. Terry Burns was very much an outsider without experience of Whitehall but with a reputation in economic forecasting and in the LBS's development of 'international monetarism'. When this appointment was announced it was openly speculated that his advocacy of a medium-term plan for monetary growth would conflict with Treasury orthodoxy. Sir Robert Armstrong's appointment as Cabinet Secretary in October 1979 can also be viewed in the wider perspective of Mrs Thatcher's careful construction of 'her' team in Whitehall, although to many Sir Robert's career had established him as a pillar of the bureaucratic status quo.

Two other key appointments reflected Mrs Thatcher's new approach to policy formation and the official Whitehall machine. John Hoskyns was made head of the No. 10 Policy Unit, formed to concentrate on longer-term problems, one of which emerged as the thorough-going reform of Whitehall itself. Hoskyns' rise in Conservative politics had been meteoric. A former Army officer, IBM executive and computer consultant, he had been introduced first to Keith Joseph and then to Margaret Thatcher in the late 1970s, when he began to play a crucial role in policy reappraisal. Hoskyns advocated a tough line on most issues. He had urged a quicker pace of union reform, the replacement of Jim Prior and the abandonment of the election commitment to the Clegg Commission's comparability study. On this last point Hoskyn's advice seems most pertinent. The government's most costly error in the first six months was the failure to jettison the Clegg awards with their current huge increases in current public spending. Hoskyn's whole approach was to query the institutional restraints, such as the Civil Service, which prevented governments taking the necessary but politically unpopular action which abandoning Clegg would have signified. Reg Prentice, similarly, recalled that 'I was worried about the Civil Service attitudes and the Civil Service unions' attitudes. In the DHSS too much stuff was being leaked and the unions within the DHSS were openly campaigning against official policy for example, the drive against fraud and abuse.'[11]

A second key appointment in relation to the mistrust of Whitehall was Sir Derek Rayner.[12] Rayner's brief was to scrutinise inefficiency and waste in Whitehall and to propose the appropriate remedies. Sir Derek and a small team of assistants were initially placed in the Prime Minister's private office rather than in the Civil Service Department, reflecting prime ministerial caution that the Rayner Efficiency Unit, as it became known, should not be 'corrupted' by the Civil Service. Sir Derek's own efficiency and energy, exemplified by his successful business career as managing director of Marks and Spencer, were soon evident. Within months of beginning his task he reported that Whitehall was wasting £70 million per year in the handful of enterprises he had already examined. The criticisms of campaigners against Whitehall waste such as Leslie Chapman seemed to have been borne out.[13] Apart from Sir Derek's task, the government also announced that it intended to reduce Civil Service manpower — a difficult policy decision that was conspicuously made to stick over the lifetime of the administration. Although the government's battles with the Civil Service were to continue throughout the administration, the initial approach of giving policy-making and policy-informing power to selected outsiders — Burns, Hoskyns, Rayner—was to set a precedent rather than an exception to the rule. One senior treasury knight recalled that 'Mrs Thatcher liked a Kitchen Cabinet. We saw a lot of Walters but Hoskyns was a loner—he was anti-politics, and impatient with the political process because it's not like business.' One Cabinet minister regretted that 'In the Cabinet room you would find yourself surrounded by Hoskyns, Walters, Wolfson, and so on. They wouldn't talk but you knew that later, when you'd gone, they'd get at her.'[15]

Following Sir Geoffrey Howe's June budget, the main battle in the first six months over policy formation concerned the proposed July £4 billion public spending cuts. Opposition in Cabinet, which became widespread public knowledge, reflected Whitehall's institutional caution at such radical measures. That the Prime Minister eventually won the battle demonstrated how important the key-personnel aspect to policy initiatives had become. The problem of Cabinet divisions dominated the run-up to the July public expenditure cuts and thus deserves further attention. On 20 July *The Guardian* confidently declared that 'the first major policy conflict for the Conservative government seemed to be developing yesterday as Cabinet ministers began the process of identifying the areas in which substantial public expenditure cuts can be found.'[16] Departmental ministers were resisting cuts relating to their departments in the time-honoured manner of representing their departmental interests in Cabinet. Mark Carlisle, the Education minister, privately warned his colleagues that educational standards would be badly affected if cuts as high as 7 per cent were implemented.[17] Yet despite the opposition in full Cabinet, the Prime Minister had the backing from the monetarists on the E committee—Sir Geoffrey Howe, John Biffen, John Nott and Keith Joseph. One backbencher on the left of the party bemoaned that 'Mrs Thatcher surrounded herself with people who would share her view. There was no one from the liberal wing of the party as a Treasury minister and this built up mistrust.'[18] Patrick Jenkin recalled that 'the PM did respect Cabinet colleagues but the important meetings might not take place round the Cabinet table. The Policy unit at No. 10 would often brief her against a department.'[19]

At the vital Cabinet meeting on 23 July 1979 a public spending cut of £3.6 billion was agreed, subsequently to be enshrined in the Public Spending White Paper published in November. Much of the attention on the cuts was more on the divisions in Cabinet than on the specific measures themselves. Thus, according to one report:

The Cabinet yesterday reached broad agreement on a large package of new expenditure cuts intended to penetrate not only into the coming financial year but on a continuing basis into successive financial years thereafter.

There was some dispute last night over who had won the argument over the spending cuts, with the hawks insisting that they had won everything that they wanted thanks to the support of the Prime Minister, and with the doves claiming some marginal successes in holding off a few of the more horrendous proposals foreshadowed by Sir Geoffrey Howe, the Chancellor and his Treasury team...

However the Cabinet argument spilled over last night into a dispute among MPs and ministers over just how well the spending departments had done in their rear-guarded action against the

Treasury. Neutral ministers insisted that the alliance between the Prime Minister and her Treasury team had prevailed, but some of the doves argued that significant inroads had been made in the original Treasury proposals.[20]

Thus, although the Prime Minister's wishes had prevailed, the manner in which they had done so was less than satisfactory. Cabinet disputes had been openly aired and Denis Healey taunted in the Commons that there had been a blizzard of leaks. The leaks process was repeated again in October when ministerial opposition to an aimed-for 20-per-cent cut in Civil Service manpower became known. Even after the publication of the November White Paper detailing cuts across the board totalling £3.6 billion, allowing for increased spending on defence, law and order and social security, and the 'wets' versus 'dries' labels intensified the divisions within the government. Mrs Thatcher's speech in November 1979 to the Lord Mayor's banquet was aimed as much at her own party opponents as at the assembled City dignitaries. She warned, perhaps rightly, that unpleasant and painful remedies were necessary to cure the British disease and that it was a herculean task not to be deflected by a stony path.

As Sir Leo Pliatsky has recalled, the Keynesian commitment to full employment had been completely abandoned:

The Conservative victory in May 1979 was more than just another change of government; in terms of political and economic philosophy it was revolution. The first victim of this coup was the commitment to full employment...

The new administration was the first government since the 1944 White Paper on Employment Policy not to make full employment one of its objectives. In November 1979 it published a short White Paper on the Government's Expenditure Plans 1980–81 (Cmnd. 7746) showing the results of its first scrutiny of spending plans after six months in office. Opening with the statement that 'Public expenditure is at the heart of Britain's present economic difficulties', the White Paper set out the government's 'three central objectives'. The first was to bring down the rate of inflation by reducing the growth of the money supply and by controlling government borrowing. The second was to restore incentives by holding down and if possible reducing taxes, particularly on income. The third was to plan for spending which would be compatible with the objectives on borrowing and taxation, and with a realistic assessment of the prospects for economic growth. Thus there had ceased to be any trade-off in government policies between the counter-inflation objective and the employment objective. The counter-inflation objective was overriding. Not only was there no mention of full employment as an objective; the word 'employment' did not appear at all in the short White Paper except in the section-heading 'Industry, energy, trade and employment', and in one of the paragraphs in that section which stated that 'No provision is made for the extension of the Small Firms Employment Subsidy'.[21]

The political-monetarist policy on which the government had been elected had been translated into policy reality in the first six months of office. Given the strong opposition from both influential figures in the Cabinet and the Civil Service, this fact alone marked down for the future the determination of the Prime Minister. How far Mrs Thatcher was able to tolerate such internal dissension was to be demonstrated during the remainder of her first administration.

END OF CORPORATISM

As well as the location of the key personnel to see through economic policy against her political friends, the first six months witnessed a fundamental change in relations between Mrs Thatcher's government and the trade unions compared to that of previous post-war governments. The attempted close relations between governments and unions that had dominated the post-war period of consensus Keynesianism was simply jettisoned.[22] The idea that the unions had a role to play in formulating government policy—the essence of the corporatist approach—was repudiated.

This change of attitude was arguably more fundamental a change than that proposed in the 1979 Conservative manifesto to amend trade union law. The significance of the end of the corporatists approach cannot be overstressed in understanding both economic policy sources and the nature of contemporary Conservatism under Mrs Thatcher's first administration.

Mrs Thatcher's hostility to trade union power was part of the legacy from both the Heath period and the 1974–79 Labour government. The Prime Minister was determined that her administration would not be humiliated in the way that events had overtaken the two previous administrations.[23] She had taken office, moreover, with the public heartily sick of the excessive use of trade union power and sympathetic to attempts to restrain, and even control, it. Central to the government's new non-corporatist approach was the discarding of incomes policy as a policy tool. The institutionalised and cumbersome bureaucratic nature of successive incomes policies had greatly increased trade union power and prestige. The unions had fed upon the entrails of incomes policy for several decades. Negotiations with governments, deliberately conducted in the glare of maximum media publicity, had given union leaders the impression that such negotiations were an end in themselves by establishing union power at the very centre of the policy process. But also, when incomes policy targets or norms broke down because of union power as monopoly suppliers of labour, the victors in this process were also the unions who could be portrayed as virtually omnipotent. The process would then begin again with the governments attempting to 'talk to' and 'negotiate with' union leaders to find an incomes policy 'agreement'. As one Cabinet minister put it 'there comes a point when the unions decide that incomes policy is a challenge to their virility—that's what happened to Callaghan for example.'[24]

The Thatcher government in repudiating this approach to economic policy was taking a revolutionary step. One senior Treasury knight recalled that 'the government never got involved with incomes policy. It just said all you're having is x per cent, and I don't regard that as an incomes policy.'[25] The machinery of incomes policy operation was never established. In June 1979, for example, the Prime Minister, Sir Geoffrey Howe and Employment Secretary Jim Prior agreed to a meeting at Downing Street with the TUC leaders, but although the occasion was not hostile, there was no agreement or common communique as had been the case in, say, Mr Heath's premiership. A further meeting with the Chancellor in July was more frosty, although most senior union leaders, who had taken corporatism for granted for so long, were reluctant to cease a dialogue, however meaningless meetings with ministers had proved.

Union leaders were hoping that Jim Prior's moderating influence would win the day as far as legislation to curb union power was concerned. Prior was a leading 'wet', sympathetic to consensus politics, aware of the limits of legislation and an advocate of a corporatist-style 'pay forum', which he indeed offered the unions, unsuccessfully, in November 1979. However, it was the Prime Minister, not Prior, who was the source of policy formation. Consequently, in July 1979 Mrs Thatcher spoke with enthusiasm of plans to curb trade union power which were embodied in a consultative working paper published on 9 July 1979. In it the familiar objectives of redefining the legal position of the closed shop, picketing and providing support from public funds for union ballots were reiterated. On picketing, which during the Winter of Discontent had emerged as the most disliked abuse of power by unions, the document noted that:

The Government is committed to introducing early legislation to amend the law on picketing. The Government believes that the function of the law in the case of picketing as in the case of other forms of industrial action is to describe with clarity the rights, immunities and liabilities of those who take part...

Workers involved in a dispute have a right to try peacefully to persuade others to support them by picketing but we believe that right should be limited to those in dispute picketing at their own place of work...

We shall ensure that the protection of the law is available to those not concerned in the dispute but who at present can suffer severely from secondary action (picketing, blacking and blockading).

This means an immediate review of the existing law on immunities in the light of recent decisions followed by such an amendment as may be appropriate of the 1976 legislation in this field.

We shall also make any further changes that are necessary so that a citizen's right to work and go about his or her lawful business free from intimidation or obstruction is guaranteed.

Not surprisingly opinion hardened. The TGWU pledged 'maximum resistance' and the TUC expressed 'total opposition'. Even a meeting with Mr Prior could produce no measure of consensus, and Len Murray melodramatically stated that the Prior proposals 'could have as serious and disastrous an effect on the country's industrial relations as the 1971 Industrial Relations Act'[26] With hindsight Mr Murray's remarks could not have been more inaccurate. Further union attacks on the government were made at the TUC conference which restated TUC objections to government economic policy and to the changes proposed in trade union law. Subsequently, legislative proposals were announced in December 1979 in the form of Jim Prior's Employment Bill, which Mr Murray again warned would lead to industrial strife.

Countering the TUC's attacks, the government was equally critical. The corporatist approach was light-years away from the comments of the Chancellor and Industry Secretary Keith Joseph. Sir Geoffrey spoke of the 'dream world' of the unions by which union militancy had been 'making a bonfire of the nation's wealth.' In this 'dream world' the unions expected:

a better future without having to do anything different or difficult about it; a dream world where we can have more public spending without higher taxes, higher interest rates or greater inflation; a dream world in which all this can be delivered by an economy whose productivity is hardly growing and whose manufacturing output is below its level of six years ago.

It is a dream world in which there is no such thing as cause and effect... in which people can be paid more without producing more; where earnings always go up in good times but never down in bad; where profits can be reduced but investment and living standards increased...

Trade union rights are not God-given. They are given by society, by the law, by the elected government. If they are used to do economic damage and inflict human suffering, is it not legitimate and necessary to question their scope?'[27]

Sir Keith Joseph was, if anything, more scathing in his remarks about Britain's unions, which had, after all, participated for so long in the governmental process. Sir Keith described the existence of a politicised trade union movement 'associated with Luddism' as one of six 'poisons' responsible for Britain's ills. Sir Keith warned, as other ministers had also done, that one of the effects of trade union monopoly power was to price people out of jobs, and that trade union members would not follow union leaders down such a path.

This analysis was central to the government's approach to incomes. Free collective bargaining—which the unions had begged the Callaghan government to restore—was not challenged by the Thatcher government. However, the government was not prepared to reflate the economy to reduce unemployment if such free collective bargaining resulted in workers being priced out of jobs. To the Keynesian corporatist incomes-policy orthodoxy, such an a, proach was anathema. To the Thatcher government it was an attempt to restore reality to pay bargaining and to place responsibility for unemployment where it actually belonged. Time and again during the first six months this point was made by ministers. Moreover, the abandonment of the corporatist approach established during the early life of the government was not to be reversed during the remainder of the period 1980–83.

It would be far from the truth to argue, however, that the government was indifferent to pay settlements in the public sector. No government can adopt such a posture, as it is ultimately the paymaster. As Leon Brittan recalled, 'the government has to have a view on pay because it has to pay so many people. In economic terms pay settlements aren't inflationary in themselves, though they may lead to higher unemployment. But in political terms pay claims can put pressure on a monetary stance or on the budget deficit and taxes.'[28] The Thatcher government which had inherited rising inflation from Labour, and the Clegg commission during the election, faced a difficult situation in implementing the non-incomes-policy approach to pay in both the private and public sector. The automatic pay-rise mentality of much of the incomes policy approach had proved damaging over a decade or more. As one economist, who was later elected as a Conservative MP, summarised it, 'In manufacturing, output is no higher now than it was fifteen years ago. Yet wages are five times higher. That is not a sensible way to proceed and never will be. If money wages rise faster than output there will be inflation because there is nothing to buy with the extra money. So it just drives prices up.'[29] The Thatcher government was determined to break this seemingly inevitable spiral of wage expectations.

Contrary to Keynesian orthodoxy, however, such a reform is more likely without a formal incomes policy than with one. In Chapter 3 it will be argued that the government's success in reducing inflation by 1983 invalidated the incomes policy hypothesis that wage rates only decline if artificially made to do so. Similarly, the non-corporatist approach, contrary to the conventional wisdom of the time, was to lead to fewer rather than more industrial disputes and lost production. It can be argued that the absence of pre-set incomes policy norms and targets enabled the government to negotiate threatened and actual strike action with skill. By the time the Conservatives faced the electorate in 1983 working days lost because of strikes were at their lowest post-war level. Following the Winter of Discontent and the initial militant stance of some union leaders to the Thatcher administration this achievement is considerable. But in its first six months the government faced a number of tests.

The miners' 65 per cent wage claim had seemed destined to lead to strike action, especially since the NUM executive in December's ballot recommended it. However, not for the first time in the Thatcher administration, the miners voted to reject their leader's advice and to accept a 20 per cent pay offer from the NCB. Noticeably delighted, the Prime Minister said that the result had come without government interference and by letting people make their own decision. A repetition of the Heath government's bungling of the 1972 and 1974 miners' disputes had been skilfully avoided.[30] Similarly, the government competently handled strikes in the Civil Service, and in the last days of December, it rightly refused to sanction more than the British Steel Corporation's 2 per cent rise in an industry where financial reality had long been absent. Nor when prolonged strike action resulted did the government panic or surrender. On the whole the new non-corporatist approach worked well and a winter of industrial disruption was avoided despite the many predictions since May 1979 that it was inevitable. This success may well have been in part due to the new mood of realism which ministers had called for, arguing that big wage claims would lead to redundancies. As Patrick Jenkin, the Social Services Secretary and a political-monetarist supporter of the Prime Minister, put it in September, 'It is folly to believe that striking, or going slow, or working to rule, or banning overtime, can make people better off. If it could why don't we all go on strike until we have a standard of living as high as Germany's?'[31]

The end of the corporatist approach to trade union power and the incomes-policy mentality established in the first six months was to have far-reaching consequences as the Thatcher administration ran its course. In Chapter 6 these issues are examined in further detail.

EMPHASIS ON MARKETS

A central and important tenet of Mrs Thatcher's Conservatism was the emphasis put on the use of markets and free enterprise to produce and distribute goods and services wanted by consumers. Furthermore, the rolling back of the state and the ending of the socialist ratchet effect decreed not only an encouragement of the existing private sector but its expansion. Denationalisation, or privatisation as it was to become known, was seen as ideologically desirable and as a way of reducing state spending and waste. During the first six months the government made a number of significant steps towards rationalising the existing nationalised and state sector or towards ultimate transfer by sale to the private sector.

In July 1979 the election promises to transform the pattern of home ownership by allowing council house tenants the right to buy their own homes began to be translated into reality. As Housing Minister John Stanley put it, the plan 'Would be a giant stride toward the creation of the genuine property-owning democracy which the government wishes to see.' The scheme was known to be popular among council tenants, and during the 1979 election the biggest swings to the conservatives had been in many council house and New Town constituencies. By 1983 its electoral magnitude was to be in no doubt.

An equally bold start in reducing the role of the state was made by Industry Secretary Sir Keith Joseph. Over a long period of time and under both Conservative and Labour governments taxpayers' money had been squandered on vote-buying 'regional aid', fossilised nationalised industries and utterly uneconomic co-operative enterprises. The 1974–79 Labour government had been particularly wasteful in such industrial grants and subsidies.[32] In July 1979 Joseph announced a cut in industrial aid of £233 million with a downgrading of areas previously designated as worthy of special assistance. He also refused to waive the £1.2 million loan-interest payable to the government by the Meriden motor cycle co-operative, which had been assiduously fostered by Tony Benn, the then Industry Minister between 1974 and 1975. Sir Keith explained that 'Investment and expansion do not flow from regional policy, which can only guide such investment there is where most labour is available. To some extent, it has succeeded in doing this, but the better an area's reputation for productivity the more chance there is for expansion'.[33] Nevertheless, both sides of industry criticised the package, no doubt reflecting the dependence on regional aid that had been developed over the years. To the Labour Opposition the cuts were designed simply to finance tax cuts for the very rich.

Sir Keith also faced controversy over his policy relating to the National Enterprise Board. Unlike the Industrial Reorganisation Corporation in 1970, the NEB was not abolished; indeed, Sir Keith's statement in July 1979 that the NEB should keep its role of 'company doctor' where no private buyer emerges was regarded as a moderate approach. A number of Conservative MPs thought the government had not gone far enough in limiting the NEB's role despite Sir Keith's instructions that the NEB should raise £100 million by dispersing some of its assets. This 'sale of the century', as it became known, did indeed restore assets to the private sector worth about £130 million between May 1979 and March 1981. However, given Sir Keith's own strong beliefs in reversing the socialist ratchet effect, the NEB can be considered to have got off lightly. As Grant has argued:

The guidelines eventually issued to the Board showed a further softening of the Government's position. The draft guidelines required that the Board should develop projects only in partnership with the private sector, but the financial version was modified by the insertion of the words 'wherever the board consider it practicable to do so'. The original draft referred to the NEB being 'restricted to' four specified areas of activity, but the final version used the phrase 'especially in connection with', thus allowing the NEB to undertake projects outside the four main areas. The four areas in which the NEB was to pursue what was termed a 'catalytic investment role' were companies in which the NEB already had an interest; companies engaged in the development or exploitation of advanced technologies; companies operating (or intending to operate) industrial undertakings in the English regions; and the provision of loans of up to £50,000 to small firms.[34]

In November 1979, however, Sir Keith's relative generosity to the NEB was of no avail when its entire board resigned after the decision to transfer responsibility for Rolls Royce—nationalised, ironically, by the Heath government—to the Department of Industry. The Chairman, Sir Leslie Murphy, had been determined to make the transfer a resigning matter, and his successor, Sir Arthur Knight, was more amenable to the government's wishes that the NEB should not be hampered by being at the centre of the political limelight. Given the conflict between Sir Leslie and Sir Keith, which had steadily built up to the November resignation, Sir Keith may have ruefully mused that perhaps outright abolition would have been wiser in the first place.

Sir Keith also made it clear that the government wished to reform the organisation of the Post Office. In July Sir Keith told the Commons that the government would review the Post Office's mail-carrying monopoly unless efficiency was increased and two months later it duly unveiled plans to split the Post Office into two corporations, one for postal services and the other for telecommunications. Sir Keith later recalled that 'I'm very proud of separating Telecom from the Post Office. It was a giant step.'[35] In October 1979, following instructions from the government, the Post Office Chairman, Sir William Barlow, emphasised that the aim 'is to get ahead with the administrative reorganisation as quickly as possible.'[36] In a similar efficiency drive Sir Peter Parker, the British Rail Chairman, announced in October 1979 a £300 million scheme involving 40,000 job redundancies, and the NCB recorded a £19 million loss with pleas for further government aid. Both these long-term problems were to recur more starkly during the Thatcher administration.

Restoring market efficiency to the steel industry was another industrial headache.[37] In July 1979, faced with the need to eliminate a massive £327 million loss, BSC announced its intention to accelerate closure of its Shotton and Corby works, threatening 11,000 jobs. In December the BSC Chairman, Sir Charles Villiers, warned that there would have to be more redundancies if the industry was to become profitable and speculated that a total of 50,000 jobs were involved. To those aware of the chronic overmanning and inefficiency in the industry, such a figure was not surprising. In fact, a week later Sir Charles announced that 53,000 redundancies were required in the next nine months, which would have a 'terrible effect on steel communities'.[38] Such effects, of course, had been made far worse by the artificial subsidisation of non-jobs for so long. Ironically, in the same month—December 1979—the private steel producers, with a third of national capacity, stated they were in the black, in contrast to BSC.

A similar story faced the Thatcher government in the nationalised shipyards. Privatisation of former warship yards, while considered in Opposition, was immediately impractical as the prospects for profitability were very low. Rationalisation of the existing nationalised structure, in the hope of minimising losses, was the governments's initial policy. Thus, in August 1979 British Shipbuilders put forward a proposal to cut 10,000 jobs in an effort to reach the government's deadline for the industry to pay its way within eighteen months. Needless to say, this problem was to emerge again during the government's lifetime.

In no other sector of state-supported industry was the need for greater market orientation more imperative than in British Leyland. BL's problems had stemmed essentially from a failure to satisfy customers, a failure compounded by strikes and industrial militancy.[39] Overmanning was a chronic problem, and in September 1979 the BL Chairman, Sir Michael Edwardes, announced that the workforce was to be cut by 2,500 over two years with the part closure of thirteen plants. However, Sir Michael made it clear that he expected government money to be made available for capital investment once a plan was available to put the company on a sound commercial and profitable basis.

It may be argued that receivership would have been the best solution for BL, but the government was not prepared to countenance this option. This may have been, as John Burton has argued, because of the widespread misunderstanding of the economics of bankruptcy. As Burton put it:

First, when a firm goes into liquidation the physical assets of the company are not 'destroyed'—they are simply revalued downwards. If British Leyland or British Steel (etc.) were liquidated, their car assembly plants and steel rolling mills would remain. The purpose of the downward revaluation is to find a purchaser for the assets of the company. And the assets are usually more valuable if they are not sold together—as a complete working organization, or perhaps as a number of separate working plants—than separately, as a large number of separate lots of equipment, buildings etc. Thus, for instance, if British Leyland were to be liquidated, the likelihood is that a large part of the present company would remain in operation, in the hands of new owners (perhaps, however, split up into a number of smaller companies).

However, the more speedily the winding-up proceeds, the easier it is to sell as a complete working organization, with a full complement of trained managerial personnel and skilled employees. It is not impossible to visualise ways in which the workings of the bankruptcy mechanism could be improved, so that the likelihood of organizational maintenance of bankrupt enterprises is enhanced.[40]

However, this option, though mooted, was not tried. Eventually, despite both threatened talk of the company being put into the hands of the Receiver and despite the Longbridge strike in November 1979 after the sacking of Derek Robinson, the senior shop-steward convenor, further government money was indeed forthcoming. In December BL was transferred from the orbit of the NEB to the Department of Industry, and a £450 million injection of taxpayers' money was sanctioned by Sir Keith. Sir Michael's corporate plan was accepted by the government as an ultimate way back to profitability and a rationalisation, involving a new product range, did indicate that market disciplines were not to be overriden by limitless supplies of state aid.

The emphasis on markets for most of the nationalised and state-subsidised sector essentially meant an efficiency drive, reductions in overmanning, profitability targets and greater customer satisfaction. However, there were areas in 1979 ready for actual privatisation plans. In October a 5.1 per cent holding in BP was sold to raise £290 million with 80 million shares offered at 363p each. In July 1979 the government announced that British Airways was to be partially denationalised with a sale of shares to the public saving the government £1,000 million on new aircraft investment. The Trade Secretary, John Nott, explained that:

The socialists talk about public ownership, but if that means anything at all, it means those who work for a firm sharing in its future. We also expect that pension funds representing many millions of people will want a stake, which will widen the basis of interest... It is inevitable that as it is at present constituted BA will be subject to the vagaries of wider public expenditure constraints. But once it steps away from government it will have greater management flexibility and enhance its future. The Treasury will no longer be crawling over its investment programmes.[41]

Ultimately, the Civil Aviation Act provided for the sale of 49 per cent of the shares in a new company controlling British Airways to the private sector. The BP and British Airways sales showed the government's resolve in its past six months to return to the private sector, where possible, public sector assets. The policy was to be further extended during the next three years. In contrast to the unhappy experience of the Heath government, the early emphasis on markets was to be sustained not abandoned.[42]

PART II

The Thatcher Government
and Economic Change

3 Contemporary Conservatism and Inflation

Demand inflation is not a new phenomenon. It has shown itself again and again in history. If there is anything new it is the intellectual climate in which it has taken place. It has been the fear of deflation, inherited from the 1930s, which has often inhibited governments from taking action to prevent it, lest they should be accused of policies inimical to employment and growth. The insistence of Beveridge that a policy of full employment involved a condition in which there were 'always more vacant jobs than unemployed men', that is a position in which the demand for labour was always in excess of supply, although he would have denied the reproach, was in fact a prescription for non-stop demand inflation. But the general climate of public opinion tolerated such conceptions as if they were obvious good sense.

Lord Robbins, 1976[1]

OVERALL STRATEGY

Inflation control had been at the centre of Mrs Thatcher's economic thinking in Opposition, during the 1979 election campaign and during the first six months of her government. The 1979 election manifesto had stated that 'to master inflation, proper monetary discipline is essential, with publicly stated targets for the rate of growth of the money supply. At the same time a gradual reduction in the size of the government's borrowing requirements is also vital'.[2] Such a policy, in contemporary Conservative terms, was a restatement of the 1970 manifesto commitment whereby 'in implementing all our policies the need to curb inflation will come first'.[3] According to the critique of the political monetarists it had been the failure of the Heath government to stick to its original anti-inflationary intention that had led to the U-turns and subsequent electoral defeat. Mrs Thatcher was determined not to repeat the Heath experience.

49

Over the course of her government she kept to the priority of reducing inflation above all else. The methods of pursuing this policy were flexible—money-supply targets, public spending cuts, tax increases, tight cash limits within which pay deals had to be concluded—but the strategy of lowering inflation was consistently adhered to. Moreover, she was determined to change the continued expectation of inflation whereby, as Sir Walter Salomon accurately put it, 'both sides of industry were in unholy alliance: management thought a little bit of inflation would increase profits, while labour was persuaded that a little bit of inflation would maintain employment. It was as though a little bit of pregnancy need not lead on to bigger things!'[4] To claim, as critics of the Thatcher policy have done, that monetarism was abandoned when M3 became too volatile and unpredictable to control, is to misunderstand Mrs Thatcher's—and Geoffrey Howe's—approach to inflation. Essentially, the central policy was to resist reflation and any shift towards Keynesian demand management aimed at reducing unemployment. 'Technical' or 'economic' monetarism would be used as a means to the end and would not constitute an end in itself. Not all members of the government made this distinction. One Cabinet minister recalled that 'the monetary thing was too dominant and monetary policy pursued in too legalistic a way.'[5] The consequent shifts in policy means, away from the preoccupation with M3, for example, did not indicate shifts in the overall strategy or a change of intention. Thus, because of the government's steadfast attitude to the overall strategy, inflation fell from a 21 per cent peak in 1980 to 4 per cent by the time of the 1983 election, providing a factually accurate background for the 1983 Conservative manifesto's assertion that:

Steadier prices and honest money are essential conditions for recovery. Under the last Labour government, prices doubled and inflation soared to an all-time peak—despite the existence of a battery of controls on prices, profits, dividends and pay.

Today there are no such controls. Yet prices are rising more slowly than at any time since the 1960s. During the last year, inflation has come down faster in Britain than in any other major economy. With lower inflation, businessmen, families, savers and pensioners can now begin at last to plan and budget ahead with confidence.

In the next Parliament, we shall endeavour to bring inflation lower still. Our ultimate goal should be a society with stable prices.

We shall maintain firm control of public spending and borrowing. If Government borrows too much, interest rates rise, and so do mortgage payments. Less spending by Government leaves more room to reduce taxes on families and businesses.

We shall continue to set out a responsible financial strategy which will gradually reduce the growth of money in circulation—and so go on bringing inflation down.[6]

The government's success on the inflation front is challengeable on the often advanced criticism that it was achieved at too high a cost in unemployment or lost manufacturing output. That is a matter for legitimate debate. But it will not do to argue that the reduction in inflation was nothing to do with monetarism if by that it is meant the overall political-monetarist strategy. Similarly, the government's consistency in repudiating U-turns, and neo-Keynesian solutions did make a significant change in the nature of post-war Conservatism. This is not to argue that technical monetarism is now synonymous with Conservatism; instead, it is to argue that the values which Mrs Thatcher holds have now come to be strongly associated with Conservative government. When Mrs Thatcher recalled that savings had been 'plundered' by reflation and that £100 in 1935 is now worth only £8.70, she was expressing a horror at inflation which predated monetarist economics. Mrs Thatcher's moral belief that savings should be protected and sound money respected are more important to understanding the insistence on reducing inflation during her first administration than the complex theorems of Milton Friedman. As Riddell has accurately observed, Thatcherism is essentially an instinct, a series of moral values and an approach to leadership rather than an ideology. It is an expression of Mrs Thatcher's upbringing in Grantham, her background of hard work and family responsibility, ambition and postponed satisfaction, duty and patriotism. Her views were 'born of the conviction which I learned in a small town from a father who had a conviction approach', as she put it in an interview in January 1983 on London Weekend Television's *Weekend World* programme. The striking feature of Mrs Thatcher's approach has been its consistency. The same themes have cropped up again and again in speeches and interviews throughout the past decade—personal responsibility, the family and national pride. The key lies in her use of language, especially in off the cuff interviews. Words like freedom, self-respect, independence, initiative, choice, conviction, duty, greatness, heart and faith recur.[7] Thus, as Lord Thorneycroft recalled, 'M3 being central stemmed from the advisers, not from Mrs Thatcher. She thought it made no sense to spend money you hadn't got—this was the Grantham approach—and mistakenly allowed to be inserted into speeches references to monetarism that were academically correct but politically foolish'.[8] For this reason we can again see that the best term to describe the economic outlook of the Thatcher period is 'political monetarism'.

The policy against inflation was made more difficult because, as previously noted, the government inherited a strongly rising inflation rate from its predecessor. During 1980 and 1981 the government therefore found itself taking tough and necessary measures to reduce inflation without the benefits being obvious. In February 1980 the inflation rate rose to 18.4 per cent, or a doubling of the rate since May 1979, as Mr Hattersley gleefully pointed out for the Opposition, so that the March budget was presented with an unfavourable background. Mrs Thatcher, aware of the criticism of the Tory wets—of which there will be more in this chapter—wisely emphasised the long-term nature of her policies stating that 'basic economic laws (cannot) somehow be suspended because we are British... For government, facing our national problems entails keeping the growth of the amount of money in line with the growth in the amount of goods and services. After years of printing too much money, to which the economy has become addicted, this will take time, but it must be done'.[9] Similarly, prefacing the tough budget the Prime Minister pointed out that her programme did not spring from 'some complicated economic theory' and that it was a fact that 'If we shrink from the task of cutting public spending the result will be breakneck inflation. We are not going to be frightened off. *What happens to other governments shall not happen to us*' (my emphasis).[10] Sir Ian Gilmour has attacked this approach by criticising the analogy between curbing government spending and how individual households curb their own spending. Gilmour states that 'if a housewife cuts her household expenses she does not thereby cut her income. Not so a national government...A government which cuts its spending on goods and services reduces national income and increases unemployment'.[11] The evidence, however, suggests that the government, not Sir Ian, was more accurate in its analysis. A government does not necessarily cut its income if, say, it reduces spending on Civil Service manpower levels. It may be that manpower is redeployed into the private sector, which increases government revenue through taxation. However, on the balance between government revenue and spending—which is the crucial factor—a government which cuts wasteful spending may increase beneficial areas of public spending, or may cut taxes, by the appropriate amount saved.

Similarly, reductions in government spending may allow interest rates to fall, thereby increasing the possibilities of private sector profitable investment to create jobs. The reflationists' fallacy is to assume that all government spending is beneficial, economically or socially, and that there is no overmanning in the public sector. It was the government's approach that was more realistic.

The deflationary 1980 March budget did not come as a surprise. In it Sir Geoffrey Howe launched his four-year Medium-Term Financial Strategy (MTFS) outlining a progressive reduction in the money supply. Alan Walters described the aims of the MTFS as follows:

The central focus of Mrs Thatcher's administration in reforming the finances of Britain was the Meduim-Term Financial Strategy (MTFS). This took a four-year view of public spending, the budget deficit (or the PSBR in our much wider terms) and the rate of growth of the money supply (the broader aggregate sterling M3 was adopted). The idea, based on the concepts of rational expectations, was that the announcement of these target rates of growth of the money supply etc. would induce entrepreneurs, investors and workers to adjust their behaviour to the new policy as though it were a *new* reality. Much—perhaps the pain of adjustment—could be eliminated by a sea change of expectations.[12]

One senior Treasury knight recalled that 'I argued against the

MTFS on the grounds that it gave no extra credibility to government policy. My argument was that the government would lose credibility if it did not meet its targets'.[13] Such objections, however, were ignored.

To realise the MTFS, the 1980 budget contained a number of measures. Public spending was cut by £1 billion to reduce the PSBR, and Sir Geoffrey Howe envisaged public expenditure as being 4 per cent lower by 1983–84.

Income tax thresholds at the bottom of the scale were raised in line with inflation, but the lower 25p rate of income tax was abolished. The prospect of future tax cuts, central to any Conservative electoral appeal, as had been shown in May 1979, was relegated behind inflation control as the Chancellor's priority. Indeed, this had been implicit in government policy, given the inheritance on taking office. One senior Treasury official recalled that 'In May 1979 on day one I asked Geoffrey Howe whether tax cuts or cutting the PSBR had priority and he said cut the PSBR. It was the only Tory government I knew that didn't cut taxes'.[14]

One innovation concerned the introduction of six experimental 'enterprise zones' in inner city areas, where businessmen could invest with such tax concessions as 100 per cent capital allowance for building and an exemption from rates. This scheme was very important to Geoffrey Howe. One economic adviser commented that 'Geoffrey was a convinced enterprise man. He really does believe jobs will be created by small businesses. We took 107 measures to make life easier for small businesses'.[15] The emphasis of the budget was, however, on a determination to reduce inflation. As Sir Geoffrey put it:

It will be clear from what I have already said that the Government continue to regard the fight against inflation as the first priority. It is an illusion to suppose that we have any real choice between defeating inflation and some other course. It is quite wrong to suppose that inflation is something with which only Treasury ministers need be concerned. And in the defeat of inflation, monetary policy has an essential role to play. Other countries recognise this very clearly. They recognise, too, that sustained monetary restraint is not an easy, automatic or painless solution. But they are struggling to get back towards more balanced budgets, as we must. The level of spending is planned to fall steadily throughout the next four years. Without these economies, a coherent policy to reduce inflation would be unattainable...

At the heart of the medium-term strategy is the need to return to a sensible level of public spending and to see government borrowing reduced. In the last 20 years the ratio of public expenditure to GDP has risen by a quarter. It would be all too easy for this ratio to go on rising indefinitely, unless we addressed ourselves to fundamentals. That is what we have done in the most far-reaching review of medium-term expenditure plans since they began 20 years ago. This review is crucial to the strategy. Crucial to success in reducing the PSBR, lowering interest rates, and bringing down inflation. And crucial if we are to find room for lightening the tax burden and so to provide scope and encouragement for enterprise and initiative...Expenditure in 1983–84 is planned to be about 4 per cent lower in real terms than in 1979–80. The effect will be a marked shift in the burdens imposed by the Government and in the balance between the public and private sectors. Above all we shall have set the volume of public spending on the right course. We shall be creating a climate much more favourable to economic growth.[16]

The budget had no shortage of critics at the time or since. Ultimately, the public spending plans were completely blown off course by the necessity to increase social security spending during the recession and the emphasis on money-supply growth proved episodic. However, the critics, either in Parliament, in the unions, or in the Cambridge Economic Policy Group[17] latched on to the paradox that with inflation rising—April's figure was 19.8 per cent—the government was deflating the economy to no avail. The CEPG simply stated that 'the evidence that inflation of both wages and prices has recently been accelerating ... entirely confutes the monetarist claim'.[18] In mid-1980 the long-term success of Sir Geoffrey's policy was not yet evident. Indeed, two months after the budget the inflation rate reached 21.8 per cent despite a reduction in the money supply to within the 7 to 11 per cent target. The incomes policy lobby, as ever vociferous, was advocating a return to artificial restraints on wages and prices, and Mrs Thatcher went out of her way to denounce such 'patent remedies' as guiding lights, pay pauses, dashes for growth, prices and incomes policy, dividend controls and social contracts.[19]

The inflationary peak of 21.9 per cent in June 1980, instead of causing any policy reversal, stiffened the government's resolve, and the following month the rate began to drop, beginning the descent to 4 per cent, which the government could put before the electorate in 1983. A tougher line on cash limits was announced, the Clegg Commission was wound up and U-turns to reduce the rising unemployment rate were expressly ruled out. The upward movement of the pound continued despite the CBI's appeals for a lower exchange rate, and interest rates remained high. The impact of the recession was obvious by August, when a 1 per cent fall in the GDP was announced. Moreover, a record and unplanned rise of 5 per cent in the money supply was evident by August. According to a number of monetarist critics such as the Selsdon Group, 'the Bank of England has been pursuing a cheap money policy all year'.[20] One Treasury adviser recalled that 'one disagreement with the Bank of England was over monetary control and the other was the MTFS. It became a joke just how a number of senior ex-directors couldn't believe they were less than perfect'.[21] Gowland, in an authoritative study of money-supply control concluded that 'in brief the government had failed to solve the essential problem of monetary control'.[22] Another Treasury official thought that 'the Bank was exerting its virility within the policy machine—as it always does—but I would disagree with the view that they were sabotaging. We had disagreements with them, but you can't sustain the charge of sabotage'.[23] In view of one senior Treasury knight, the 'Bank of England didn't try to sabotage, the Governor was a practical monetarist after all. But the PM gave the Governor and the Bank a roasting—she was critical of the clearing banks for pushing consumer credit and doesn't have a feel for what it's like to operate in private enterprise'.[24] To this economic backcloth both the expressions of government policy at the October 1980 Conservative conference and on Geoffrey Howe's November mini budget demonstrated a single-minded perseverance with tough anti-inflationary policies.

At Brighton Mrs Thatcher told Conservative agents—the most pragmatic of all Conservative strands of opinion—that successive governments had, over thirty years, tried overspending, overborrowing, subterfuges like devaluation and import deposits, all of which had failed. Similarly, the conference was told that there would be no U-turn on economic policy, coining the phrase 'you turn if you want to—the lady's not for turning'. The Chancellor's message was equally clear, declaring that 'it would be folly beyond belief to turn back now'. On taxation, always a conference favourite, he pessimistically stated that 'it would be wrong for me to arouse any great expectations today. When I am able to ease the load, I have the feeling from the debate that it is first to industry, to enterprise and small businesses that you would wish me to direct my attention'.[25] When inflation fell to 15.9 per cent in October, Sir Geoffrey was equally cautious, venturing that the battle against inflation involved substantial and painful adjustments.

The November mini-budget reinforced the declared policy line. Interest rates were cut by 2 per cent, taxation increased by £2 billion and public expenditure cut by £1 billion. The 1 per cent rise in employee's National Insurance contributions effectively displayed the choice between tax increases and public spending cuts if the government was to stick to its forecasts. Furthermore, pensions and other benefits were to be put up by less than the rate of inflation to cancel a 1 per cent overprovision, and the index-linked savings certificates scheme was extended in the hope of raising a further £3 billion. Defending his deflationary package, Sir Geoffrey argued that:

In order further to offset upward pressures on expenditure, we are making cuts in the volume provision for the majority of spending programmes. Our aim is to keep the planning total for the volume of public expenditure in 1981–82 about 1 per cent below the out-turn now expected for the current year ... We must also restrict the cost, and so the cash requirements, of the public sector. The cost of public expenditure programmes is as important as volume. It is essential to our fiscal policy, and also entirely fair, to look in the coming year for a much lower growth in public service earnings than in the recent past. It has already been announced that the Rate Support Grant limit will allow for a 6 per cent annual increase in earnings from due settlement dates in the current pay round. It will provide for an increase in prices other than pay of 11 per cent between the average levels for 1980–81 and 1981–82.

Expenditure in other parts of the public services will be subject to broadly the same financial disciplines.

He had also been considering the revenue requirements for

financing next year's expenditure:

I am determined that the PSBR in 1981–82 should be consistent with the Government's medium-term economic strategy and the need to ease the burden of adjustment at present falling on industry … Inflation had come down appreciably, and is well below the current level of short-term interest rates. In agreement with the Governor of the Bank of England I have therefore concluded that some reduction in these rates is possible. Accordingly, the Bank of England, with my approval, is this afternoon announcing a reduction in Minimum Lending Rate of two percentage points.[26]

The mini budget was extensively criticised. The 2 per cent interest rate cut was considered too small by many in industry and the further deflationary measures antagonised, as could be expected, the Tory wets as well as the opposition. Moreover, a political storm erupted over proposals published by the DHSS that there was a substantial increase in Employer's National Insurance contributions on top of that of employees. Like most Chancellors before him, the beleaguered and heavily criticised Sir Geoffrey could only appeal for patience 'to see inflation coming down and so making more room for expansion within the established monetary framework. Then we can have higher output without the government rushing into "reflationary" packages, which would serve only to rob us of the emerging hope of future prosperity'.[27] By January 1981 Sir Geoffrey was not optimistic in forecasting single-figure inflation for the year as a whole, following a further decline to 8.4 per cent over the preceding six months.

Such impending improvements did not lead to a relaxation of government policy. Indeed, following the appointment of Professor Alan Walters as the Prime Minister's economic policy adviser it was clear that the political monetarists in the Cabinet had required more congenial advice than that they had been receiving from the wets and much of the Keynesian-orientated Civil Service. Professor Walters was no lackey, and in the controversial run-up to the March 1981 budget he demonstrated an independence of thought that critics of his appointment had not assumed would be forthcoming from a monetarist who had described Mrs Thatcher in *Now!* magazine as 'the only real Tory leader since Churchill'. The battle for the

1981 budget caused a wide polarisation in the government's economic policy-forming machine.

The controversy surrounded the report drawn up in February 1981 by Professor Jurg Niehans, which argued that monetary policy had been excessively tight with the high interest rates attracting 'hot' money to London and causing a high pound. Niehans, who had been commissioned to examine government policy by the Centre for Policy Studies via Alan Walters, was supported in his view by John Hoskyns and Walters himself and strongly opposed by Terry Burns, Peter Middleton and the Chancellor. Peter Middleton's support for Geoffrey Howe marked him out for promotion, which duly came in 1983 when he succeeded Douglas Wass. One insider recalled that 'they felt in Peter they had someone they could work with'.[28] These opponents argued that a too tight monetary policy was not responsible for the recession, which they put down to a combination of wage explosion, OPEC and the rising pound. None of these had been exacerbated by monetary policy and the rising pound was attributed to the importance of petro status. One Treasury official, who took this line recalled that 'what I didn't accept was that you could explain the high exchange rate by the monetary base. I argued that high exchange rate was pressurised by oil prices'.[29] A Treasury junior minister also thought that 'Alan Walters wasn't right on monetary policy being too tight'.[30] Although the Prime Minister rejected the Niehans thesis, it did lead to changes suggested and supported by Walters in the following months. As Mrs Thatcher's biographers put it:

Hoskyns provided an abridged version of the Niehans Report for Thatcher and she, too, could not bring herself to agree with it and see that she was wrong. But the proof of his diagnosis was in subsequent action. First, despite opposition, Thatcher came round to Walters' view, suggested by Niehans, that too narrow a range of monetary measures was being used which ignored bank deposits and that a monetary base system would prove more effective. Second, a relaxation of the tight monetary control was coupled with a tightening of fiscal measures, which had been left lax because they were considered relatively unimportant.[31]

Other changes were also forthcoming following the internal

debate over the Niehans Report. The exchange rate was introduced as an additional indicator and the object of control was no longer the money supply but 'monetary conditions' or the 'underlying rate of monetary growth'. According to Sir Keith Joseph, 'We never took enough account of the exchange rate in the 1970s. The missing perception in '79 was the exchange rate'.[32] while a junior minister noted that 'we got the exchange rate wrong '80-81'.[33] One Treasury adviser recalled that 'You have to look at the arrival of Alan Walters as crucial. On monetary policy he didn't like the reliance on M3 as the measure. In my view Neihans was mistaken. Monetary policy was not the pressure on the exchange rate. There were oil-market factors. As soon as the news on OPEC in 1979 and Afghanistan and Iran came through, you could feel the exchange rate going up'.[34] The same adviser also considered that the government had been vulnerable to such terms as 'Thatcherite' and 'monetarist' as the oil crisis and world recession deepened. For opponents of monetarism such changes in emphasis were greeted with glee. However, it would be wrong to argue that adjustments of the means discredited the ends of political monetarism. As one former Treasury official critical of monetarist economics has put it:

> If in the end the British monetarist experiment were deemed to have failed because of the monetary fiasco that might be an incorrect verdict, but not an unfair one. For the monetarists, by placing so much emphasis on the money supply, have dug a pit for themselves.
>
> The most important part of monetarist philosophy is that concerned with the efficiency of markets and the need to let those markets function. Yet the monetarist salesmen have chosen to fill their shop window with the gewgags of monetary technicalities, distracting attention from the more durable goods inside.[35]

If the secret Niehans Report[36] was temporarily confined to the policy-making inner circle, the same could not be said for the Cabinet dispute over the March budget. Clear policy divisions were publicly acknowledged as the wets strove to oppose any further deflationary pressure.[37] Again, however, the key personnel won the battle and Sir Geoffrey presented his most controversial budget on 10 March 1981. There were no increases in personal allowances or widening of tax bands.

Indirect taxes were substantially increased and a total of £4.3 billion was taken out of the economy. Lord Harris of High Cross recalled that 'the 1981 budget was a triumph for Alan Walters. It was an enormous act of courage. Howe said to me shortly afterwards that we'd have inflation down to 5 per cent by 1983'.[38] Leon Brittan also recalled that the '1981 budget was an economic watershed of the first order. I thought so at the time. It was counter-Keynesian at a time of deep recession. Twenty years ago a Keynesian textbook would have told you the opposite'.[39] Similarly, in defence of the 1981 budget Sir Alan Walters has argued that:

And above all, the 1981 budget wrenched the government deficit (PSBR) back on to its original course. This meant large increases in taxes about five billion pounds or more than 2 per cent of GNP. The budget of 1981 must be reckoned as the biggest fiscal squeeze of peace time. But it did convince the markets that the government was sticking to its policies. And, at first gradually, then much more rapidly, expectations adjusted to the reduced rates of inflation. Along this hard and rocky road, however, we were treated to an avalanche of protests by the massed ranks of the economics profession led by its most distinguished luminaries. It would have been so easy for the government to ease up. But it would also have been disastrous. In a trice all the progress that had been made in revising expectations would have been undone.[40]

Despite the familiar chorus of criticism from both inside and outside the government, Mrs Thatcher stood firm. Defending the budget she said:

What really gets me is that those who are most critical of the extra taxation are those who were most vociferous in demanding the extra expenditure. What gets me even more is that having demanded that extra expenditure they are not prepared to face the consequences. I wish some of them had a bit more guts and courage than they have shown, because I think one of the most immoral things you can do is to pose as the moral politician demanding more for everything, and then say no when you see the bill ... For those who say 'yes increase your deficit spending, have this cosy reflation' I say they must face the fact that the interest rate would not have gone down, it would have gone up, and then they would have stifled and strangled at birth any expansion of industry and investment that we might have had. So

when people say that this is a no-hope budget, I can only say to them
that this budget is the only hope for Britain.[41]

Nigel Lawson, the financial Secretary to the Treasury also
attacked those who thought it possible to boost the economy by
more borrowing and described as nonsense the argument that
there could be a trade off of unemployment or inflation. One
senior Treasury knight who was sceptical of monetarist policies
recalled that Lawson 'was the thinker behind Howe's
Chancellorship'.[42] A similar argument to Nigel Lawson's was
also forthcoming from Mrs Thatcher, who observed that 'It
once seemed obvious that so long as there were unemployed
hands and under-used plants, we could put them to work by
more or less throwing newly created money in their direction. In
practice, as governments increasingly discover, the extra money
did less to raise production than it did to push prices up even
higher and unemployment up even more'.[43]

Samuel Brittan has convincingly argued that the 1981 budget
was climacteric and Thatcherite more by inadvertance. As he
observed:

The intention was to resume the path of gradual reduction in the PSBR
as a proportion of the national product. Treasury advisers thought
they had made allowance for the recession in budgeting for a higher
PSBR for 1981–82 than that set out in the Medium-Term Financial
Strategy (MTFS) formulated the previous year. But this was a subtlety
that failed to penetrate outside the dusty yellow corridors of the New
Public Offices which house the Treasury and did not even penetrate
into every room there.

The impression of 'tightening up' was increased (a) by the abortive
revolt of a group of Conservative ministers and MPs glorying in the
name of 'wets', (b) the faster than predicted rise in unemployment (the
Treasury's output forecasts were reached, but its productivity
forecasts were much exceeded) and (c) the 2 billon undershooting of
the PSBR behind its planned level in the 1981–82 financial year. The
main aim of the government in tightening fiscal policy was not,
however, to restrict further overall, but to shift the monetary-fiscal
mix so that interest rates could fall.[44]

One Treasury adviser thought that 'the perfectly simple
argument for the 1981 budget was that without it our strategy
would not have been believed by the financial markets. A group

of us—John Hoskyns, Alan Walters, Terry Burns and myself—played a role in the '81 budget with the Chancellor keeping Mrs Thatcher informed sometimes in the face of criticism'.[45] Another senior Treasury official recalled that 'I was quite happy with the 1981 budget, which made people realise that the MTFS was for real and not to be discarded when the going got tough'.[46] According to one Treasury minister, 'the Treasury having been defeated on public expenditure in autumn 1980, Nigel Lawson convinced Geoffrey [Howe] that what had been foregone must be recouped'.[47] One Treasury knight who opposed the tough budget recalled that there were 'spirited discussions at No. 10, with Walters, Hoskyns, and Wolfson wanting a tougher budget and me not, and the Chancellor, initially, not. They thought it wasn't tough enough and they wanted a lower PSBR'.[48]

U-turns were thus explicity ruled out, as was discovered by the 364 economists whose open letter to the Prime Minister and Chancellor rejected monetarism and called for alternative policies. The letter even went as far as to say that 'there is no basis in economic theory or supporting evidence for the government's belief that by deflating demand they will bring inflation permanently under control'. It may be argued that when inflation fell to 4 per cent in 1983—its lowest level for fourteen years—the government had won that particular intellectual debate. Indeed, the evidence of the success of government policy was available in 1981. In July 1981 inflation fell to 11.3 per cent—having peaked at 21.9 per cent in May 1980—and the government's repudiation of any U-turn indicated that an even lower rate was a matter of time.

However, the pressure for a U-turn was to reach its height in the summer of 1981 when riots erupted in a number of British cities, seemingly indicating that unemployment was causing civil unrest. Although the available evidence showed that there was no correlation between high unemployment areas and the rioting—for example the absence of rioting in the depressed Tyneside or Glasgow—the wets in the Conservative party pushed their case with increased vigour. To head off this dissent Mrs Thatcher conducted a major reshuffle in September. Jim Prior, while retaining his position on the E Committee, was made Northern Ireland Secretary and his Employment portfolio given to the Thatcher loyalist Norman Tebbit. One Thatcherite junior minister recalled that 'Prior, having come to the conclusion that his attitude to the Department of Employment and the Prime Minister's were irreconcilable, was happy to go to Northern Ireland, but when he discovered that Tebbit was to be his successor that's what he really objected to'.[49] Mr Prior has since denied this.[50] Mark Carlisle and Lord Soames were sacked, which was not unexpected, but the dismissal of the most articulate wet, Sir Ian Gilmour, showed the Prime Minister's resolve to stick to existing policies. Gilmour's resignation letter became the most quoted document for months after, containing the paragraph 'Every Prime Minister has to reshuffle from time to time. It does no harm to throw the occasional man overboard, but it does not do much good if you are steering full speed ahead for the rocks. That is what the Government is now doing'.[51] As well as Tebbit's promotion, other appointments reflected the Prime Minister's need to balance her administration with more of her defenders. Nicholas Ridley, a long-time monetarist, became Financial Secretary to the Treasury, Norman Fowler became Social Services Secretary, Nigel Lawson became Energy Secretary, and Lady Young, leader of the Lords.

Strategically those appointments were well timed to tip the scales against the wets at the 1981 Conservative conference.[52] Mrs Thatcher made an aggressive defence of her policies. As a Conference performance it resembled James Callaghan's 1976 speech when the Labour conference was told a number of honest truths very bluntly.[53] Indeed, Mrs Thatcher's style was remarkably similar to that used by Callaghan in 1976. She argued:

We are dealing with one of the most complex and sensitive problems of our time. Neither rhetoric nor compassion is enough. There have been many voices in the past few weeks calling on us to spend our way back towards a higher level of employment, and to cut interest rate at the same time. It is a familiar treatment and it has been tried by many different governments these past thirty years. In the early days it worked well enough. In the 1950s a few million pounds of what we learned to call 'reflation' earned a swift reward in jobs and output. But as time went on the dose required grew larger; and the stimulus achieved grew less. By the 1960s it was needing hundreds of millions of extra spending to lift some hundreds of thousands of our people back into employment. By the 1970s we found that after thousands of extra millions had been spent we still had unemployment at levels which ten or twenty years ago would have been unthinkable.

The trick has been tried too often. The people, as earners and consumers, had rumbled what the government was doing to their money. They took that into account in their wage demands, so all the extra money went into wages and prices and not into more jobs. And so, today, if we were to heed the calls to add another thousand million pounds to our plans for spending, we might, thereby, create an extra 50,000 jobs in two years' time. And even those would be all too swiftly cancelled out by the loss of other jobs in private industry as the result of what we had done. For a good chunk of the higher taxes and the higher interest rates needed to find the money for the extra spending would come from the tills of every business in the land. Ah, but we are told, then don't put up the taxes or the interest rates; put them down instead. In other words, print the money. That way I must tell you, lies the collapse of trust in sterling both at home and abroad; the destruction of the savings of every family. It leads to suitcase money and penury as the sole reward for thrift. That is not what this Government was elected to do.[54]

A similarly defiant message was delivered to Parliament in response to the Opposition's censure motion on 28 October, scorning the Labour party's proposals as leading to financial crisis and renewed inflation. By the end of 1981 the government had established its credibility in putting inflation control as its permanent economic objective, but a growing political worry was the implementation of tax cuts rightly regarded as being electorally popular. The March 1981 budget had raised taxation substantially, so when the opportunity presented itself in late 1981 in the form of increased government revenue from the sale of North Sea assets and a falling level of public spending as a share of national output, the political opportunity was too tempting to resist. Moreover, the government needed to recover its popularity following the victory of Mrs Shirley Williams in the Crosby by-election in November 1981, when a Conservative majority of 19,272 had been reversed to a 5,289 SDP majority.

Accordingly, in March 1982, against a background of optimistic predictions of 7 per cent inflation by March 1983 (which turned out to be a pessimistic prediction), Sir Geoffrey presented a budget injecting £1.3 billion back into the economy.

Personal income tax allowances were raised by 14 per cent—2 percent more than required to compensate for inflation—and the higher rate thresholds and tax bands increased. Excise duties were raised only in line with inflation, and while the budget was far from the reflation advocated by many, it did represent a political appreciation of the unpopularity of high taxation. It was a budget aimed at the opinion polls, without abandoning the centrality of anti-inflation policy. As Sir Geoffrey put it in his speech:

Thanks to last year's budget, public borrowing has gone down as a percentage of gross domestic product, giving us interest rates lower than they would otherwise have been. In the six months following the budget, our rates were on average four points below American and French levels, and on a par with German rates, in spite of the difference between German and British levels of inflation. And output started rising from the middle of the year. Inflation has been almost halved since the spring of 1980. It should be in single figures during this year, and lower still in 1983. Productivity has been rising sharply. In manufacturing industry last year, output per man rose by about 10 per cent.

Lower pay increases combined last year with fast productivity growth, meant that unit labour costs in manufacturing rose hardly at all. Our performance was comparable with Germany and Japan, and better than all other major competitors. And exports were rising again by the end of 1981. In the last four months, their value and volume was well up on a year earlier. Business surveys, and most economic forecasts, point to a further rise over the next year. In the economy as a whole we now expect output to grow by 1 per cent in 1982 and by rather more in 1983. This gives the lie to all those who argued, not least at the time of last year's budget, that our policies were foredoomed. The recovery that we foresaw, and worked for, is now taking place. My aim in this budget is to nurture and help sustain it.[55]

Following the budget the economic indicators continued to move in the government's favour. Public borrowing turned out to be lower than expected; the May money supply figures showed the government to be on target; inflation fell to single figures in May for the first time in more than three years, and Geoffrey Howe told the Commons in July that a gradual recovery had begun and was expected to continue. Moreover, the Falklands War had revived government popularity[56] and in June the Conservatives won the Merton, Mitcham and Morden by-election from the SDP incumbent Mr Bruce Douglas-Mann with an impressive 4,274 majority. By September Sir Geoffrey was forecasting 6.5 per cent inflation by 1983, and the fall in inflation and booming North Sea oil revenues encouraged speculation of a March 1983 tax-cutting budget. In October 1982 the Chancellor, somewhat uncharacteristically confident, spoke of Britain entering a new phase of low inflation, as the month's figures showed inflation at 7.3 per cent, and most significantly, prices actually falling between August and September.

The November 1982 mini budget confirmed the optimistic mood—despite the fall in sterling, which was much appreciated by manufacturing industry but which held long-term implications for inflation control. National Insurance Surcharge was cut by 1 per cent, economic growth of 1.5 per cent and 5 per cent inflation predicted for 1983 and overpayments of social security benefits clawed back. On public spending the Chancellor declared that for the first time since 1977 the annual review had not led to an increase in planned spending which was kept within the figure of the 1982 White Paper. Nevertheless, tight control over nationalised industry borrowing would remain.

By the time of the 1983 budget, electoral considerations were scarcely suppressed. The inflation success was evident and widely trumpeted by the government. In January the inflation rate was at a thirteen-year low of 5.4 per cent, and Norman Tebbit stated that the government 'is set to be the first in over twenty years to achieve in office a lower average increase in prices than that of its predecessor'.[57] The February Public Expenditure White Paper opened the clear possibility of a tax-cutting budget by announcing that public spending in 1983–84 would be £500 million less than planned the previous autumn following a £1.7 billion shortfall in 1982–83. On 15 March 1983 Sir Geoffrey Howe presented his last budget. Not surprisingly *The Times* headline of 'Election flavour budget aims for everyman' summed up the response.[58] Income tax thresholds were increased, releasing 1.75 million people from tax altogether, mortgage tax-relief limit was raised to £30,000, child benefits raised, and excise duties increased broadly in line with inflation in a package injecting £1.7 billion back into the economy. This modest boost—although bitterly disappointing to the reflationists—was accompanied by figures showing industrial and manufacturing production at a two-year high amid widespread talk of a sustainable economic recovery.

Unlike other Chancellors who have only been vindicated by hindsight, for example Peter Thorneycroft, Sir Geoffrey had the satisfaction in his last budget of announcing the success in reducing inflation which he had steadfastly aimed for since May 1979. In his speech he could rightly claim that:

Inflation was on a rising trend when we came to office. It peaked at some 22 per cent in 1980. The reduction since then has been dramatic with retail price inflation now down to 5 per cent. The benefits of this transformation are felt throughout the country—it results from the firmness and consistency of the policies we have pursued in the past four years. We shall not change course. Downward pressure on inflation will be maintained. With the lower exchange rate some check in our progress now is unavoidable.

In the fourth quarter of this year inflation in retail prices may for a time be running at about 6 per cent, a little above what it is now, but still substantially below its level of a year ago. And it seems likely that the rate of increase of the GDP deflator—which is a measure of prices across the whole economy—will continue to fall, from 7 per cent in 1982–83 to 5 per cent next year. The trend of rising inflation that appeared irresistible has been decisively broken. We are now certain to be the first Government for a quarter of a century to achieve a lower average level of inflation than did its predecessor.

In the next Parliament it will be our purpose to do even better.[59]

That next Parliament was merely a few months away, and during the election campaign the May inflation figures showed inflation at 4 per cent, the lowest for fifteen years. The overall record on inflation control is the single most impressive economic achievement of the first Thatcher administration. Moreover, it was achieved without resort to the incomes-policy delusion and in spite of tremendous pressure from the wets, both inside and outside the Cabinet, to abandon the strategy and reflate. These two facets of the government's inflation record deserve further consideration.

THE QUESTION OF PAY CLAIMS

As previously mentioned in Chapter 2, the Thatcher administration was determined to dismantle the corporatist incomes policy approach to the question of pay claims. The incomes policy approach of flat-rate or percentage increases for all, irrespective of productivity, market forces, of labour supply and demand, profitability, efficiency or merit was officially repudiated. This clear rejection of incomes policy corporatism—and the trade union co-operation it implied—did not mean that the government had no policy on pay claims. In an economy with such a large public sector the government, as the ultimate paymaster, cannot be indifferent to public sector pay claims, and the Thatcher government was particularly tough in not sanctioning pay rises which broke either cash limits or which bore no relation to the supply and demand for labour at the existing pay rate. In effect, this flexible approach is the antithesis of the across-the-board mentality of incomes policy corporatism. Thus as one senior Treasury official put it:

the cash limits approach was not the sort of thing people had in mind by incomes policy. You forced people to live within cash limits and you have to make the pay bill come inside those limits. The benefit of not having an incomes policy is that we didn't get the amalgamation of costs of paying back increases for earlier apparent success. The absence of that meant there was no build-up of pressure from that direction and the government could stay out of that sort of involvement.[60]

The government's early policy was made more difficult by the refusal to disavow the 1979 election pledge to respect the Clegg comparability awards, which continued into 1980 dispensing wage rises with regard to matters totally irrelevant to such crucial criteria as labour supply and demand. Moreover, as Lord Thorneycroft recalled, 'with Clegg there was no vestige of connection between comparability and anything the Conservative party stands for. But we had Clegg signed sealed and delivered and we should have had that battle in the days of Opposition'.[61] One Cabinet minister disagreed commenting that 'I wanted to scrap Clegg from the start'.[62] According to one junior minister, 'the Clegg decision was a catastrophe. Public sector pay went straight off the deep end'.[63]

As inflation reached nearly 22 per cent in mid 1980, so pay claims roughly kept pace. Water workers settled for 21.4 per cent, power workers for 19 per cent, Post Office workers for 15 per cent, Rail unions for 20 per cent, white-collar civil servants for 18.75 per cent, doctors and dentists for 31 per cent, teachers for 25 per cent, bank employees for 29 per cent and agricultural workers for between 19 and 24 per cent. However, Talbot car workers settled for 5.5 per cent, BL workers for between 5 and 10 per cent and many private sector workers for equally small increases. In May 1980 Sir Geoffrey Howe had argued that 'It is for everyone involved in pay bargaining to decide whether their role is to make that task longer and harder, or quicker and easier. Moderation in pay demands is not doing a favour to the Government, but helping those who work in the industry to keep their employment and to prosper'.[64]

However, by July 1980 the public sector pay bill was being augmented by 40 million with each percentage point on pay settlements thus threatening public expenditure programmes previously budgeted for. A 6 per cent pay rise for the 1980–81 wage round was thus written into the cash limits as a rough approximation of total pay costs. However, the 6 per cent did not operate as a 'norm' or 'target' and was not advanced as a political virility symbol as had been Mr Callaghan's ill-fated 5 per cent.[65] Explaining the government's policy, Mrs Thatcher made this clear with regard to local authority spending. When questioned in the Commons Mrs Thatcher said:

The government has no locus in the negotiations. They are conducted between the firemen and the local authorities, and the government has no standing. The Government comes in in two ways only—first by deciding the total increase in the total pay bill for the local authorities and secondly in those duties of the Home Secretary through the Fire Inspection Officer about the numbers in the fire service. Otherwise, the matter is wholly one for the local authorities. Last year when it came to the Rate Support Grant, the government fixed a cash limit of 13 per cent. No one called that an incomes policy. It wasn't. This year the government has fixed the cash limit on the pay bill of 6 per cent. That isn't an incomes policy either. How the local authorities allocate that 6 per cent is a matter for them, as it was a matter for them how they allocated the 13 per cent. It has not and never has been a pay limit.

Consultations took place with the local authorities and the government took the decision that all that the ordinary people of this country could afford to contribute to the increased local authority pay bill was 6 per cent.[66]

Equally emphatic was Employment Secretary Jim Prior who declared that 'What we are doing is to set out assumptions about how the wages bill should rise over the coming year. There is no question of the government setting a single flat-rate pay norm. There are no criminal penalties for failing to observe it, nor penalties of the kind devised by the Labour government to police their norms'.[67] Similarly, one junior minister commented that:

'the difference between cash limits and incomes policy is that with the former you have to trade-off remuneration and employment as in the private sector and make the bargaining like that in the private sector. That is completely different to an enforced incomes policy. We avoided the Commissions of Enquiry approach that had previously snatched defeat from the jaws of victory.[68]

Those who thought that government pay-claims policy was to impose an incomes policy in all but name were thus to be disappointed. With the exception of one or two highly publicised disputes, such as the Civil Service strikes, there was no repetition of a Winter of Discontent (as had been widely forecast) and the 6 per cent figure did not emerge as a 'norm'. In the private sector many pay deals were very low or non-existent as the recession began to bite, as the CBI pay databank survey in August 1981 revealed.[69] Without resorting to the incomes-policy alternative, pay rises were cut in half between June 1980 and 1981 and in the public sector, as Table 1 shows, a wide diversity of actual settlements was evident in contrast to any blanket across the board award.

For the 1981–82 pay round the government adopted the same flexible approach except that the cash limit anticipation on public sector pay was set at 4 per cent. Again, explaining the rationale of the policy the Treasury statement argued that 'The pay factor does not imply that all public service pay increases will or should be 4 per cent. Some may be less and some may be more. There is no automatic entitlement to any particular pay

Table 1: *Settlements in the 1980–81 pay round*

Number	Group	Settlement (%)
Public Services		
1,000,000	Local authority manuals	7·5
540,000	Local authority white collar	7·3
530,000	White-collar civil servants	7·3
470,000	Teachers	7·5
400,000	Nurses	6·0
319,000	Armed forces	10·3
270,000	Hospital ancillaries	7·5 (over 15 mths)
140,000	Industrial civil servants	7·5
120,000	Police	13·2
30,000	Firemen	18·8 ('comparability' deal)
17,000	Ambulancemen	7·5 (over 15 mths)
Public Sector		
225,000	Coalminers	13·0 (over 10 mths)
180,000	Railwaymen	11·0 (two-stage deal)
96,000	Power workers	13·0
73,000	BL	6·8 (plus productivity)
70,000	Steel workers	7·0 (after 6 mths freeze)
50,000	British Airways	8·0 (after 3 mths freeze)
42,000	Gas workers	12·7
32,000	Water workers	13·0

increase; each must be justified on its merits'.[70] The repudiation of automatic entitlement increases—central to incomes policy corporatism—was significant in that this was already a fact of life for many in the profit-orientated private sector. A similar stress on flexibility was made by the Prime Minister, who told the Commons that a 'comprehensive incomes policy was not a practicable possibility in our society. In other societies it had happened only with direction of labour and the extinction of freedom'.[71]

As with the 1980–81 pay round, that for 1981–82 did not produce uniform, imposed increases. Nor did a wave of strikes result, despite occasional threatening talk by a few union leaders. In 1981–82 over 70 per cent of all public sector workers received more than 4 per cent cash-limit anticipation. The police settled for 10.3 per cent, teachers for 6 per cent, doctors, dentists and civil servants for between 5 and 6 per cent, water workers for 9.1 per cent and nationalised industry chairmen for 6 per cent. In the private sector the CBI reported in June 1982 a level of settlements in manufacturing industry averaging only 7 per cent; engineering manual workers settled for 5 per cent and some workers had no increase at all to save jobs threatened by the recession.

For 1982–83 the government set the cash-limit anticipation level at 3.5 per cent, brushing aside with confidence the 'ritual incantations' of trade union opposition. Mr Tebbit pointed out that with low pay settlements had also come the rejection by workers of union leaders' strike calls, increasing productivity, and an all-time low level of industrial disputes. In the debate on the Queen's Speech Mrs Thatcher stated that there could be no surer vote of confidence in the government's economic policies than that for the first time for more than a decade trade union negotiators were willing to put their signatures to pay deals which were to last for two or even three years. Despite what was regarded as a victory for the water workers—a 10 per cent settlement following a strike—other pay deals still showed signs of decline, and in April 1983 it was reported that the rise in average earnings was the lowest for five years. Public sector settlements were low and the CBI reported a 5.6 per cent average in manufacturing industry.

The Thatcher government's overall record on pay claims policy is one of sustained success. Without a formal incomes policy, without corporatism, norms and artificial restraints pay settlements had been brought to low levels undreamed of by incomes policy advocates. Critics who had maintained that free collective bargaining would result in a free-for-all spiral of increasing wage costs had been proved decisively wrong. Moreover industrial disputes were at their lowest levels since the 1940s largely because the unnecessary strikes caused by pay norms and restraints had been avoided.[72] These successful conclusions marked a fundamental change in economic behaviour brought about by the Thatcher government. It is inescapable to mention the contrast between the end of the Heath government and the end of the first Thatcher

administration. The repudiation of incomes policy corporatism
had proved even more successful than long-term opponents of
incomes policy had predicted.

BATTLE WITH THE WETS

The single-minded pursuit of low inflation by the Thatcher
government brought about a fundamental division of opinion
within the Conservative Cabinet, backbench MPs and the party
itself. The conflict between the political monetarists, or dries,
and the left-wing Conservatives, or wets, was a marked feature
of the whole of the period from 1979 to 1983. The ideological
disputes which had to only a limited extent surfaced in
Opposition now became central not only to policy
determination but to the nature of the modern Conservative
party itself. At no time since the 1940 confidence vote which led
to Neville Chamberlain's resignation had the Conservative
party been so divided. The inter-party disagreements during the
1956 Suez crisis were dwarfed by the scale and persistence of the
ideological war during the first Thatcher administration. One
prominent Cabinet wet recalled that 'the right wing smelt blood
and with Mrs Thatcher they got tacit support from No. 10. Time
after time we were told you've had twenty years in charge, now
it's our turn. I strongly disagreed with the policy strategy but
the PM had a remarkable grasp on government—there was no
faltering from day one'.[73]

During 1980 the divisions in the Cabinet and party became
blatantly obvious. As unemployment rose so the critics who had
never believed in monetarist remedies of whatever description,
pressed for 'reflationary', 'pragmatic' measures to reflect 'One
Nation, compassionate Conservatism'. Ian Aitken in *The
Guardian* put it that the wets:

believe that the party will store up serious trouble for itself if it fails to
respond to the social problems created by mass unemployment. A
rigid adherence to the present policy will prove disastrous, they
believe, and they are urging their colleagues to accept that the broad
basis of the Government's strategy can only be saved if ministers are
willing to bend. 'I always thought politics was the art of the possible'
said one. At the moment we are pursuing the art of the impossible.[74]

Yet the wets' position was not a strong one. They lacked a coherent alternative strategy and a political appeal. As Riddell has argued:

Almost by definition, they gave only a series of ad hoc responses. Moreover, as Mrs Thatcher's earlier quotations noted, they did not disagree with the need for a change of direction in policy. Their concern was about the pace of change. So their criticisms and suggestions seemed limp in the face of the certainty and confidence of the Thatcherites. Moderation was not a strong rallying cry.[75]

The electoral angle was also significant. Many wets believed, as Terence Higgins openly declared, that high unemployment would lead to electoral defeat and that the party must be, above all, a party of government. In September 1980 Cabinet conflict was echoed by Edward du Cann, the Chairman of the 1922 Committee, and further controversy emerged at the 1980 Brighton conference. Mr Heath in a veiled attack (compared to later conference performances) told BBC's television programme *Panorama* that the government should not rely on the control of the money supply as the single means of economic management. He argued that 'the essential thing is to keep the right balance between the different aspects of economic policy, which of course means that you have to take into account what happens to unemployment. If the public is upset about unemployment then they won't give you their support in the other things you want'.[76] Similarly, later in October Mr Heath attacked the high exchange rate of the pound, a common criticism by industry of government economic policies. By 5 November Mr Heath was describing government policy as 'catastrophic', bitterly commenting that 'people are recognising the merits of the last Conservative government compared with the catastrophic things they see happening to them today'.[77]

Mr Heath's attacks at least were expected and, given the antagonism between Mr Heath and the Prime Minister, the latter could ride the storm without undue worry. One wet backbencher recalled that 'we on the liberal wing didn't have a leader, Ted was carrying out a vendetta'.[78] However, the same could not be said of Geoffrey Rippon's remarkable attack on government policy in the Commons. A former member of Mr

Heath's Cabinet, he asked, referring to public borrowing and the money supply, 'will you agree that the reason why both are rising so sharply and that public borrowing is so high and the cost of unemployment is so high is because interest rates are so high? Are we not in danger of creating a society in which moneylending is the only profitable venture?' [79] The question provoked a major split and Mr Rippon repeated his criticisms on television a few days later, describing the government with an interesting mix of metaphors, as being like 'motorway madness' and the 'Gadarene swine'. Moreover, as the tensions heightened within the Conservative party, Sir Harold Wilson openly predicted that Mrs Thatcher would be 'ditched' as leader and 'it will be as though she's never been. She will become a non-person'. Indeed, there had been private talk by Conservative wets about such a scenario. Thus one backbench wet recalled that 'It's true that had the Falklands not happened she may have gone. The men in dark suits would have called to see her. I wouldn't have ruled out a 1940-style rebellion'.[80] Mrs Thatcher's position was strong constitutionally as Prime Minister in an era of prime ministerial government, but in the Conservative party her hold was less secure.

The Cabinet wets now began a concerted attack on the way that the key personnel of monetarists were preparing budget policy and effectively bypassing the full Cabinet. In the run-up to the 1981 deflationary budget the Cabinet wets tried, unsuccessfully, to influence policy formation by a mixture of private lobbying and leaking. However, when the scale of the budget's deflation was actually first made clear in Cabinet on the morning of 10 March the wets were horrified. They had no sympathy for the anti-inflationary policies, preferring reflation to attempt to reduce unemployment. Yet they had been outflanked and faced the choice of either rebellion or acquiescence. As Wapshott and Brock described it:

They also took their own counsel, for resignation in any party, but particularly the Conservative party, is rarely forgiven quickly. That option might mean the beginning of a frustrating political career of internal opposition, waged from the back benches, or the end of a career altogether. If all three resigned at once and persuaded some others to join them, they would be able to form a significant rump around which opposition to the government's economic policy could be rallied. But that would be open rebellion against the Prime Minister. As she had guessed, they decided to stay. They felt impotent to change the budget proposals, so no immediate good would come of resignations, and opposition from within the Cabinet was more effective—and more comfortable—than opposition from outside. It was a Thatcher victory and she celebrated it by sharing it; she allowed the extent of the dissent within the Cabinet to be conveyed to the press, in order to make the point that few government ministers were opposed to the measures. At the same time, the leak looked as if it had come from the three principal critics, making them appear to be disloyal as well as defeated. It was a clever political coup.[81]

As one backbench MP put it, 'Cabinet colleagues were loyal, given the pressure they were under. They didn't feel they were able to contribute. They had to like it or lump it'.[82] Similarly, one Cabinet minister recalled that 'in 1981 we had taken some hard measures and were not able to see the results yet and there were those who had profound differences with Mrs Thatcher. However, so much of the argument had shifted on to her ground'.[83] Another minister, later sacked by Mrs Thatcher, simply bemoaned that 'it was an unhappy Cabinet 1979–81, I don't miss being in this government'.[84]

It was in the Commons rather than the Cabinet that the Prime Minister faced the greatest challenge. A backbench rebellion over petrol tax increases was followed by the widely publicised defection of Christopher Brocklebank-Fowler, the MP for Norfolk North-West, to the fledgling Social Democrats. Other dissenting MPs were prepared only to attack the budget, and Peter Walker, whilst counselling against defections to the SDP publicly and pointedly stated that there should be less concern with economic theories and more stress on compassion. In May the Commons rebels against derv tax successfully defeated the government, and Geoffrey Howe had to halve the 20p increase in duty. However, this defeat, as one backbench MP correctly recalled, was 'more a call from the backwoodsmen, the shires, than a call from the wets'[85] The pressures on the government to inaugurate the predicted U-turn had been great, but the political-monetarist strategy was still intact. Furthermore, many of the potential dissidents among the 1979 intake of MPs were to climb on the ministerial ladder. One backbench wet recalled that 'we started the Blue Chips—15 or so of us—to have an influence on government, but I hadn't realised how much people were prepared to temporise and fudge to get up the political ladder. Backbenchers are at the margin and it's extraordinarily difficult to have any effect. It takes two years to get sufficient confidence to challenge the accepted wisdom'.[86] Another backbench wet bemoaned that 'we Blue Chips sat around and said there will be a Winter of Discontent but it never actually came. We thought that we'd get a Winter of Discontent followed by a Summer of Discontent on the streets as unemployment went up. But the figures went up like a fruit machine and it never came 1, $1\frac{1}{2}$, 2, $2\frac{1}{2}$, 3 million'.[87]

Although the front line of the battle between dries and wets was in the Cabinet, it was attacks from outside that caused Mrs Thatcher and her supporters the greatest worry. Unlike the Cabinet wets, who were still to a large extent restricted by the conventions of collective Cabinet responsibility, Mr Heath was not. During 1981 his attacks on government economic policy increased. In July the strategy was a 'disaster' and he advocated a return to 'consensus politics'.[88]. He pledged further opposition, 'just going on telling the country home truths which the great majority of people recognise. I shall not be stopped in the House of Commons and I shall not be stopped by No. 10'.[89] However, as one MP put it:

the relationship between the wets and Mr Heath was an interesting one. Ted used such funny tactics—he only once attended a backbench committee and then he sat at the back six rows behind everyone else. It fitted in with his behaviour as leader towards the party. He sought to pursue his campaign at party conferences giving the odd snide TV interview beforehand or a private lunch for selected political correspondents. He spread his venom that way.[90]

One junior minister thought that 'rebellions were quite disproportionately in Cabinet compared to the backbenchers. You often felt that the wets were to be found in the ranks of government ministers. Heath's role was helpful to the government because whenever wets mustered for rebellion, Heath would say something outrageous and they'd go back to their shells'.[91] Reg Prentice recalled that 'on most matters I was on the side of the PM and critical of the wets. I felt they didn't have an alternative strategy and that in a way it was a tribute to our policies that we were unpopular'.[92] Similarly, Leon Brittan thought that 'Cabinet ministers could raise a subject if they disagreed, but those who were unhappy didn't have the capacity to put an alternative. The wets just didn't have a strategy'.[93]

Following the September 1981 reshuffle, which sacked three Cabinet wets—including Ian Gilmour, who claimed that the majority of the Cabinet opposed Mrs Thatcher's policies—Mr Heath launched a further attack at the 1981 party conference, calling for a complete change of direction. His criticisms of the government's 'dreary path' were echoed by Norman St John Stevas, who had been sacked from the Cabinet in January 1981, and who told a conference meeting that:

to subordinate politics to economics and within that thraldom to select a single economic end, the abatement of inflation, as the one to be pursued regardless of all other values and considerations is not only to turn politics into a gamble on ground which since the war has been marked not by success but even worse, it is to subscribe to a false and distorted view of human nature...who would have thought that we could live to see the day when economic materialism could deck itself out in Tory colours and claim to be not only the authentic voice of Conservatism but its only legitimate manifestation, yet this is precisely the theme of what has been arrogantly styled 'The New Conservatism'.[94]

However, one Cabinet minister recalled that 'the party at conference was animated with impatience at the wets and the activists lined up with the party leadership'.[95]

Whatever would have been the consequences of adopting the wets' alternative approach, the abandonment of the reduction of inflation would have been the first casualty. Nor did the wets have a convincing response to Sir Geoffrey's argument that there was not a choice between measures to combat inflation and measures to combat unemployment. Turning directly to Mr Heath, the Chancellor quoted the 1970 manifesto 'in implementing all our policies the need to curb inflation will come first, for only then can our broader strategy succeed', which went to the heart of the internal battle in the Conservative party. Consequently, as Sir Geoffrey logically argued regarding the 1970 commitment, 'if it was true then, as it was, when inflation was half as high, it is twice as true today',[96] One former Cabinet minister thought that 'the split 1979–83 was not wholly ideological—there was a lot of personality in it too. Dissentients like Pym don't put forward refutations of monetarism which threaten socialism head on. That was the strength of (the government's) approach. No one can protect socialism against it. Gilmour was intellectually pathetic, his arguments don't meet socialism head on'.[97]

The battle continued over the December 1981 mini budget when Mr Heath claimed that there had never been any practical or intellectual justification for monetarism and Ian Gilmour led a rebellion of fourteen MPs against the government's spending plans. One dry backbencher recalled that 'the wets really lost out all along the line. The standard pattern annually was to get the pre-budget stories into the press about their threatened rebellion. The next stage was apprehension about the budget and the third stage was to threaten a major revolt. But the wets could only win if they established an alliance with one of the other groups in the party, as with the derv rebellion in 1981 with the agricultural lobby'.[98] Similarly, a Cabinet dry thought that 'summer of '81 was a slightly awkward period with some flapping going on, though the cooler and older heads were less likely to get up and make speeches. The September '81 reshuffle marked an implicit step because from then the Cabinet pushed together and operated much more as a team'.[99] Patrick Jenkin, recalling the reshuffle, noted that 'no member of the Cabinet actually resigned, 1979–83, although there was some antipathy towards the PM. The critics like Gilmour were pushed, they didn't resign'.[100] Another senior minister thought that 'before the '81 reshuffle I was aware—as someone who spoke at the end of Cabinet—of a balance of views that was too close for comfort. Norman St John Stevas, for example, was much too indiscreet about colleagues and did not get a proper balance between representing the Commons as a whole and getting the government's case across as Leader of the House'.[101]

The rebels' criticisms were also, arguably, accorded greater relevance and respect because of the internal turmoils of the Labour Opposition, which had moved so far to the left to have lost political legitimacy. The threat of the SDP and the Liberals also was a factor. The Tory wets' policies were remarkably similar to the 'moderate' Keynesianism of the Alliance (as it was to become), and many wets saw such an approach as electorally persuasive. However, this kind of approach is an illusion. On the economic side the inescapable truth is, as Sir Leo Pliatsky has argued:

A policy of reflation through higher public expenditure is inevitably bound up with the question of the limits on government borrowing. Some of the supporters of an expansionist policy tend to talk of putting the nation's savings to use, or some such phrase. But it is a critical question how much higher an already high PSBR could be pushed up without recourse to money creation by borrowing from the banking system and without raising interest rates, which would run counter to the expansionary objective'.[102]

Similarly, in terms of Conservative philosophy, as Patrick Jenkin recalled, 'the One Nation approach was never about *consensus*; it was representing everyone in the nation. We've never been less of a class based party than we were 1979–83'.[103]

On the political side the wets' argument was equally unconvincing. In countering such thinking Archie Hamilton, a Thatcher loyalist and PPS to the Transport Secretary, addressed a remarkable open letter in *The Times*:

Dear Wet Colleague,

I thought I would write to try to cheer you up as you seem to have been very nervous and unhappy lately. On the surface, things do not look too rosy. The economy seems to be taking longer to turn around than anyone expected. Unemployment remains stubbornly high. The SDP has done remarkably well despite the absence of any very visible policies. Your seat looks increasingly vulnerable, and it may be that you are hoping, for the first time in your life, that the Labour vote will hold up in your constituency, and so keep out the SDP at the next election.

You have suggested to me that we steal the clothes of the SDP and watch the voters return. I can quite see the temptation to make a dash for the apparent safety of what you call the centre. But the SDP have no clothes. They appeal to the electorate because they have not yet settled their policies. When they do, they will suffer an inevitable alienation as many people find they disagree with them.

In any case, drifting towards the position of the Opposition parties is hardly likely to do us any good at the polls. If we adopt the policies of the Opposition, we're endorsing their claim to govern and inviting the voters to follow our example and support them.[104]

Whatever the merits of Mr Hamilton's letter—and with hindsight his argument proved accurate—it was the Conservative wets that were proving more troublesome to the government than the official Opposition. This was demonstrated in February 1982 when a pessimistic speech by Francis Pym was the most embarrassing thing Mr Foot could produce with which to attack the government.

However, it was arguably General Galtieri who came to Mrs Thatcher's aid. Following the Falklands crisis and war, which began in April 1982, the Conservative dissidents remained largely silent—Jim Prior's coded plea for 'some additional [economic] activity' being one exception. Cyril Townsend recalled that 'before the Falklands she was the most unpopular Prime Minister since the war, and then the Falklands came along. She is the luckiest lady alive because of the Falklands and Labour's problems'.[105] At the 1982 conference the mood of unity was apparent and the 'resolution' of the Falklands campaign the dominant feature. Nevertheless, Peter Walker did criticise the rise in unemployment and the one-fifth slump in manufacturing output. He advocated: above all refiring the engines of economic growth. We accept too readily that stagnation must be our lot in the 1980s. It leads to some esoteric and unhelpful exercises in how to scrap part of our welfare system in order to live within our means. The Tory tradition, however, is to produce the economic goods so that we can afford the welfare services of a civilized society'.[106]

The major battles between the key dries and wets had now been fought, and between the end of 1982 and the 1983 June election, as the inflation rate success became more evident, the wets were less prominent. True, Sir Ian Gilmour made a strong attack on the 1983 budget, despite its small tax-cutting and reflationary flavour, as doing nothing to reduce unemployment, but by then the government's euphoria at the lowest inflation for fifteen years and the disintegration of Labour's challenge, temporarily at least, put the internal Conservative disputes into the background. One backbench dry thought the wets' defeat had come earlier, arguing that 'when the 100 backbenchers sent the letter to Mrs Thatcher before 1982 budget supporting her, it pulled the rug from beneath the wets' feet. Mrs Thatcher, I'm told, waved it at anyone who expressed fears about how the backbenchers would act'.[107] Similarly, Michael Brown recalled that:

I was very conscious that Mrs Thatcher was anxious to keep in touch with the backbenchers. Ian Gow was the eyes and ears. If you mentioned anything to him you'd get a letter from the PM a couple of days or so later. I think the problem wasn't with the backbenchers but with the ministerial team, many of whom had not supported her in 1975'.[108]

One backbench wet thought that:

the PM didn't promote the far right—Winston Churchill would hang on her every word but he never had a job. Of my intake in '79 those promoted were from the pragmatic centre and none of the talent at the lower levels was from the right. But she's promoted her own men into Cabinet and left out Kenneth Clarke, Douglas Hurd, and Ken Baker, all of whom would have served in any other Tory Cabinet'.[109]

Despite their criticism of government policy, the wets lost the policy battle between 1979 and 1983. There was no U-turn. The middle-way consensus Toryism of Butler and Macmillan based on Keynesianism and corporatism was not reintroduced. The Heath government's U-turns were skilfully avoided. The Cabinet wets, for their initial numerical superiority, had been outmanoeuvred by the 'political monetarists'. Cabinet reshuffles had, in any case, strengthened the Prime Minister's hand as influential wets had been dismissed and replaced with Thatcher loyalists. In the Conservative party as a whole as the administration's term of office developed Mrs Thatcher became an electoral asset and the internal critics increasingly irrelevant. It can be argued that when inflation fell, as the Chancellor had intended, the wets had lost the intellectual battle as well.

4 Contemporary Conservatism and Unemployment

> We used to think that you could spend your way out of a recession and increase employment by cutting taxes and boosting spending. I tell you in all candour that the option no longer exists, and that insofar as it did ever exist, it only worked by injecting a bigger dose of inflation into the system.
>
> James Callaghan, 1976[1]

THE PRIOR YEARS

The issue of unemployment has long been a focus of Conservative economic and social thinking. In the post-war period, many Conservatives came to blame their 1945 election defeat on the 1930s association of Conservative rule with high unemployment, and consequently the party in the 1950s and beyond was eager to adopt Keynesian fine tuning and demand management. However, central to Mrs Thatcher's critique of the errors of the 1970–74 Heath government had been the overreaction to the one million unemployment threshold which had caused the abandonment of the 'Quiet Revolution' and the move leftwards to considerable state intervention.[2] Mrs Thatcher was as determined not to repeat the Heath mistake as the wets were not to reintroduce the old association in the electorate's mind of Conservative rule and mass unemployment. To many wets, believing there existed a trade-off, low unemployment was preferable to anything else including low inflation. Thus Ian Gilmour has argued, quite incorrectly, that 'the unemployed are the innocent casualties of the battle against inflation',[3] as if there was a choice or trade-off that governments could decide or predetermine.

The period from 1979 to 1983 therefore saw continuing re-examination of the nature of contemporary Conservatism as the unemployment figures moved steadily upwards both under Jim Prior and then Norman Tebbit as Employment Secretaries. In January 1980 the unemployment figure stood at 1.4 million and with further increases forecast Jim Prior launched the first of a number of palliatives provided by the Thatcher administration. He told the Commons that 'We are extending for a further year the job-release scheme, which opens up vacancies for unemployed workers by enabling older workers to leave their jobs early. The scheme will continue to be open to women aged fifty-nine, but for men who are not disabled the age of eligibility under the scheme will revert from sixty-two to sixty-four.'[4]

Such measures were soon deluged by the political outcry as the unemployment figures continued rising. For the Labour Opposition the problem was perfect for making political capital with maximum political emotion. Bruce Millan speaking in June 1980 was typical of Opposition ministers, warning Mr Prior that he was:

presiding over the biggest employment disaster since the 1930s and if you had a conscience at all you would resign from the Government because we are told you don't believe in its policies...The worsening employment figures are a deliberate and inevitable result of Government policy. They have not arisen as a side-effect of the main thrust of the Government's economic policies. They were inevitable right from the start, when the Government adopted their monetary policy. The Government is deliberately trying to squeeze inflation out of the economy by reducing output and increasing unemployment. What we have seen yesterday is only the start of the process and it is going to get worse'.[5]

Nevertheless, the percentage rate in June 1980 was only 10 per cent, leaving 90 per cent in work. Arguably, such figures did not represent a serious imbalance in the economy, although the gross figure 1,659,676 was the highest since the 1930s. It may also be argued that the excessive overmanning in manufacturing industry and much public service employment was not reflected in the official figures and that the inherited situation was therefore more perilous. As Walter Salomon has put it:

The present recession has clearly begun to cut into the chronic overmanning which has bedevilled our economy. My estimate is that taking the spectrum of private firms, nationalised industries and the public sector, overmanning before the government came to power could have been running at at least 15 per cent. If the present policies have only reduced this by, say, 4 per cent, then 1,006,000 'non-jobs' would have been eliminated from the system. The most recent figures available on labour productivity per man-hour show a rate of current annual increase of at least 10 per cent in the manufacturing sector. This figure supports my view.[6]

Mrs Thatcher when pressed for explanations for rising unemployment was rightly reluctant to blame herself. In July 1980 when a 1.9 million total was announced she argued that workers were pricing themselves out of jobs. She told Independent Television News that the key factor was how much workers demanded in pay claims, adding that 'If they take out more than the value of what they produce, we shall have increasing unemployment because we shall not be able to sell the goods'.[7] Moreover, she told the Commons that those in depressed areas should be willing to move to find work, a reasonable assumption made less practicable by Britain's feudal council-house rent system, which has always restricted labour mobility.

In November 1980 with the unemployment figure at 2.1 million, Jim Prior announced a £250 million 'new deal' for the young jobless who had been particularly swelling the official figures. The Manpower Services Commission which had initially been told to reduce its spending by £114 million in 1980 was to provide an extra 180,000 training or work experience places for sixteen and seventeen year olds next year in addition to the 260,000 already planned. The aim, Mr Prior said, would be to provide a place on the scheme for every young person unemployed before the Christmas of the year they leave school.

Help for the long-term unemployed was also announced. The Special Temporary Employment Programme would be replaced by a new scheme called the Community Enterprise Programme, which he pledged would 'continue for at least three years', though it would be subject to annual review. Essentially, such measures were political window-dressing aimed at countering Labour's objective to 'destroy at the ballot box...the party of unemployment'.[8] Mr Prior hinted at the electoral aspect himself in January 1981 when he spoke pessimistically about the long-term prospects. David Howell the Energy Secretary and then Thatcher loyalist also candidly stated that when recovery came 'It will be uneven. Areas of new prosperity will flourish. Areas of former prosperity will be bypassed. More money will go into advanced automated equipment; less into employing people in manufacturing industry'.

During 1981 there was a growing political outcry with each month's figures, including the TUC's 'People's march for jobs'. The August unemployment figure stood at 2,940,000 and followed another package from Mr Prior who had rightly argued that 'the underlying causes will not be solved by spending even more public money. It has been tried before and it has failed'.[9] However, while reflation was ruled out, the £500 million package involved weekly payments of £15 to firms for each employee under eighteen years old employed at under £40 or less per week, the establishment of twenty inner city training centres, the provision of an extra 110,000 places on the Youth Opportunities Programme (YOP), an additional £60 million to encourage 50,000 more youngsters to stay at school or college, and further government funds of £12 million for voluntary work under the Community Enterprise programme.

The jobs package was predictably ridiculed by the opposition and was also insufficient for the Tory wets. Mrs Thatcher adamantly told both groups in Parliament that reflation would accelerate inflation, leading to still higher unemployment. Recalling the Labour party's stance, Sir Keith Joseph noted that 'the Labour party were pathetic in the sense that they would not recognise reality and fought with a conservative—with a small 'c'—passion to keep all as it was. Callaghan, when we quoted what he'd said in 1976, and Foot said it was not Labour party policy. They jeered'.[10] The government's refusal to go further than palliative measures was confirmed by Trade Secretary John Biffen's remarks. Analysing the wider picture rather than the politically sensitive monthly figures, he noticed that:

unemployment has concealed a significant fall in the labour force of manufacturing industry, with considerable implications for future improvement in labour productivity. Overmanning has been replaced by unemployment, a change which is miserable in human terms in the short run but eventually carrying a potential for national advantage...But let no one suppose there is not a national advantage—always provided the government has the stamina to stick with the policy and the compassion to temper its sharp and personal effects.[11]

In looking at unemployment in such terms rather than as a function of the party battle at Westminster, Mr Biffen had performed a service to intelligent debate. Similarly, Lord Thorneycroft recalled that 'nothing would have altered the underlying fact that we had been grossly overmanned and we were in the worst position as the full force of the recession hit us'.[12] One Treasury official observed that 'I was surprised by the level of unemployment that resulted, but we got the profile of the level of output very close—productivity rose by so much more. The Cambridge group got the unemployment forecast right but were way out on output'.[13] A senior Treasury knight recalled that 'what happened was that industrialists ran for cover and couldn't borrow, so they had to get rid of labour and stocks. The discussion of policy, though, was never in terms of unemployment or the balance of payments'.[14] Samuel Brittan has also observed that:

The particular severity of the British unemployment problem was due to a combination of severe structural change and an ossified labour market. The British economy has had to adjust to (a) sharp fluctuations in energy prices which have made many processes and products obsolescent; (b) the drift in the most efficient location of many traditional manufacturing industries towards the newly industrialising countries; (c) the rapid reduction in inflation; (d) the effects of North Sea oil in crowding out non-oil exports; and (e) the long-delayed attack on overmanning. The first three were common to other industrial countries in varying degress the last two unique to Britain. They combined to produce very heavy manpower losses in manufacturing industry.[15]

By the time Mr Prior was replaced by Norman Tebbit as Employment Secretary in September 1981, the unemployment figures were still increasing, but the government's determination not to be panicked into a reflationary U-turn was still clear. As has been said, the Thatcher government had been right—and continued to be so—not to voluntarily take the blame for unemployment's rise. The pricing of workers out of jobs by high pay rises, skills mismatch, overmanning and restrictive practices, high levels of inflation compared to Britain's foreign competitors, strikes, bad management, labour immobility, the world recession, high taxation and low profitability had all contributed over a number of decades, to many different sorts of unemployment. Whatever the alternative solutions may suggest,[16] the Thatcher government was right not to believe that huge increases in public spending would have solved the problem. This was a view strongly held by Norman Tebbit, the Employment Secretary appointed in September 1981.

THE TEBBIT YEARS

By the time Norman Tebbit had become Employment Secretary he was already a hate-figure for the British left wing. He was a known supporter of tougher legislation against abuses of trade union power, a keen advocate of 'political monetarism' and, being from a modest social background with a career as an airline pilot, did not receive the deference the Left often paradoxically shows for Tory aristocrats. As the unemployment total continued to mount, Tebbit became a particular target of the Labour left, a position he actually seemed to relish. Although in private a civilised and humourous man, he seemed content in public to play up to the ogre image Labour had created.

In December 1981 Mr Tebbit unveiled another package of palliative measures as the gross unemployment total was just under 3 million. Every sixteen-year-old school-leaver would be guaranteed a year's basic industrial training from September 1983, aiming at a comprehensive system of apprenticeship provision. The YOP allowance was raised to £25 per week, 30,000 extra places were to be created on the Community Enterprise Programme for 1982–83, and the MSC was to develop an 'Open Tech' technical training programme. The proposals which were, according to Mr Tebbit, 'the most far reaching and ambitious set of proposals on training ever laid before Parliament', stressed that:

Our major competitors lay much greater emphasis on training young people than we do. In France and Germany 80 per cent or more of young people reaching minimum school-leaving age receive further education or training of some kind. In Britain in 1979 on the most favourable interpretation the figure was less than two-thirds.

Who has the responsibility to train? At the moment the position is muddled. Individual employers, local education authorities, joining negotiating bodies, industrial training bodies, the Manpower Services Commission and government departments are all involved.

...The young unemployed will remain a priority group. The Youth Opportunities Programme was introduced in 1978. Since then it has become clear that we need a full-scale training programme that provides for an increasing number and range of unemployed young people.

A new and better Youth Training Scheme should be introduced by the commission to cover all unemployed minimum age school-leavers by September 1983.[17]

But as usual in British politics it was the gross unemployment total, the politically significant total, though with little economic merit to it, which caused the greatest controversy. In January 1982 the three million unemployment threshold was passed amid a stormy reaction in the Commons. The Opposition, however, singularly failed to make political capital out of the fact. Labour was vulnerable throughout to the charge that it had no real alternative and that the policies it advocated had been tried before and found wanting. One Cabinet wet recalled that 'in debate after debate they never got it together. Geoffrey Goodman of the *Daily Mirror* said to me that it had tried to get a campaign on unemployment off the ground but had failed to do so'.[18] The consumer decided where jobs went, Mrs Thatcher told Michael Foot, adding with reference to the Opposition leader's tenure of the Employment portfolio in the Wilson government from 1974 to 1976 that 'Mr Foot got unemployment down temporarily at the cost of reflation which puts unemployment up later'.[19] Similarly, Mr Tebbit in the debate on the 3-million figure argued that 'when the

Conservatives came to office they had faced stored-up problems of poor industrial performance, years of stunted and inadequate growth in productivity and years of excessive growth in wages as compared to productivity. Contrary to what was implied by the economic illiteracy of Labour's plans for expansion, unlimited spending out of limited resources was a recipe for economic disaster, not recovery. There were no short cuts. Britain's industry and commerce must provide the goods and services the customer wanted at the price he could afford, or someone else would. Jobs would be created in Germany or Japan and lost in Britain. The signs were that the economy was growing and that the returns on the efforts and hardship were coming through. To throw that away in a wave of self-indulgence, mistaking that for constructive help, would be economic madness and disaster for both the 12.7 per cent unemployed and the 87.3 per cent employed alike. To the Labour Opposition, however, the £13 billion being spent on unemployment pay should have been used as a fund to finance long-term and secure jobs. This simplistic and naive remedy was to surface, equally unconvincingly, during the 1983 election campaign. One Cabinet minister recalled that 'there wasn't a lever in Whitehall marked "full employment" and another marked "unemployment" which we had deliberately pulled. I think we managed to get this across to the electorate'.[20] Another Cabinet minister, Patrick Jenkin, put it that 'there were a number of people who found themselves out of a job but who told me 'Maggie's right'. We went round factories that had multiplied productivity five times in three years. We succeeded in the end in winning the argument that unemployment would come down only if we were more competitive'.[21] Leon Brittan similarly recalled that 'I quoted in speeches that a constituent of mine had come to see me after being made redundant, complaining about the level of redundancy pay. He turned to me at the end and said, "It had to happen as there were so many of us not doing a proper job". People realised that unemployment wasn't inspired by monetarist governments or wicked employers—that perception was very widespread'.[22]

As well as the Opposition's criticisms, Mr Tebbit faced discontent from the Tory wets. In March 1982 thirteen Conservative MPs rebelled and voted to restore the 5 per cent that had been cut from unemployment benefit in 1980, supporting an Opposition clause during the report stage of the Social Security and Housing Benefits Bill. The rebels were led by Sir Ian Gilmour, whose style of aristocratic paternalism was far removed from Mr Tebbit's self-made attitudes of independence and self-reliance. In July the government's majority sank to only eight, from 291 to 283, after a further rebellion on the benefit cut.

Further palliative measures to offset the effects of unemployment were also forthcoming in July 1982. Mr Tebbit announced grants would be available to employers to give part-time work to those on the dole. The 'job splitting' scheme meant that 'the larger savings in benefit payments should mean a net saving in public expenditure'.[23] Moreover, special aid for the long-term unemployed would provide 130,000 temporary and part-time jobs to enable people to 'regain the dignity of a job, to remain in work, even on a part-time basis'.[24] Sir Geoffrey Howe also announced the creation of eleven new 'Enterprise Zones' to add to the existing eleven. Nevertheless, the Chancellor, characteristically pessimistic, conceded that 'unemployment on this scale is here for a long time. . .The scale of the thing is much larger than can be adjusted by government response. I think it is very important for the debate not to suggest that there is, lying around, some prescription or solution that, for some perverse reason, the government. . .is putting on one side'.[25] In August 1982 one in seven, 3,292,702 were signed on the unemployed register.

One sensible reform made by Mr Tebbit in October 1982 concerned the compilation of the aggregate unemployment total. The count was henceforth to be based on computerised records of those claiming benefit, instead of the numbers registered at employment offices. The new system, which enabled £13 million to be saved a year, could also more quickly identify those people who find jobs, so that the number counted would be more accurate. However, about 20,000 disabled people would be included in the figures for the first time. The net effect of these improvements was to remove about 100,000 from the aggregate, politically sensitive total. The Department of Employment had in any case, estimated that between 10 and 20 per cent of the registered jobless were not actually looking for work. In December 1982 the Economist Intelligence Unit in a wide-ranging survey found that 8 per cent of those unemployed were prepared to admit to receiving payment for casual work—a criminal offence.[26] The same report, incidentally, showed that only 38 per cent of the unemployed blamed the government for their plight, with 47 per cent blaming the world situation or nobody in particular.

During 1983, as the government consolidated its lead in the opinion polls prior to the general election, it was clear that the high unemployment total of over 3 million registered would not automatically lead to a Conservative defeat, as many, (including Conservative wets) had predicted only a couple of years previously. Even Michael Heseltine's statement that the armed forces were to offer voluntary training places for the young unemployed brought a mild Opposition rebuke instead of a 'conscription' outcry that may have been anticipated. As Mr Heseltine put it:

We have offered to sixteen year olds a guarantee of work experience at that age. Therefore there is no way in which they are going to be told there is only an opportunity in the armed services. It will be their choice, if rather than taking a civilian opportunity, they opt for an armed services opportunity. A very large number of them would like to do just that. I have been considering the role of the armed forces in the government's programme to provide training and work experience for unemployed school-leavers. The high quality of the training provided by our Armed Forces has convinced me that they should play a part.

I therefore propose to make available some 5,200 places for the young unemployed volunteering for such opportunities which will be on the same basis as the Youth Training Scheme. The precise number of places available in the first year will depend on the number of applications and the capacity of the Services training organisation. The young people will volunteer to join one of the Services on a twelve months engagement, part of which will be spent in formal training and the remainder in work experience. All volunteers will receive the same basic training as regular Sevicemen and women and some will go on to learn skills and trades.[27]

Whatever the value of such schemes, which will be discussed later in this chapter, the government had successfully diffused the unemployment issue as an electoral threat. Indeed, the 1983 Conservative manifesto proudly boasted that:

This government has an impressive record in helping the unemployed, who usually through no fault of their own, are paying the price of these past errors.

We have committed over £2,000 million this year to training and special measures for the unemployed. This is supported by substantial help for the European Community's Social Fund, amounting to over £250 million in 1982. As long as unemployment remains high, we shall maintain special measures of this kind, which bring effective help to many of those who have no job.

This year some 1,100,000 people are being trained or helped by the most comprehensive programme of its kind in Europe.

For the first time the new Enterprise Allowance Scheme offers many thousands of unemployed people the support they need, but previously could not get, while they start their own businesses. We will maintain special help for the long-term unemployed through the Community Programme, and for the older unemployed through early retirement schemes.[28]

Arguably, however, the greatest service done to the creation of real jobs by the first Thatcher government was in its refusal to reflate and bring about a temporary and insecure reduction in the aggregate total. As James Callaghan had once put it, 'that was the history of the last twenty years'. The Thatcher administration had shown itself determined to face economic realities and in doing so to accommodate contemporary Conservatism to economic change.

ALTERNATIVE REMEDIES

One particular aspect of the debate on how to reduce Britain's unemployment has been the question of numbers. As this account has shown, the politically sensitive number—which governments are naturally inclined to watch closely—is of dubious economic value as it aggregates in a misleading way many different types of unemployment. School-leavers, redundant steel-workers, housewives, unemployable chronic alcoholics, job changers, and so on are all lumped together and referred to by Opposition politicians as victims of government policy.[29] This has been as true for Conservative as for Labour Oppositions, and consequently, intelligent debate on the political level has been almost entirely replaced by party political point-scoring. Such political pressure forced the Heath government into a series of major U-turns, and the Thatcher government was, from the outset, determined to avoid repeating that experience.

The greatest objection to the Keynesian reflationary remedy to unemployment advanced by Labour, Liberal and SDP leaders between 1979 and 1983 relates directly to the numbers aspect. The inadequacy of such a remedy has already been argued in this account and evidence over thirty years or so has suggested that Keynesian reflation can only reduce unemployment temporarily in the short run before higher inflation damages the economy and leads eventually to a higher unemployment plateau. Keynesian reflation tends to treat unemployment as if it all stems from demand deficiency and is all of the same kind. The gross aggregate figure is central to the Keynesian remedy and hence is its central weakness. Reflation will not help specific types of unemployment and eventually may make them worse.

Reflation does not remove restrictive practices or slothful management; it does not price people into jobs; it does not assist the steel-worker or coal-miner whose industry or pits have become uneconomic compared to international competitors; it does not loosen the monopoly labour power of trade unions to force up wage costs; it does not help in the promotion of exports, which account for one-third of all production. Nor does reflation help either the unemployables or those who already moonlight. Moreover, the reflationary alternative fails to appreciate that the unemployed are not the same number of people chasing the same few jobs. Only one-third of all job vacancies, for example, are notified to Job Centres, according to the Department of Employment. Miller and Wood rightly argue that:

In spite of every difficulty in its way, the labour market continues to absorb people on a sufficient scale to belie the picture, widely assumed amongst journalists, broadcasters and politicians, of a massive, stagnant and expanding pool of permanently unemployed people. Even at the present time of high unemployment there remains a substantial flow into and out of employment. The flow statistics for unemployment and vacancies onto and off their respective registers are a better guide to the state of the labour market than any 'snap-shot' total of the unemployed. On 12 March 1981 for example, total vacancies outstanding were 97,000—a bare 3.8 per cent of the total unemployed. But the flow statistics tell a different story. In that month 348,000 people joined the unemployment register and 277,000 left it for new jobs, while 149,000 vacancies were notified and 150,000 were filled. This is a corrective to the popular misconception of nearly 3 million unemployed endlessly chasing only 100,000 vacancies.[30]

In short, reflationary Keynesian economics, though the most vociferously trumpeted alternative against the Thatcher government, is one of the least convincing remedies.[31]

A number of more plausible alternatives and suggestions come from close analysis of the different types of unemployment. It has been argued, for example, that wages councils cause unemployment by pushing up labour costs and thereby discouraging the hiring of unemployed workers. The Thatcher government showed itself sympathetic to this approach but did not take it to its logical conclusion—the abolition of wages councils themselves. One Cabinet minister put it that 'we were stuck with the ILO convention on wages councils, so we couldn't abolish them'.[32] However, in March 1983 Mr Tebbit reduced from 8 per cent to 6 per cent a pay award for half a million shopworkers, recommended by the industry's wages council, because some businesses had claimed they could not afford the costs. As Mr Tebbit put it in a letter to Raymond Sun, the council's chairman:

It is abundantly clear that if they [the proposals] are not modified, they will have damaging effects on employment in the retail industry.

Should you ignore the representations and confirm the proposed increase, I would be driven to conclude either that the council does not recognize any links between wages and jobs, or that it does not see it as part of its responsibility to take this clear indication into account when making proposals about minimum rates.[33]

Further confirmation of the damage of wages councils because they were a cause of unemployment also came from the

National Federation of Self-Employed and Small Businesses in a report in 1981. Mr James Woolsgrove, the chairman of the Federation's wages council sub-committee, reported that wages councils had forced up the real cost of labour considerably by insisting on increases well above average for younger workers and by reducing the length of the working week. The effect had been to cause unemployment, with the worst affected being women, school-leavers and ethnic minorities, who had all found themselves priced out of jobs.

The councils required an expensive secretariat and enforcement arm, adding further costs to businessmen and consumers because of increased paperwork. Awards were difficult to understand and interpret, causing further administrative difficulties for traders.

They were inefficient and often allowed far too little time for those affected by their decisions to lodge objections, and awards could be back-dated so that businessmen did not know where they were on labour costs. This made efficient budgeting impossible, driving down profit margins and reducing the number of new firms entering each industry or adding to the cost to the consumer. 'There is an overwhelming pressure from small businessmen for longer periods of consultation, a less offhand approach from inspectors and the ending of back-dated awards', Mr Woolsgrove argued.[34]

Academic analyses have also confirmed such evidence. Professor Patrick Minford has advocated that the government should act in its own 'backyard' by putting an end to the councils. Minford has argued:

Wages Council awards are also inconsistent with other aspects of current employment policy, e.g. the Young Workers Scheme (YWS), whereby lower wages for youth are encouraged and subsidized so as to stimulate employment, or the New Training Initiative (NTI) where some low allowances are paid for those participating in it.

Abolition of the Wages Council system would, it can be confidently postulated, serve to expand employment, offer competitive wages for the socially disadvantaged, create an incentive for youth training, remove inconsistencies with other parts of present employment policy and alleviate rather than promote poverty. In short, if a Wages Council comes to be regarded as effective, it is therefore harmful; it is therefore otiose and useless. Both counts add up to a positive case for steps towards the removal of minimum wage legislation, namely through the eventual abolition of Wages Councils. The declaratory effects, as well as the economic ones, would be a firm signal to all concerned.[35]

Closely allied to the strong evidence on the disadvantages of wages councils is the evidence that trade union monopoly power to supply labour has created unemployment. This is not a new analysis but is none the less powerful for that. Thus, Samuel Brittan has argued that:

Union monopoly raises wages per hour at the cost of reducing the number of man-hours worked in the unionised sector. There is a conflict of interest between people who have jobs and expect to retain them—who gain from successful union monopoly action—and the unemployed or new entrants, who would do better with less payment and more jobs.

The danger to employment has nothing to do with extremism or subversion. It is in the nature of labour monopoly and can be exercised just as much by rational self-interested moderates. The socially beneficial role of unions is to represent individual employees and protect them from harsh treatment or discrimination. The monopolistic collective bargaining function is at best a promoter of a dual labour market—a better paid unionised sector and a secondary submerged sector into which the less fortunate are crowded. If the displaced workers are unwilling or unable to find places on the secondary labour market, unionised pay settlements serve to increase unemployment.[36]

During the first Thatcher administration it became politically possible to claim that workers could price themselves out of jobs rather than claiming demand deficiency, as in the post-war Keynesian era. In November 1979, for example, Geoffrey Howe stated simply that 'if workers and their representatives take pay decisions which are unwise because they seek too much, they will find they have crippled their employers and gravely harmed themselves by destroying their own jobs'.[37] During the course of the next four years ministers constantly warned that the government would not resort to reflating the economy if workers did price themselves out of jobs by increasing labour costs to damaging and self-destructive levels.

As Samuel Brittan observed, 'while in other countries unions accepted that wages could just keep pace with prices during the second oil-price shock, no such restraint was shown in the UK until union leaders learned by bitter experience and millions of people had been priced out of jobs'.[38] To reflationist critics such as Ian Gilmour, the 'rise in unemployment to a record level . . . has been the most spectacular result of monetarism',[39] an argument of beguiling, yet unconvincing, simplicity.

The evidence, however, suggests that during the Thatcher administration, and also during previous administrations, trade union monopoly power to fix wages above market levels had been leading to unemployment. Miller and Wood have argued that:

Insofar as the trade unions can and do set wages above the market rate, they will tend to cause or perpetuate unemployment unless the workers kept out of work can find jobs in the non-unionised sectors.
National wage bargaining, too, has unfortunate effects upon unemployment. National bargaining sets wages without any adjustment for the relative value of the same work in different parts of the economy and the country. The enforcement by trade unions of national rates will concentrate unemployment where employers in competitive markets cannot pay the national rates, because they cannot pass them on to consumers in higher prices.[40]

A particularly detailed microeconomic study of this phenomenon has been conducted by Professor Minford, who has argued that the inability of wages to fall in the non-unionised sector below the levels of income provided by social benefits explains why workers priced out of jobs in the unionised sector are unable to find alternative work. Minford argues that, as trade union power has sharply increased in the 60s and 70s, so the number of unemployed as a result of labour-market failures has increased. To Minford the monopoly power of unions is the key factor:

A union exists to raise the wages of its members to an 'optimal' amount, given first, that higher union wages means fewer union jobs, and second, the wages that their members could get in the non-union sector. The union typically determines an optimal union wage which is some way above the non-union wage. A monopolist raises his price to the point at which his profits are maximized; this point will be above that which would have been set by free competition and will reduce the size of the market—so with a union monopoly.

Workers who lose their jobs as a result of their monopoly power will then seek jobs in the non-union sector. These additional supplies of labour, force wages down there, until supply is equal to demand. But at this point we note that the social security system guarantees a minimum income regardless of work and that taxes apply to workers with very low incomes. As wages in the non-union sector fall, they become progressively less attractive (after tax) to workers forced out of the union sector. Some, perhaps many, will not be prepared to take the jobs on offer for such rewards. They will go on the dole.[41]

Not surprisingly, Minford, and others, have argued for tougher legislation to deal with trade union power and particularly to erode their monopoly position by instituting a Labour Monopolies Commission. Such a body would be empowered to investigate any apparent breaches of the public interest in labour market competition and to bring actions under common law to obtain enforcement of the investigations proposed remedies. In the fullness of time the Commission would build up a body of case law that 'should have the same effect as the Restrictive Trade Practices Court and the Monopolies and Mergers Commission have had in the goods market under existing laws'.[42]

Although the relationship between the Thatcher government and the unions will be discussed in Chapter 6, suffice it to say at this juncture that the Minford proposals, while correctly analysing the major cause of unemployment, arguably overestimate the efficacy of legalistic remedies to trade union power. Even if a Labour Monopolies Commission were to work without legal complications, there would still remain social factors mitigating in favour of union monopoly power. It is these cultural aspects of workers' behaviour that are crucial to the breakdown of monopoly power. For example, the terms 'scab' and 'blackleg' still have stigmatising effects in many parts of Britain. Workers who would take jobs at below unionised rates in a previously monopoly unionised factory may find huge social pressures upon them, including ostracism and personal abuse. To make what is known to the unions as 'blackleg' or 'scab' labour acceptable in many working-class communities involves a long-term change in attitudes. Legislation may assist the change but it cannot decree it.

Of course, there are occasions when employers, including the government or its agencies, should sack strikers and recruit new workers at market wage-levels rather than submit to the blackmail that monopoly power induces—particularly with Fleet Street printers, for example. But it would be much better if the winds of change in the economy and society would break down abuses by trade union by altering attitudes to the relationship between wage increases and unemployment. It can be argued that this process has already begun under the first Thatcher administration as workers refused—as in the coal-mines—to support strike calls by union leaders. A moderate, economically literate union membership, refusing to adopt the militancy of salaried union officials, would do more to break down trade union abuses, including monopoly power, than legislation, however well intentioned. With the decline in pay settlements after 1980 and the reduction in the number of strikes to their lowest level since the 1940s there is evidence that attitudes are changing. In the long run this would bode well for increased employment levels.

One alternative remedy to reduce unemployment that has long been advocated has been the elimination of the 'why work?' syndrome. High benefit levels and other social security payments, it has been argued, deter the unemployed from seeking work, and consequently a wider incomes differential between those in work and those unemployed has been suggested. Reform of the tax system to prevent penal taxation rates on those on low incomes is often advanced as a way of achieving this end as is the more direct reduction in the real level of unemployment benefits which the Thatcher government undertook. Miller and Wood thus argued that:

in future unemployment benefit rates should be coupled not to the retail price index as at present but to the lowest decile of average earnings, even if they were falling, in effect reintroducing the principle of the 'wages-stop', abolished in 1975, which ensured that supplementary benefit was less than an individual could be expected to earn in work. Similarly, the supplementary benefit scale rates, or at least the short-term rates which apply to the unemployed, should be linked to the price of a basket of 'essential' goods, as for national assistance rates until 1948.[43]

Similarly, a tougher attitude to 'scroungers' who claim benefit while actually working is urged to prevent fraudulent claims. These remedies if enacted, may reduce unemployment but only so marginally as not to make the trouble and cost worthwhile. A far more sensible approach would be to effectively remove this particular category of people from the unemployment register altogether. First, rather than investigating and prosecuting scroungers, which is expensive, such people should be officially tolerated but not regarded as actually seeking work. They would receive as Sam Brittan has advocated a 'social dividend' rather than unemployment benefit, so that 'people would then have the choice of opting out temporarily or permanently from commercial society, with no attempt either to hunt them down as scroungers or to pretend that they are genuinely "unemployed"'.[44]

Second, along with those receiving 'social dividend', those working part-time should be put on a separate register from those who are genuinely involuntarily unemployed. Instead of penalising the unemployed by deducting benefits if, and when, part-time work is uncovered, the regulations should be changed so that the declaration of extra income would not lead to less benefits. Those working part-time or moonlighting on an ad hoc basis, would be put on a 'part-time working' register and not counted as unemployed. Moreover, it would still be an offence not to declare extra income, but with the sanction of loss of benefit removed the incentive to lie would disappear. This reform would effectively admit the truth of the present situation—that many of the unemployed work part-time, swelling the black economy, and are forced to claim incorrectly, that they are unemployed.[45]

Two registers would replace the present one and would further help to weaken the useless notion that all registered unemployed are in the same situation. It is long overdue for governments to come to terms with Britain's black economy and the part played in it by some of those now registered as unemployed. Professor A.L. Ilersic, for example, has estimated that those officially unemployed but moonlighting were evading tax amounting to £1.3 billion.[46] In Arthur Seldon's view the black economy is nearer 20 per cent of GDP 'because of barter, which is unrecordable'.[47] This money can never be recovered—partly because the cost of inspectors and administration would make it counter-productive—and represents a genuine and beneficial source of economic growth. It is this aspect of moonlighting rather than as Heertje *et al.* put it, 'hidden jobs constitute the major part of tax evasion',[48] which should guide public policy. Furthermore, a two-registers policy, with the moonlighters taken out, would enable closer scrutiny of those actually unemployed to take place and ultimately allow more effective remedies to emerge.

The alternative remedy of subsidising employers to increase or maintain employment, rather than paying unemployment benefits also surfaced during the Thatcher administration. Indeed, the 'Walters plan' for subsidising youth employment with weekly payments of £15 for employees under eighteen years old on less than £40 per week unveiled in 1981, was an imaginative innovation in this direction. Given the high costs of dole payments, this alternative deserves further attention, not least as a way of reducing public spending. The case has been strongly argued in particular by David Bell, the vice-president for organisation and manpower planning at the Institute for Personnel Management. Bell suggested that a payment be made of £2,000 per year to employers for each new job created to encourage work-sharing and adaption to a shorter working year and working life.[49] As an alternative to the cost of unemployment benefit payments, such a scheme may have some viability.

Finally, it is worth mentioning some less beneficial alternatives in order to caution against them. The import controls solution propagated by the Cambridge Economic Policy Group, and others, would invite tariff retaliation and a decline in world trade. Moreover, such philosophy is incompatible with a free society.[50] National Service or conscription would be too costly and would be opposed by the Armed Forces who prefer to remain wholly professional. Public capital investment in specific projects—as opposed to a general Keynesian reflation—are also superficially attractive. But the history of such use of public money is lamentable. Indeed, Ian

Gilmour, advocating greater productive investment, as opposed to greater consumption, seems unaware of the repeated failures of such schemes.[51] In any case, investment is not of merit because it is 'productive' but because it yields a rate of return. Concorde, De Lorean, British Rail, and so on are not the models for reducing unemployment. The economics of the white elephant project is not the way to real jobs. Nor does the work-sharing or early retirement nostrum offer any solution, containing as it does the fallacy that there is a limited amount of work to be done—the 'lump of labour' fallacy.[52] Such tinkering remedies with their neo-Luddite philosophy surfaced too readily from many quarters in the period from 1979 to 1983.

In conclusion, the Thatcher government was right not to panic when the unemployment figures rose; it was not responsible for them and had no reason to act as if it was. The palliative measures which were initiated as the figures rose, while politically justifiable were of only marginal value, although some of them deserve further attention. The abolition of the wages councils, the reduction in trade union monopoly power and changes in the definitions of unemployment all have much to commend them. But the greatest hope for increased employment lies, as it has always done, in a more efficient, entrepreneurial economy where customers, not governments, create real jobs. The Thatcher government deserves credit for rightly believing this is to be the long-term objective.

5 Contemporary Conservatism and Public Spending

The chronic weakness of the public expenditure surveys of the 1960s was their tendency to underestimate future costs. The 1963 survey showed public expenditure rising by an annual average of 4.1 per cent in real terms. When the survey was rolled forward a further year in the summer of 1964 a figure well in excess of 4 per cent emerged—either as a result of new programmes adopted in the intervening twelve months, or as a result of the recosting of the earlier programmes. On the top of this were added the social benefits decided upon by the Labour government in October 1964 in its first days of office. The new government announced in February 1965 a new 4.25 per cent annual average limit for the growth of public expenditure for the five-year period 1964–65 to 1969–70. Not only was this geared to unrealistic National Plan target rates of growth for the whole economy, but public expenditure failed to stay even within the announced guidelines. After the announcement of the 4 per cent ceiling, emergency cuts were announced on no less than five occasions—July 1965, July 1966, July 1967, November 1967 and January 1968. It was only in 1968–69 that the growth of public expenditure really came under control with an increase of only 1.6 per cent in real terms; and it was expected to rise by an average of 3 per cent in the following three years under the Labour government's original plans.

Samuel Brittan, 1970[1]

OVERALL STRATEGY

Controls on public spending, as explained in Chapters 2 and 3, were central to the Thatcher government's economic strategy. By cutting state spending the government hoped to make room for tax cuts, allow interest rates to fall, help to curb inflation and, more philosophically, to reduce the role of the state in society as a whole. In the 1980 Public Expenditure White Paper it was announced that 'the government intend to reduce public expenditure progessively in volume terms over the next four years', and public spending cuts in 1979–80 brought the expected denunciations from interested parties. The Economic Secretary to the Treasury, John Biffen, recalled that 'the first requirement was to trim borrowing which did fall consistently, but the revenue base was contracting because of the recession, so that what was available for tax cuts was reduced'.[2]

However, the government's plans were soon to be blown off target. In 1979–80 general government expenditure rose by just over 2 per cent and in subsequent years, as the cost of recession increased, the task of controlling public spending proved as agonising for Mrs Thatcher's administration as it had proved for Mr Callaghan's.[3] As Sir Leo Pliatsky has argued, there are many obstacles in the way of public expenditure cuts:

> Experience shows, of course, that there is a natural tendency for plans to go wrong, and that the multiplicity of government objectives makes it extremely difficult to achieve all of them. Some of the difficulties were predictable from the outset: the commitment to increases in particular programmes which meant that the government would have had to run hard just to stand still; the improbability of a turn-round in the financing of the nationalised industries on the scale proposed; the uncertainty of those savings which required the co-operation of the local authorities; and the tendency of spending ministers to want to spend once the pressure of events became more potent than the Brownie points awarded for cutting their programmes. But on top of these factors it was the slump, gathering momentum rapidly as the year progressed, which had not been anticipated in the 1980 budget—whether or not it was foreshadowed in unpublished Treasury forecasts—and which wrecked the expenditure plans.[4]

The battle with the wets was a crucial focal point for resisting spending cuts, but other ministers also proved only too willing to fight for their department in Cabinet. The bilaterals between Treasury ministers and spending departments continued as a familiar war of attrition. As public spending targets proved not to have been attained, the pressure for further cuts became more acute. By February 1980, for example, public spending was running outside the cash limits, with the Ministry of Defence—not for the first time—the major culprit. In March 1980 the horrific overspending of local authorities was causing concern to Environment Secretary Michael Heseltine and—not for the first time—plans were drawn up to penalise the overspenders. In June 1980 the government felt forced to throw a £1.5 billion lifeline to the British Steel Corporation to prevent its liquidation, thus putting further pressure on the PSBR target. All these examples showed how difficult it was to fix public spending only a few months in advance. The view of one backbench dry was typical in considering that 'we began too timidly on the public spending control'.[5]

It was therefore hardly surprising to the policy-makers that public sector borrowing was well above the government's target. As Melvyn Westlake put it in *The Times*, 'two factors seem to be raising borrowing: the recession, which seems to be biting deeper than the Treasury had expected, and the recent high pay settlements in the public sector'.[6] On the latter point, the government was paying dearly for the ill-advised decision to adhere to the 1979 election pledge to respect the Clegg Commission's handouts. By October 1980 treasury figures showed the government had exceeded its public spending forecasts by nearly £1.5 billion in the first half of the financial year 1980-81. Thus, one Cabinet minister recalled that 'we didn't seriously get down to public expenditure until the second year. The unions were more optimistic early on and the emphasis was on tax cutting and pushing the economy forwards'.[7]

Consequently, Treasury ministers declared that fresh spending cuts were required merely to keep borrowing under control. The Ministry of Defence was a particular candidate for stringency. Prior to gaining office, the Conservatives had pledged to increase defence spending after what was considered to be years of neglect by Labour. Moreover, many Conservatives felt that there must be room for spending cuts elsewhere than defence. Francis Pym, the Defence Secretary, was prepared to fight the Treasury all the way, and in November 1980, faced with a Treasury demand for an additional £400 million cut, privately threatened to resign rather than succumb. Pym's position was a strong one, as the newspaper which carried his resignation threat assessed:

What has brought about the present crisis is Mr Pym's belief that he was appointed to defence with a commitment to increased spending but that he is now facing the fifth demand for more cuts. While the

Government has aimed at an increase of 3 per cent in real terms in the department last year, it is not widely accepted that it will not do so this year or next, and on top of the cuts the department has also had to cope with the effects of the moratorium.

It is clear, however, that Mr Pym is considering his position not only in terms of the Conservative party's attitude to defence—which is frequently over-stated without reference to the changing nature of the Conservative party activists in the last decade—but also with reference to the future of the party.

The Defence Secretary is well aware that having resigned he would become focus in the party for dissidents from the government's present line and he would have the aproval of both right-wingers who want to protect defence and others who are resisting further spending cuts.[8]

The deadlock was only broken in May 1981, when Mrs Thatcher reshuffled the Cabinet, making Mr Pym leader of the House and appointing John Nott as Defence Secretary. However, Nott's 1981 Defence Review, which rationalised defence spending in the long-term was itself overtaken by the military cost of the Falklands campaign. Defence spending between 1979 and 1983 thus proved intractable and volatile. As this was also the case with other areas of public expenditure, it was not surprising that Treasury ministers looked to the longer term. Financial Secretary Nigel Lawson envisaged—rightly as it turned out—tax cuts before the next election if public spending was curtailed. Leon Brittan, the Economic Secretary, ventured that:

As far as our public expenditure is concerned, our broad strategy is unaltered. We are still firmly committed to making significant reductions in the medium term. The pressures of recession and our recognition of its consequences have led to higher spending than originally planned for 1980–81 and will do so again for 1981–82. But we do not accept the argument that, in today's conditions, the right course is for the government to abandon totally its previous plans and add still further to the present levels of public spending.

Such levels of public spending, however, were higher than the government would have hoped, even though, as Mr Brittan rightly stated, there was to be no abandonment of the government's intentions. In October 1981 the Treasury was hoping for a £3 billion to £4 billion clawback of the public spending overrun merely to leave the total of public spending in real terms at the same level for 1982–83 as for 1981–82. Indeed, only eight weeks after the Chancellor announced the revised 1982–83 targets in November 1981, the government had to find an extra £1,250 million from the contingency reserve to finance overspending. By February 1982, government spending was taking up between 45 and 46 per cent of national income compared to only 41 per cent in the last full year before the Thatcher government came to office. It was no small wonder that ministers revised downwards their expectations of tax cuts before an election. Similarly, one Conservative party official commented that 'that's where the hope of tax cuts drained away with the 1980–82 PSBR. We could have abolished capital gains tax, investment income surcharge and restored the Capital Transfer tax bands'.[10]

Public spending policy, as a result of these setbacks, was being increasingly presented in a longer term framework. Projections and future spending options were publicly discussed and mused over years in advance, whereas previously the process had been more private. Leon Brittan, in March 1982, predicted that public spending would fall to 41 per cent of GDP by 1984–85 and that the Medium-Term Financial Strategy had an increased credibility. Similarly, Mr Brittan looked to future expenditure provision in a key speech to the Institute of Fiscal Studies in May 1982. He argued:

The real question is how much the state can afford to provide free, and still leave the individual citizen with the incentive and ability on top of that ... to provide for his own old age, his own health and his own children's education, directly.

... I believe we have to begin to rethink both the way the basic services are financed and delivered and the way that people choose, and government provides, services above the basic level.

... There may be scope for a whole range of different possibilities, with public and private facilities co-existing and supplementing each other, together with an increased reliance on private insurance, vouchers and the like.[11]

The debate among Conservatives about the nature and provision of public services was also to prove politically contentious.

The defence lobby in the Conservative party—particularly its naval wing—was strengthened by the Falklands war and by the subsequently inevitable decision to find £2.5 billion to retake and hold the islands for the British Crown. Moreover, in December 1982 a further £1 billion was authorised by John Nott to replace defence equipment lost during the campaign and also to eliminate deficiences made evident in the operation. Nott, previously the target for the backbench naval lobby, was congratulated and cheered as the Defence White Paper was unveiled. According to one prominent backbencher, John Biggs-Davison, 'it was predictable ... that defeatists ... who said Britain, could not, or should not, repossess the Falklands should now exaggerate the difficulty and expense of holding them'.[12] The option of not paying for Fortress Falklands had completely vanished by the end of 1982.

The welfare state lobby in the Conservative party was also keen to prevent long-term public spending cuts in the social services. Many left-wing Conservatives felt that swingeing public spending cuts in this area would be a fundamental betrayal of the Conservative tradition of compassion and social responsibility. Thus, when a Think Tank report recommending such cuts emerged before the 1982 party conference, the left-wing outcry forced Mrs Thatcher to publicly repudiate any dismantling of the Health Service. On the other hand, Sir Geoffrey Howe warned that the alternative to radical changes in funding the welfare state could mean a 50 per cent rise in the basic rate of income tax to 45p and a 25 per cent VAT rate. He pointed out that the government was still very far from fulfilling its last manifesto commitment to reduce the share which the state takes of the nation's income. If it kept up its present policies and the spending levels to which these committed them, it could easily end up moving farther away from that commitment rather than closer to it.

Unless ministers were prepared to look critically at their health, social benefits and defence programmes, the government could be forced into politically unacceptable cuts in other areas. Local authorities had already made a good start in opening aspects of their operations to the private sector. Central government and the health service should do the same, he said. Individuals had to be encouraged to provide more for themselves through insurance schemes.

New ways had to be found for services to be supplied without public funding. Thorough study and new insights had to be followed by radical decisions, Sir Geoffrey argued.[13] One possible future revenue raising reform which may force itself on the government despite its electoral implications is the ending of mortgage subsidies and the married person's tax allowance. Such reforms—and taxation reform in general—were not on Sir Geoffrey's agenda for 1979–83 but it is likely, and arguably desirable, that they should feature more prominently in future debates on public expenditure and revenue sources. Moreover, reductions in the high level of agricultural subsidies in relation to the CAP are long overdue.

But as 1983 brought election speculations and the budget tax cuts, the search for what the party newspaper, *Conservative Newsletter*, called 'acceptable long-term solutions to the public expenditure nightmare' were temporarily delayed. The 1983 Public Expenditure White Paper envisaged total spending in 1983–84 at £119,600 million compared with the £120,700 million planned on the 1982 White Paper. In April 1983 it was announced that public borrowing in 1982–83 totalled £9.2 billion, nearly £2 billion more than the £7.5 billion predicted in the budget only one month earlier. The long-term problems of financing high levels of public expenditure were thus as acute as ever at the end of the first Thatcher administration. However, what is certain is that without the public spending cuts undertaken by the government the public spending nightmare would have been even more frightening.

IMPACT OF SPENDING CUTS

As well as the overall strategy, the actual implementation of individual spending cuts caused the government much political anxiety and led to considerable political strife. The results of spending cuts often led to much resentment against the government because of the 'bleeding stump' tactics of those enforced with carrying out the cuts. By cutting at the limbs—and leaving the 'bleeding stump'[14]—rather than cutting at the fat, spending cuts in the Health Service, education and local government were presented as examples of government viciousness, whereas the suffering was actually caused by those agencies who, resenting any retrenchment on their spending, deliberately sought to discredit expenditure cuts. Hood and Wright accurately describe how:

As in the case of the 'rational' public service strike, which aims to do maximum harm to the public in order to force government to yield, bureaucracies and politicians seeking to resist cuts may choose to concentrate those cuts in the places where they will most hurt the outside public, be most easily noticed, and thus court the maximum political unpopularity for the government. Such actors may actively help to orchestrate the chorus of protest against 'inhuman' cuts. Hence (to put it vulgarly) the pressure for closing down the flower gardens rather than reducing the town hall bureaucracy, for cutting down on school books rather than on educational administrators, and so on. Sometimes there really is no choice but to act in this way as when, after voting down the 1979 EEC budget, the first thing that Euro-MPs discovered was that their own salaries and expenses had been cut. Far more commonly, there will be scope for bureaucratic choice. Thus in 1980 the Public Record Office chose to meet a requirement for a 10 per cent budget cut in the following year by closing down its central London public search rooms, thus making the cuts highly visible to its clientele and subjecting its London-based clients (who may include some 'influentials') to maximum inconvenience (*The Times*, 23 June 1980). Similarly, the Scottish Development Agency was coming under fire in mid-1980 for concentrating its cuts on money given away to companies rather than on its own organization. This is the 'sore thumbs' and 'bleeding stumps' tactic.[15]

Moreover, as well as the 'bleeding stump' tactic, the government found opposition to spending cuts so politically pervasive because the cuts were spread 'across the board', affecting every department's expenditure and virtually every aspect of the public sector, from the whales such as defence and the NHS to the minnows such as the Arts Council and overseas aid. Thus the wide range of cuts although sometimes only modest brought a wide range of protests to add to the confusion over the actual depth of specific cuts. A number of examples illustrate the problems faced by the government.

First, cuts in the social services proved difficult because, as with defence, which has already been mentioned, the Tory wets' sympathy would lie more often than not with Opposition critics. In January 1981 Mr Alf Morris, Labour's former Minister for the Disabled, attacked 'inhuman' cuts for the disabled in relation to the government's decision to cut invalidity benefits. The political row caused a rethink, and in April 1981 Jim Prior announced that the Manpower Services Commission had been told to withdraw cuts in facilities for blind and disabled people. The 'bleeding stump' tactic had worked as had been intended. In April 1980 the Social Services Secretary, Patrick Jenkin, rightly told the Commons that social services savings should be made on administration not by cutting services to the most vulnerable groups. Mr Jenkin noted that 'in some local authorities elected members seem too ready to accept without question significant cuts in services to vulnerable groups. It is for elected councillors to insist that savings should be found wherever possible by cutting down administration rather than attacking services'. However, the mechanics of implementing the cuts by local authorities meant that often the very opposite of Mr Jenkin's policy actually happened.[16] One Cabinet minister recalled that 'you can hardly take a safety razor to the NHS before people scream. Go into any hospital and ask to see the manager no one will know what you mean'.[17]

Nor did Health Service reorganisation, initiated by Mr Jenkin, remove the spending cuts dilemma or the need for greater Health Service efficiency. Even such measures as encouraging outside contractors to undertake cleaning and laundry at a net saving to the NHS were bitterly opposed by the NHS unions whose strike in 1982 over pay displayed the difficulty of allocating revenue within the Health Service between patient care and employee satisfaction. Not surprisingly, the government turned to alternative approaches encouraging private medicine and an insurance-based health service before the political pressure at the 1982 Conservative conference brought the commitment to continue the NHS in its existing form. However, radical reform of the Health Service finance may soon be back on the political agenda. Thus, as one Cabinet minister put it:

what is sacred is the high priority to quality health care and absolute protection for those who cannot pay bills at the point of sale. That will remain the long-term sacred aim. The cow is Health Service administration, riddled with inefficiency. The ancilliary services could be better done outside. You need to chop up the cow and it's not part of the Conservatives' One Nation tradition to keep in being every bureaucracy.[18]

Similarly, the Selsdon Group's draft manifesto in October 1982 argued that:

We would be content to see the principles of the Health Service preserved for those who are gravely ill. However, those requiring treatment for predictable and easily curable illnesses would be expected to pay for their own treatment through insurance schemes.

In this way state assistance would be concentrated upon those in greatest need while at the same time attracting increased resources into an area which is currently underfinanced because of political control and union domination.[19]

Given the difficulties the Thatcher government faced in implementing cuts in the Health Service, such a prescription seems even more relevant in the long term despite the political embarrassments caused prior to the 1983 election.

Second, cuts in education spending proved contentious, difficult to implement and were vulnerable to 'bleeding stump' opposition. Education had been particularly hard hit by the Callaghan government's public spending cuts at the time of the 1976 IMF crisis, and many insiders regarded the Department of Education and Science as Whitehall's soft underbelly of excessive public spending fat. Education cuts were no surprise, and partly because of this the opposition to any cuts was well-organised, articulate and persistent. The 1979 round of spending cuts took £240 million from education and was followed in February 1980 by the decision to cut in half the number of assisted places for private education that had featured strongly in the 1979 Conservative manifesto. The 1980 rise in student grants was 5 per cent less than the inflation rate, and in April 1980 a £260 million cut in local authority education budgets brought a reduction in O'level courses and a few new school books. However, these cuts in services were negated by the 20 to 25 per cent pay rise for teachers recommended by the Clegg Commission in April 1980. A further £50 million cut in August 1980 was accompanied by a deterioration in the school-meal service, which was criticised, ironically, by the teachers' unions who had received pay rises from Clegg bearing no relation to the supply and demand for teachers. Ultimately, despite well-orchestrated predictions, fewer teachers than expected lost their jobs. Indeed, the DES budgeted for 2,000 more teachers when £50 million for additional education for sixteen to nineteen year olds was announced in 1981.

In higher education, spending cuts arguably faced greater difficulties. The government put the task of implementing the cuts in the hands of the, albeit reluctant, University Grants Committee. The UGC, charged with allocating selective cuts worth £150 million in the budgets of Britain's forty-four universities,[20] was 'put into the position of judge, jury and executioner for the toughest financial verdict ever handed out to the universities'.[21] The government told the UGC to save money and reduce 'waste', but the opposite model, the 'bleeding stump' was forthcoming. Efficient technological universities such as Salford, Aston and Bradford were severely cut, whereas other universities seemed to escape for no better reason than their age. The worst aspect of the UGC's 'bleeding stump' was the reduction of 12,000 university places without providing for any compulsory redundancies among university staff. If the Health Service cuts had enshrined the principle that the NHS was for those that worked in it, not the patients, then the UGC cuts enshrined the principle that universities existed not for the benefit of students but for university employees.

However, it soon emerged that the situation was far worse. The generous voluntary redundancy payments made to dons brought forward many willing takers among the able and those capable of finding work elsewhere, whereas the inefficient and incompetent were able to stay put and avoid the efficiency axe. The 'golden suitcase' effect, as Norman Barry has described it, therefore led to the opposite of the efficient, well-motivated career structure that the government had intended. Barry, rightly, argued that the mechanics of voluntary redundancies had had extremely unfortunate consequencies:

Since the funds that finance these severance payments are separate from a university's general income, it is not surprising that some vice-chancellors are asking people to come forward to 'take the money'. Although hard information is difficult to obtain about the precise form of the cut-backs, intuitive reasoning suggests that *it is impossible under the present arrangements for incompetent staff to be weeded out.* Severance payments and early retirement arrangements are not likely to be attractive to the 'plodders' who have few employment prospects outside the university system. In practice, the major staff economies are being affected by the better academics in their fifties taking generous early-retirement terms, many of whom are immediately re-employed on a part-time basis. There are examples of much younger individuals taking severance payments; and some of these find employment elsewhere in polytechnics or even the better government services for a time.

In effect, highly competent and employable academics are being offered suitcases full of used and untraceable 'fivers' to leave the profession, while the less competent stay on under no more onerous conditions than before.[22]

Whether or not the government's overall approach to education spending was flawed will be discussed later in this chapter. However, suffice it to say at this juncture that it was not the government that was 'barbaric', as Mr Foot put it, in seeking public spending cuts in education but the implementation of the cuts that was counter-productive. Ultimately, the Thatcher government ended up with many universities losing their better dons, with the incompetent more entrenched and with the economically and academically unjustified system of tenure still intact. No wonder that Sir Keith Joseph, Mark Carlisle's successor as Education Secretary, bemoaned that he heartily wished universities were financially independent, at least in part.[23]

A third major area of public spending cuts concerned local government finance. Here an intractable and endemic problem became more visible during the lifetime of the first Thatcher administration. For Environment Secretary Michael Heseltine the problems seemed to become larger the more attentively he sought solutions. Local government had long been the subject of administrative debate. The Redcliffe-Maud report, the Peter Walker reorganisation of the early 1970s, the Layfield Report and the intricacies of the Rate Support Grant had all witnessed a growing local government crisis of inadequate funding chasing ambitious spending plans. Where once local government was a mundane matter of street lights, parks and pavements, it had by the 1980s become a complication of services some more readily appreciated by ratepayers than others.[24] Where once local government was more often than not politically bipartisan and salaried officials confined to little more than the Town Clerk and an assistant, by the 1980s local government had become a bitter political battleground particularly sought after by the professional 'hard left' in the Labour party. Moreover, the number of local authority employees had increased to astronomical levels encompassing several layers of bureaucracy assisted by numerous leisure officers, planning officers, housing officers, welfare officers, environmental health officers, and so on.[25] Senior local authority employment was no more than a blatant waste of money, as only a cursory look at *The Guardian's* public appointment page testifies. In September 1983, for example, Lewisham local authority was attempting to recruit two employees for a Racism Awareness Unit, and the GLC allegedly required two Deputy Unit Heads of the 'Women's Committee Support Unit'.[26] Such employment creation was at the heart of the local government financial crisis. Even useful jobs providing legitimate services had been vastly augmented. No one doubted that certain local authority jobs should exist in the right quantities; but the proliferation of such employment without economic justification had long been overburdening ratepayers, both industrial and private, before Mrs Thatcher came to power.

Mr Heseltine, in short, inherited a grim situation. Council overspending, particularly by Labour authorities, was to be a perpetual problem, ultimately passed on to Mr Heseltine's successors. By April 1980 rate rises were averaging 26 per cent and Mr Heseltine already faced a number of rebel authorities, such as Lothian and Newcastle-upon-Tyne, when he threatened to cut the Rate Support Grant of councils setting rates above a notional 119p in the pound. Jack Smart, Labour Opposition leader of the Association of Metropolitan Authorities, declared in April 1980 that 'this is the nearest local government has been to...bankruptcy. Local authorities are going to have to make people redundant or go bankrupt. They will just not have the cash to pay people. They will also have to put up the rates again'.[27]

However, the evidence showed that some local authorities had brought severe problems on themselves. Between 1979 and 1980 local councils did cut manpower by 17,500 jobs. But 108,000 new employees were recruited, so that redundancies represented a minute 0.6 per cent decrease compared to an 8.5 per cent decrease among civil servants at Mr Heseltine's own department.[28] Furthermore, salaries of local authority officials increased with no regard to ratepayers' ability to finance them. Salary tables compiled by the Fulham and Hammersmith Ratepayers Association showed that in the two years from May 1979 officials' salaries increased between 75 and 130 per cent compared to an overall inflation rate of 24 per cent for the period.

Table 2 details the exact increases.

Table 2: *Increase in salaries of officials of Hammersmith and Fulham Council, 1979–81*

Position	1 July 1979	31 March 1981	% increase
Chief Executive	15,240	26,588	74.46
Housing Director	12,114	21,222	75.19
Engineering Director	12,114	20,783	71.56
Development Planning Director	11,832	20,705	74.99
Finance Director	10,704	20,342	90.04
Leisure and Recreation Director	8,682	20,210	133.18
Social Services Director	8,667	20,002	130.38
Borough Valuer	10,704	19,620	83.03
Assistant Chief Executive	9,333	19,066	104.29
Head of Personnel	10,704	18,928	76.83
Borough Solicitor	8,715	18,928	117.19
Assistant Director of Social Services	9,231	18,752	103.14
Borough Architect	8,037	18,615	131.06

Source: The Times, 21 January 1982.

Given the failure to reduce overmanning and the high salary awards in local government as a whole, it is not surprising that spending cuts, falling on actual services, are a perfect example of 'bleeding stump' tactics. It is therefore difficult to agree with Bosanquet that 'one way of improving collective choice would be to strengthen local government and to give it greater responsibility, both for its spending and for raising revenue'.[29]

One problem which proved particularly intractable was that of local authority spending under section 127 of the Local Government Act. This enabled local authorities to spend up to a 2p rate for the benefit of residents. However, in effect, this form of public spending became a major abuse as councils poured ratepayers' money into politically motivated activities, the most notorious of which were associated with Ken Livingstone's GLC. In August 1980, under section 127, Labour-controlled Wakefield Metropolitan District spent £350,000 on 'job creation for 120 young people', in an open challenge to the government's cash restrictions.[30] Mr Heseltine only one month earlier had cut local authority spending by £200 million—the fourth round of cuts—and was soon to be criticised by Conservative as well as Labour-controlled authorities.

In October 1980 both Labour and Conservative local authority leaders criticised a further 1 per cent cut in the Rate Support Grant and reduction of local spending by 3.1 per cent. As Mr Heseltine put it:

If local authorities plan for that target, and budget in line with the cash-limit assumptions, increases for ratepayers should be contained within reasonable levels and be much lower than this year.

This will place severe demands on local government—on councillors, on local government management and local government employees. There is no alternative but to ensure that local government plays its part in the reduction of public expenditure.[31]

The problem, however, was soon back again. In March 1981 13 local authorities were told to cut their spending by 20 per cent and 199 by 5 per cent to return to the target levels of expenditure.

In May 1981 Mr Heseltine docked £800 million from

overspending councils after rent rises averaging 20 per cent had further demonstrated local authorities' financial incontinence in April. After one alternative approach—mandatory referendums by local authorities to seek approval for rate rises—had been voted down by a backbench revolt, Mr Heseltine reverted to the war of attrition and £300 million was withheld in September 1981 because of further council overspending. But Mr Heseltine could announce a minor triumph at the end of 1981 when figures showed that English local authorities had finally cut their workforces, though by only 2.2 per cent, between September 1980 and September 1981. Nevertheless, councils still employed 1,891,630 full-time workers and the rate of job decline was less than that implied in the government's spending plans.

By 1982 a minority of Labour authorities were still defying government policy, and to penalise them Mr Heseltine sought Parliamentary approval for the Rate Support Grant Increase Order, explaining to the House that:

The fact that so many authorities are now demonstrating that with sensible manpower and recruitment policies savings can be made, demonstrates again the reasonableness of what I asked for. But though the shift is happening, it is late in the day and unless the pace of the last quarter is maintained, is still below the level needed overall to meet the current spending targets.

Instead of an overall reduction in real terms in current spending, there was a budgeted cash overspend of perhaps £1,300m this year. While the upward spiral had been stopped, thanks to the minority, the direction had not yet been reversed.

I have therefore decided that I must confirm the withholding of £200m from the 1980–81 Rate Support Grant, and it is for this reason that the first order for which approval is sought today provides only an additional £84m grant. This increase is mainly for increased loan charges in that year.[32]

This action was followed up by a 9 per cent cut in council spending for 1983–84 before figures confirmed that local authority spending was 7 per cent above target for 1981–82. However, it was proved that Mr Heseltine's targets were not draconian, as was often alleged, but the fact that council savings of £45 million were made after the Conservatives took control of many councils in the May 1982 local elections. In particular, in Birmingham the new Conservative council had agreed a £12.3 million savings package. Such successes were rare, however. Despite the government's strenuous efforts, for which it deserves credit, local government spending was still a jungle of waste, inefficiency, overmanning and overspending when the Parliament ended in 1983. One Cabinet minister lamented that 'local government was a failure of democracy as rates fall on businesses that don't have votes. Local government spends £10 billion on education that I would transfer to the Department of Education and Science. In 1979–83 we went round and round and never came to any answer on local government'.[33] For 1983–84 English councils were still planning to spend £780 million in excess of the government's target, and actual spending cuts had fallen more often than not on services of real value. The 'bleeding stump' had become institutionalised among local authority waste.

A fourth area of public spending retrenchment concerned the Whitehall Civil Service. Here the government's efforts proved more successful. The 1983 Conservative manifesto was thus able to proclaim:

This country is fortunate to have a Civil Service with high standards of administration and integrity. The Civil Service has loyally and effectively helped to carry through the far-reaching changes we have made to secure greater economy, efficiency and better management in Government itself. It is a tribute to this spirit of co-operation that the number of civil servants has been reduced from 732,000 to 649,000 with the minimum of redundancies and with higher standards of service to the citizen. This has saved the taxpayer about £550m a year, and is helping us to improve the civil service working conditions.

The efficiency 'scrutinies' launched by Lord Rayner and other money-saving techniques have now identified savings worth £400m a year to the taxpayer. We have abolished 500 quangos and done away with no less than 3,600 different types of government forms.

We are successfully putting out to tender more services needed by central government. We shall press on with this wherever public money can be saved and standards of service maintained or improved.

Public spending is now planned in terms of hard cash instead of so-called constant prices, and the discipline of cash limits on spending has been extended. As a result, public spending is firmly under control.[34]

However, this success had not been easy to achieve, bearing in mind it involved reversing the long-term trend towards greater bureaucracy and consequent overmanning. The cut in the number of quangos was less than that advocated by such backbench quango opponents as Philip Holland, and Sir Leo Pliatsky's White Paper on '*Non-Departmental Public Bodies*' presented in January 1980 recommended only modest savings in the total public spending bill. Similarly, the Prime Minister's personal hope of reducing the cost of Civil Service index-linked pensions proved abortive when Sir Bernard Scott's committee failed to recommend the dismantling of the system, ironically created by the Conservatives under Mr Heath's premiership.

However, these setbacks may be regarded as offset by the spectacular success in actually reducing Civil Service numbers. One Cabinet minister recalled that 'the Civil Service was reduced to the smallest size since the war, contracting by 100,000. It would be blinking at human nature not to expect some resistance, yet the contraction was actually done by the Civil Service as a whole. Privately many civil servants have said it's tightened things up and you needed to set a number to concentrate minds'.[35] Here Mr Heseltine's cost cutting was most effective. By June 1982 staffing cuts at the Department of

Table 3: *Change in staff numbers in government departments, 1979–82*

Department	% change in staff, 1 April 1797 to 1 April 1982*
Defence	−12.4
Education and Science	−6.1
Employment (including Manpower Services Commision)	+9.4
Energy	−10.2
Environment	−24.9
Foreign and Commonwealth	−8.2
Home Office	+3.3
Industry	−12.6
Health and Social Security	−2.9
Transport	−6.3

* = Full-time equivalents

Source: The Times, 16 February 1982.

Environment were higher than in any other government department, supplementing the efficiency drive initiated by Mr Heseltine known as Management Information for Ministers, or MINIS.[36] The Department of the Environment was thus already close to the 26 per cent manpower cut intended by the government between 1979 and 1984. Table 3 shows the effectiveness of Mr Heseltine's measures compared to other departments.

Mrs Thatcher also threw her political weight behind the Heseltine reforms. In a letter to Timothy Eggar, the Conservative MP for Enfield, she stressed with regard to programmes for improving financial management in Whitehall that:

I shall need to be satisfied that the programmes submitted by departments conform to the principles established so successfully in the Department of the Environment, and that they are sufficiently consistent with each other to permit the ready movement of officials.

We are increasing the emphasis laid on managerial skills in promoting and training throughout the Civil Service generally. I shall also be looking for an increased proportion of candidates with business experience amongst those selected for the Civil Service.

There is still a very long way to go. Managerial skills, as you rightly say, have not developed anything like far enough in the Civil Service.

The use of MINIS in the Department of the Environment has, however, shown what can be achieved, and this lesson must not be lost on the rest of the Civil Service.[37]

One Cabinet minister recalled that 'Margaret had an obvious loathing for the Civil Service, she hates officialdom—it's the same syndrome as Hoskyns'.[38] Public spending cuts were not confined to the known areas of high-profile spending or just to departments with major budgets. Indeed, the overriding nature of the cuts was that they were, as has been said, 'across the board', 'sharing the misery' as Hood and Wright put it, rather than 'quantum' cuts 'terminating specific programmes'.[39] As a result, the scope of 'bleeding stump' tactics increased and political opposition to expenditure restraints was often greatest for comparatively low-profile cuts. Thus, £130 million cuts in the BBC's budget, involving the disbandment of five orchestras and reductions in World Service Broadcasting brought about fierce political opposition, much of it from Conservatives horrified at the government's apparently philistine approach. Regional radio news and weather programmes were also scrapped in a classic example of the 'bleeding stump'. Similarly, the Arts Council implementing £1.25 million worth of cuts, ostentatiously cut the grant to the Royal Shakespeare Company, forcing the abandonment of its tours to areas with no live theatre.

Other areas of spending cuts offended entrenched vested interests, not so much in the amount of the cut but in the decision to cut in itself. The Third World lobby was outraged by Foreign Aid cuts, even though Lord Carrington's lobbying on the Foreign Office's behalf kept them to a minimum. Cuts in the provision of legal aid, despite much evidence of its abuse,[40] produced a similar outcry. In short, the principle of public spending cuts was often as contentious to interested minorities and pressure groups as the extent of the cut itself. As a result, public spending cuts proved difficult to implement in the way intended by the government, and 'bleeding stump' tactics brought political opprobrium to ministers allegedly wielding the spending axe insensitively. One Cabinet minister recalled that 'there was no way round the bleeding stump problem—we shouldn't have had the trees from which the stumps could bleed'.[41] Moreover, as the rising cost of the recession forced successive rounds of spending cuts, the dilemma of reconciling high aggregate levels of public expenditure to the need for lower interest rates and taxes became seemingly more intractable.

THE ALTERNATIVE APPROACHES

Given the need for public spending control, which the Thatcher government rightly regarded as central to its economic strategy, the obvious question raised by the difficulty described so far in the chapter was how should spending cuts be allocated by cuts 'across the board' or by quantum cuts in specific programmes? The government adopted the former approach, as had its predecessors at the time of the IMF crisis, and found the practical problems of implementation of many different cuts considerable. One economic adviser commented that 'we'll never get public spending down from say 44 to 34 per cent of GNP by across-the-board bilateralism'.[42] Similarly, one ministerial member of the 'Star Chamber' Cabinet committee formed to adjudicate between the Treasury and spending departments put it that 'You've got to look at the big options—it's a fallacy that you can save big amounts out of administration. After the bilaterals you're left with the hard nuts to crack, and we spend considerable hours in the Star Chamber, which is bound to lead to compromise'.[43]

The alternative quantum approach is therefore worth considering in more detail. David Howell, since his dismissal from Mrs Thatcher's government, has attacked the government's cuts in the 'wrong targets'. Howell's critique is that 'across-the-board cuts have a habit of being eroded. The cash and manpower broad-brush squeezes have to go hand-in-hand with the systematic questioning of functions and objectives which was initiated in 1970 but which lost momentum during the decade'.[44] While descriptively accurate, this view is less prescriptively persuasive. Howell argues:

It is now a high test of balanced Conservative government, which will result in much political peril if failed, to bring more precision and selectivity into its efforts to cut back public expenditure-generating activities in other words, to hit the right targets. By the "right" targets I mean the 'big four' ballooning current spending generators which work ceaselessly in the health, welfare, defence and education areas. Together with agricultural support, these are the big eaters of public funds and the areas where policy objectives (what are we really getting for it all?) have been least systematically and rigorously questioned.[45]

The objection to Howell's 'big four' is that they are central to Conservative philosophy and current policies. The obvious targets, nationalised industry fossilisation and local government overspending, are omitted.

The quantum approach should seek as targets areas not regarded as central to Conservative policy. The quantum approach seeks as much to preserve the good areas of public spending though within normal bounds of efficiency as much as it seeks to actually reduce public spending in real terms. This approach, therefore, should commend itself to Conservatives of both right and left as a way of allocating public money to those areas traditionally reserved in Conservative philosophy for state provision. Conservatives have long advocated a strong defence policy based on NATO, plus Britain's own independent nuclear deterrent. The Thatcher government committed itself to NATO's 3 per cent increase in defence spending and spent, when the need arose, £2.5 billion retaking and holding the Falklands. Leaving aside internal improvements in efficiency which are common to operations of government departments and agencies the defence cuts between 1979 and 1983 ran counter to the government's own policy of strengthening defence policy.

Similarly, education and the social services have traditionally been areas considered by Conservatives as legitimate and desirable for adequate public funding. Arguably, the education cuts were contrary to this philosophy. A better-educated workforce, as Professor Stonier has argued, with more not fewer graduates will be better suited to translate knowledge into wealth and to find real employment.[46] Ken Baker, the Information Technology Junior Minister, recalled that 'I launched the Stonier book, which was very good. I kept saying that when the oil runs out we shall have information technology, so we must have an educated workforce to take advantage of the micro-chip revolution'.[47] Mr Baker's argument is sound and persuasive. Graduates are among the most employable of all educational groups, being able to adapt more easily to different skills and job opportunities. Moreover, cuts in school budgets were more likely to produce more unemployable semi-literate sixteen year olds as fodder for YOP schemes. Investment in education can reduce unemployment in the long run and is totally compatible with the provision of the right framework for employment that Mrs Thatcher has proclaimed.[48] This is not an argument for negating improvements within the educational system. There still exists a strong case for making teachers' and lecturers' pay respond to market forces, given the oversupply of labour and an overwhelming case for the abolition of university tenure. But these arguments should not be confused with the principle of state-provision of a highly educated workforce, a principle with a long history of support from Conservatives.

The Health Service also has been central to Conservatives' concern with the less fortunate in society. It has also become the favourite target for quantum cuts by many. According to Lord Harris of High Cross, 'the welfare state is the big arm for cuts'.[49] Nevertheless, it may be argued that a healthier society will be more productive and wealth creating. Cuts which close hospitals or increase waiting lists are incompatible with this aim and can be seen to be counter-productive. Again, this is not an argument against efficiency drives. The privatisation of hospital services, the resistance to the unjustifiable wage demands of the hospital unions and the encouragement of the private health-care sector are all laudable aims. But spending cuts which inconvenience patients are not and should not be a measure employed by any government committed to a safety-net NHS.

Public spending cuts in the arts budget and for the BBC were also unwise for a government aiming at wealth creating. Both the arts and the BBC earn large sums of foreign exchange, either from visitors to Britain attracted by its cultural excellence or in the sale of high quality television programmes overseas. Spending on the arts and BBC represents investment in one of the growing areas of export earnings.[50]

Defence, law and order, education, the Health Service, the arts and broadcasting should all commend themselves to Conservatives as worthwhile public spending, within the normal requirements of efficiency of course, and as such the last candidates for public expenditure cutbacks. However, there are other areas of state spending less deserving, either economically or within Conservative philosophy. It is in these areas that the argument for quantum cuts is strongest.

The obvious candidate is the huge level of state spending on the nationalised industries and on subsidising manufacturing employment. Although this will be examined in greater detail in Chapter 7, suffice it to say here that much Department of Industry spending is difficult to justify on any grounds. John Burton in an excellent and comprehensive study of industrial subsidisation has noted that:

The most serious damage to the process of economic evolution is caused by certain large, loss-making, state-owned enterprises. The discipline of corporate bankruptcy has for them been virtually suspended, and the taxpayer has been dragooned into becoming an unlimited liability guarantor of all their losses. Moreover, the costs of their activities are hidden from the taxpayer because the losses are funded from general taxation. Furthermore, their losses are often so huge that the enterprises are difficult but not necessarily impossible to privatise.[51]

Nor should the legislative and constitutional difficulties of making nationalised industries bankruptable be seen as insurmountable. Although the Thatcher government moved in the right direction in insisting on greater efficiency in the nationalised and state-supported sector, it did not seriously consider the option of bankruptcy for chronic loss-making industries perpetually consuming public funds. The subsidisation of thousands of railway, shipyard, steel and coal-mining jobs is a sad commentary on the effects of nationalisation that Conservatives, at the time, opposed. One MP, although on the left of the party, commented that 'we were appalled at the excessive money going into steel, mines and BL. The £6 billion in BSC was way beyond limits. What we needed was carefully costed capital projects, like repairing the sewerage pipes in Lancashire'.[52] The government's policy of selling off to the private sector only the profitable, or potentially profitable, parts of state enterprises is worthy in itself. But it does not remedy the central deficiency of much of the nationalised sector the production of goods that customers do not want because of high costs, changing tastes or preferable alternatives. Nor is the commonly advanced jobs argument persuasive. Many nationalised industry jobs are artificial in the first place, a delusion practised by both governments and workforce. Moreover, even the costs of dole or redundancy payments would be far less than the maintenance of such industrial fossils as British Rail, British Steel, British Shipbuilders and the NCB. As Burton rightly argues, continued and prolonged subsidisation increases costs by lessening the impetus for efficiency measures and thus perpetuating the original problems. As Burton notes:

An ailing company which is facing potential bankruptcy knows that it must reorganise its activities and improve its performance. It is the very urgency of the situation which provides the stimulus to contemplate and implement drastic recovery measures. A company that is bailed out by government subsidies has, by comparison, much less incentive to reorganise: the threat of imminent disaster for its owners and controllers is suspended or at least diminished. The subsidised enterprise is consequently less likely to contemplate and undertake the requisite corrective measures. Moreover, subsidies encourage union negotiators to resist slower wage growth (or wage reductions) and de-manning, whilst taking the pressure off management to push for them as a component of the reorganisation and recovery strategy.[53]

A bankruptcy policy for the nationalised loss-making sector would enable potentially profitable parts to be quickly transferred to the private sector while the public expenditure saved could be better employed elsewhere by cutting taxes, lowering interest rates as the PSBR falls, or increasing spending on defence, education, the Health Service or the arts, all of which would boost real employment. One should not forget within the context of nationalised industry spending that each £1 billion reduction in public spending allows 1p to come off the standard rate of income tax, an argument that should commend itself to both Conservatives and the electorate as a whole.

Ultimately, the aim of such a quantum cut would be to strengthen private sector rather than public sector employment by changing employment patterns in keeping with world-wide technological change and Britain's international comparative advantage. This key point has been overlooked by Michael Nevin, for example, who, while making the valid distinction between current and capital public sector spending, suggests 'investment' capital spending on British Rail and a channel tunnel.[56] Such public sector 'investment' has been the cause of huge expenditure problems from Concorde, which Nevin fails to mention, to BSC, De Lorean, Meriden Motorcycles and the Kirby Manufacturing Workers' Co-operative. There is no merit in investment, public or private, for its own sake. It is the rate of return on investment that really matters. To neglect this fact makes any distinction between capital and current spending worthless or even positively misleading. The quantum-cut approach advanced in this chapter would lead to less rather than more economically dubious public spending spuriously justified on capital account.

On the political level, one long-overdue reform would be the abolition of the present Department of Industry and the creation of a Department of Science and Technology, with its Secretary of State a Cabinet member. The appointment of Kenneth Baker as an Information Technology Junior Minister was a step in the right direction by the Thatcher government, but a bolder reform should not be prevented by the political memory of Frank Cousins as Harold Wilson's Minister of Technology in the 1960s. Indeed, the considerable success, with limited resources, of Ken Baker in promoting a climate where information technology could blossom was one of the most laudable achievements of the first Thatcher government. Baker's energy in encouraging industrial robots, CADCAM (computer aided design/computer aided manufacturing), the Software Products Scheme, Micros in Schools, the fibre optics and Upto-Electronics Scheme, Micros for GP's, Electronics CADMAT and Biotechnology in Industry Scheme all demonstrated the wide scope of investing in new technology. Such government aid was the very opposite to industrial fossilisation based on yesteryear's manufacturing base. Quantum cuts in the nationalised sector would release further funds for information technology support. Moreover, the bilateral system of negotiation between Treasury ministers and Whitehall departments over public spending, while unavoidable, would work better under the quantum expenditure-cut proposal outlined above, as well as avoiding the 'bleeding stump' and multiplication of political opposition to each spending restraint.

A second candidate for quantum cuts is local government spending. The difficulties encountered by Mr Heseltine have already been described, and a more radical approach is required to restrain the rise in the rates burden on industry and the citizen. The 1983 Conservative manifesto, recognising this, advanced many extremely desirable reforms stating:

we shall legislate to curb excessive and irresponsible rate increases by high-spending councils, and to provide a general scheme for limitation of rate increases for all local authorities to be used if necessary. In addition, for industry we will require local authorities to consult local representatives of industry and commerce before setting their rates. We shall give more businesses the right to pay by instalments. And we shall stop the rating of empty industrial property. The Metropolitan Councils and the Greater London Council have been shown to be a wasteful and unnecessary tier of government. We shall abolish them and return most of their functions to the boroughs and districts. Services which need to be administered over a wider area such as police and fire, and education in inner London will be run by joint boards of borough or district representatives.[55]

One senior CBI official recalled that 'rates were the biggest single tax on business. We had cases of roofs being taken off factories to avoid rates. Local government isn't subject to market pressures and it has grown since 1939 in an unorganised way. Business has no vote over rates our only vote is with our feet'.[56] Such sentiments accurately reflected the burden borne by industry and created by local authority waste and overmanning.

Further action, therefore, to curb overmanning is as necessary in local authorities as it is in British Steel or BL. To achieve this the government may have to consider a legislative freeze on all local authority recruitment at the discretion of the Environment Secretary. If this undermines local government autonomy, it would be justifiable, if public expenditure can be properly controlled and rates kept within the limits of financial discipline. Local government has become the last refuge of the professional hard left, and reversing this trend with the consequent saving of public money should override the traditional freedom of local government to essentially spend on any project or employment however unjustified or irrelevant.

These two quantum cuts suggestions are not easy options; nor are they without political risks. However, they may prove a more effective way of both effectively and correctly controlling public expenditure, keeping it to levels that the country can afford and also in preserving the beneficial areas of public spending which Conservatives have a history of promoting. The Thatcher government's overall strategy of reducing total public spending was economically justified; the methods of carrying it out proved more difficult than most observers had expected and the alternative quantum remedy may be the next best solution given the long-term nature of the public expenditure dilemma.

6 Contemporary Conservatism and Trade Union Power

some employees have opposed and obstructed the spread of collective bargaining to new sections of the workforce, especially those increasing numbers employed in 'white-collar' jobs. Unions too have often failed to involve their members closely enough in their work, or to tackle with sufficient urgency the problems of overlapping membership and unnecessary rivalry, which always diminish their effectiveness and sometimes their reputation. Many employers' relations with unions have been greatly complicated by the large number of unions that may have members in a single factory.

In Place of Strife, Cmnd 3888, 1969

SCOPE OF LEGISLATION

Reform of the abuses of trade union law had been made a central issue in the 1979 election, not so much by the Conservatives' Opposition proposals but by the highly unpopular and gratuitous trade union behaviour towards the general public during the 1978–79 Winter of Discontent. Nevertheless, the Thatcher administration moved by stealth in this area, mindful both of Jim Prior's preferred low-key approach and of the failure of all-encompassing trade union law reform under the Heath government's Industrial Relations Act.[1] As Chapter 2 outlined, the main casualty of the Thatcher government's new approach was corporatist policy-making in the incomes policy mould rather than wholesale and immediate legislative changes.

Jim Prior's legislative plans, which culminated in the 1980 Employment Act, reflected the judicious and careful approach to the limits of what legislative change could actually achieve—a view which, from the start, was not wholly shared by right-wing backbenchers or by Cabinet hard-liners. Indeed, Mrs Thatcher in February 1980 told Robin Day on BBC's

Panorama that she and her Cabinet colleagues would now have to wait and see whether Mr Prior's softly-softly approach to the hotly disputed difference over individual or corporate trade union liability in cases of secondary picketing was likely to work. If it did not, she said, then the government would have to go much further in the direction of attacking trade union funds.

Mr Prior's consultative proposals, unveiled in February 1980, centred round legislation to curb secondary picketing by removing immunities from pickets unless they picketed their own place of work plus restrictions of the operation of the closed shop. Mr Prior cautiously insisted from the outset that 'What matters above all is that the much-needed changes we are making will stick and will work. It's no use rushing in with tough-sounding measures which then won't work or can't be enforced'.[3] Such reticence was unacceptable to some Conservative backbenchers, who called for the outlawing of not only secondary picketing but secondary strikes, ballots on strike action and immediate rather than proposed legislation. Forty-four backbenchers tabled a critical motion to that effect facing Mr Prior with a Commons battle on two fronts, given the ritual protests of Labour Opposition. One critical backbencher recalled that 'I was a leading rebel in trying to tighten up the 1980 Act. The Bill was too slow in coming forward and did allow for all the lessons of the Winter of Discontent. The backbench employment committee—to a man Priorites—were out of touch with backbench feeling, particularly among the 1979 intake'.[3] Reg Prentice noted that 'I would have been inclined to move more quickly with the legislation. During 1981 the backbenchers wanted a second Act and signed a motion. Further action wouldn't have come naturally from Jim Prior'.[4] In April forty-five Tory rebels duly voted in the lobbies for a tougher legislative stance. Similarly, a Bow Group memorandum, *The Next Employment Bill: Agenda for Action*, written by George Gardiner, argued strongly for tackling the question of trade union immunities and for further measures to curb the closed shop.

Consultations with the TUC proved abortive, however, despite Mr Prior's efforts, and worsened as the TUC held its 'Day of Action' protest at the government's policies. The miners at their 1980 conference declared that they would rather go to prison than recognise the government's industrial relations legislation, and Arthur Scargill openly advocated defying the law. The NUM executive in July reaffirmed this line, and at the 1980 TUC conference Moss Evans of the TGWU echoed the sentiments, declaring that 'I think the unions at some time will find it necessary to break the law, and I suppose they will have to put up with the consequences'.[5] Trade union opposition even to Mr Prior's cautiously modest legal reforms was thus outright.

Mr Prior's most difficult defence of his 1980 Employment Act came at the Conservative party conference, where advocates of abandoning the step-by-step approach raised their voices. Mr Prior's argument in his own defence was:

It does not make sense to act as though we're taking part in the charge of the Light Brigade. We're not Wedgie Benn in blue. . . We mean to deal with abuses as we identify them and as we think the time is right. But our main objective must be to go at a pace acceptable to public opinion to carry with us the support of the shop floor, and in that way to make our changes in the law stick. It's easy to pass laws but nothing is more damaging for Parliamentary democracy than to pass laws you can't enforce. For too long now there's been a widespread feeling that union leaders have been playing politics rather than doing their job. But they couldn't unite against the Employment Bill, could they? And that's what they'd love to do. They would love to have something which would get the moderates on their side. By God, I'm not going to give them that chance.[6]

The 1980 Act was indeed a modest and moderate reform. It widened an individual's right not to be unfairly dismissed where he objected to being a member of a union subject to the closed shop. Secondary picketing was outlawed, section 17 removing immunity for secondary industrial action that induced the breach of a commercial contract. This reform had been particularly awaited following the violent secondary picketing during the 1980 steel strike. Section 18 stated that immunity is also removed from pickets unless they picket at their own place of work; from most forms of secondary industrial action, unless it is targeted specifically to interfere with the supply of goods or services to or from the employer in dispute, with his first supplier or first customer; and from industrial action to compel trade union membership, except where employees work for the same employer or at the same work place as those taking such action.[7]

The 1980 Act was quickly followed, however, in January 1981 by Mr Prior's Green Paper on trade union legal immunities,[8] the next stage in the step-by-step approach. The characteristically Prior approach was confirmed and difficulties in legislating against abuses highlighted rather then played-down. For example, it stressed that there were 'practical limits to the extent which long-standing practices such as the closed shop can be eradicated by law' and similarly that 'Powers to declare strikes unlawful if they threaten the community could put almost every major strike at risk and mass prosecution of strikers for breaking such a law could hardly be regarded as a practical proposition'.

By the time the period of consultation on the Green Paper was over at the end of June 1981 there was considerable pressure for tougher legislation. The CBI favoured the ending of the closed shop, considering the existing voluntary collective agreements as difficult to operate; a large increase from £16,910 to £30,000 in compensation to closed-shop victims was also advocated. Mr Prior himself admitted in reference to the decision of Sandwell Council to sack a poultry inspector, Joanna Harris, that:

One thing that is not acceptable is that the closed shop should continue to allow people to be dismissed in the manner of Sandwell and Walsall and a number of other cases where obviously the deterrent powers introduced in the 1980 Act are not proving sufficient to deter an employer who is determined to follow that course.[9]

But if pressure was building in the Conservative party and industry for further legislative reform, Mr Prior was not the man to pilot it through the Commons. In September 1981 he was demoted to the Northern Ireland portfolio and replaced by a hard-line opponent of trade union abuses, Norman Tebbit.

The pace of reform quickened with Mr Tebbit's appointment, but there was still to be no return to the Industrial Relations Act mentality of all-embracing legislative change at one go. In the 1981 Queen's Speech further legislation was given priority, and in November 1981 a consultative document, outlining the details of legal changes, aimed to diminish the powers of unions to mount successful industrial action. The proposals included making unions liable up to £250,000 for unlawful actions through injunctions and damages, the dismissal of strikers fairly for refusing to return to work after a brief set period, the subjection of existing closed shops to periodic ballots, increased compensation for closed-shop victims and the exclusion from immunity of any industrial action motivated by political or personal considerations. Sir Raymond Pennock, the CBI Chairman, purred that 'we at the CBI think he has got it just about right. He has not missed out anything of importance'.[10]

Trade union and Labour party opposition was, as expected, forthright, but with the union membership becoming less militant there was to be no repeat of the successful sabotage of the 1971 Industrial Relations Act. The TUC warned that unions accepting government money, as provided for in the Bill, to conduct ballots for union leadership elections would be expelled and the Labour party promised a total repeal. A number of trade unionists, particularly the NALGO leadership, predicted dire industrial consequencies if the Bill reached the statute book,[11] and the TUC's special conference in April reiterated this line. At the 1982 TUC conference an overwhelming vote was passed to defy 'anti-union laws', and Arthur Scargill bluntly put it that 'There is only one response. Faced with this legislation we should say we will defy the law. It is the only action we can take and it is the only response this movement can give. If there is an attempt to use this legislation then you defy it not as an individual union but as a movement'.[12] These threats were to no avail, however, and the 1982 Employment Act duly became law on 18 October, embodying the changes presaged by the November 1981 consultative document. The 1982 Act meant a substantial increase in the compensation for people unfairly dismissed for not belonging to a union in a closed shop. It outlawed union-labour-only contracts drawn up by local authorities and allowed unions, as opposed to merely trade unionists, to be sued for damages of up to £250,000 if strikes are unlawful. Moreover, there were curbs on political strikes by restricting immunity from civil action to industrial action 'wholly or mainly' about pay and conditions. One senior CBI official recalled that 'Tebbit played with consummate skill and we supported him. The justification for the legislation was that the unions enjoyed immunities and we had felt that there was more to be done in that field and that Prior felt he hadn't wanted to go any further'.[13]

But Mr Tebbit was not prepared to call it a day on legislation forms. In January 1983 a Green paper on union democracy was published which stated:

Much public concern has been voiced about the need for trade unions to become more democratic and responsive to the wishes of their members. In the case of many unions, the role and influence of the rank and file seems to be minimal, and all too often it is evident that the policies which are being pursued do not reflect the views and interests of the members ... There is undoubtedly widespread concern about the electoral arrangement of trade unions. In many trade union elections the proportion of the eligible membership who actually vote is extremely low. Union rules differ widely on election procedures and some are quite unspecific on the subject. This opens up the possibility for example of a union's governing body having power under the rules to draw up its own preferred method of election procedure and then selecting one best suited to securing its own re-election. The more undemocratic the arrangements, the more difficult it must be for the union members to secure the rule revisions needed to introduce more democratic processes. The courts can and do provide remedies on proof of particular malpractices. But unless trade union election procedures are as far as possible proof against irregularities, suspicion will remain.[14]

Furthermore, following the water-workers strike in 1983, Mr Tebbit hinted that he was considering the outlawing of strikes in essential industries by 'legislation specifically directed in the area of essential services. My mind is not closed to that'.[15] As a result of the government's success in reducing trade union power and in vastly reducing the number of strikes, such plans seemed more plausible in the new climate of trade union weakness. Not surprisingly, therefore, the 1983 Conservative manifesto promised that:

Our 1982 Green Paper, Democracy in Trade Unions, points the way to give union members control over their own unions. We shall give union members the right to: hold ballots for the election of governing bodies of trade unions; decide periodically whether their unions should have party political funds. We shall also curb the legal immunity of unions to call strikes without the prior approval of those concerned through a fair and secret ballot. The proposal to curb immunity in the absence of pre-strike ballots will reduce the risk of strikes in essential services. In addition, we shall consult further about the need for industrial relations in specified essential services to be governed by adequate procedure agreements, breach of which would deprive industrial action of immunity. The nation is entitled to expect that the operation of essential services should not be disrupted.[16]

In summary, the Thatcher government had avoided repeating the major debacle of the 1971 Industrial Relations Act by legislating step-by-step with a modestly increasing pace of reform aimed at specific abuses of union power. Taken as a whole, the 1980 and 1982 Employment Acts were modest reforms, given the great increase in trade union power in the preceding decade. Partly because of this, and partly because of the changed economic climate, the legislation did not produce industrial chaos and may have helped to prevent it by removing certain legal immunities. Leon Brittan thought that 'we got the pace of union reform right. Part of the unions' weakness was the recession but we made sure that there wasn't a *causus belli*'.[17] One Cabinet minister recalled that 'Prior's brief before the '79 election was to persuade the public we wouldn't be in conflict with the unions. Jim Prior was the Geoff Boycott figure, not giving any chances to the opposition and [Norman Tebbit] was the Ian Botham coming in at about no.6'.[18] The legislation record between 1979 and 1983, in contrast to that between 1970 and 1974, was one of unspectacular achievement, but achievement nonetheless.

THE HANDLING OF DISPUTES

In a pluralist society where the right to strike by free trade unions is legal, no government can hope to avoid a number of industrial disputes during its time in office. Strike action is a voluntary measure by unions, and governments have to react to strikes as a fact of political life. The first Thatcher government, however, contrary to the expectation widely expressed when it took office, did not preside over an increase in strikes caused by confrontation politics. In fact quite the reverse occurred. Strikes, and working days lost thereby, declined to their lowest level since the 1940s, and trade union militancy, which had scarred the 1970–74 Conservative government, was conspicuous by its absence. In the private sector, strikes were rare and in the public sector less numerous and prolonged than under previous governments.[19] The Thatcher government can take credit for this record. First, the absence of formal incomes policy reduced the number of disputes typically caused by government intervention to prevent a mutual agreement between unions and management. Second, the absence of formal incomes policy eliminated the need for a wave of strikes to 'restore' free collective bargaining. Third, the government did not encourage the belief that strike action would succeed by surrendering once strikes had begun to take effect, and fourth, the government successfully appealed to moderate union membership to reject strike calls by militant union leaders. The handling of the public sector disputes that occurred between 1979 and 1983 demonstrates these four points.

The first test for the government was the 1980 steel strike. The initial 2 per cent offer was increased during negotiations to 17 per cent in January 1980 and the final settlement in April on 18 per cent was below the going rate in the public sector and was regarded as a vindication of the government's decision to sit out the strike rather than capitulate. The government's rationale was well expressed by Industry Secretary Sir Keith Joseph who told the Commons that:

The BSC is bankrupt. If it were not nationalised it would be bankrupt. It is quite wrong to suggest there is any more money available except in what is either provided by the steelworkers or provided in addition to that already provided by our long suffering taxpayers.

The taxpayer is paying £4,000 million for the steel industry. That is over £200 per British family towards British steel. That surely is enough involvement.

... BSC estimate that their offer will bring the average earnings of a steelworker next year up to at least £124 a week. Is it fair that other workers should be asked to give the difference from their taxes or is it right that the difference should be earned by the steelworker himself from improved productivity?[20]

Moreover, long-term aspects of the dispute did not deflect the government. The violent picketing of private steel-works not involved in the dispute made reform of trade union law on picketing more relevant; and the restructuring of the steel industry to reduce overmanning and eliminate loss-making capacity was brought into more urgent focus, as will be discussed in Chapter 7. Reg Prentice recalled that 'the whole balance changed as soon as Mrs Thatcher entered Downing Street; beer and sandwiches were out and the unions were not seen as an estate of the realm to be treated specially. There was a new attitude to industrial disputes and the government didn't let Bill Sirs off the hook in the steel strike as he'd expected'.[21]

Further encouraging signs for the government were the rejection by BL workers of a strike call over pay urged by their shop stewards in April 1980 and the miners' vote not to strike to save jobs in the mining and steel industries, again in defiance of their leaders' recommendation. A similar strike threat at BL in November 1980 was quashed with the acceptance of a 6.8 per cent pay offer approved by twenty-nine out of thirty-six plants, an outcome for industrial peace that would have been regarded as extremely unlikely in the period of the 1974–79 Labour government.

In February 1981, however, the government suffered its only major defeat in an industrial dispute when it backed down over the threat of a miners' strike against the NCB's plans to close twenty-three pits. But the issue was more complicated, and in the long run the government showed that though they lost this battle they were winning the war. In the February 1981 climbdown, the pit closures were withdrawn and cash limits relaxed in return for what Energy Secretary David Howell described as a thorough examination of the coal industry. But political intrigue rather than the miners' might was responsible for the government's retreat. The NCB's chairman, Sir Derek Ezra was widely considered to have provoked the NUM as part of a wider battle with the government to increase cash limits for the industry. Ezra had not concealed his hostility to the government, not only with regard to the coal industry but in his capacity as Chairman of the Nationalised Industries Chairmen's group. In July 1980 he had pointedly told a Commons Committee that 'we would be most reluctant to be saddled with financial objectives which we believe cannot be achieved'.[22] According to a Treasury adviser, 'we were going forward with the closures until Scargill and Gormley met Ezra and Ezra referred—inadvertently I think—to the exact number of pits on the list prepared by the NUM delegation'.[23] One Cabinet minister who was close to the crisis thought that 'Ezra didn't do it deliberately—but I could be wrong'.[24]

It was also speculated that Jim Prior had not been adverse to a government climbdown over the pit closure issue, an accusation that Prior rejected. The *Daily Express* considered that Prior had secretly plotted with Gormley to enable cash limits to be increased and proclaimed that 'Jim was to blame for surrender'.[25] The evidence for this allegation is less than convincing. More accurate is the explanation of Fryer and Jones who argued that:

Prior did have a role in the climbdown but it was different. He met Gormley not last week but on January 21, in one of a regular series of informal encounters he arranges with union leaders. Gormley warned Prior of the probability of a national strike if the NCB came up with a package of closures.

Last weekend, when the unofficial action was beginning, it was Prior's job to assess its importance. Were the strikes for real? Was the NUM serious? There was no doubt about it, Prior told his colleagues. To risk a confrontation with a united union would be madness.

Additionally, Prior was more sensitive than his colleagues to Gormley's position inside the union. With the NUM executive due to meet on Thursday, Gormley would have no alternative but to back the call for a ballot and a recommendation for a strike, despite the cautionary noises he kept uttering when the Welsh and others came out unofficially. It would be the only way he could assert his authority.

Prior saw that the moment for the government's intervention, planned with very leisurely timing for the next Monday (i.e.tomorrow), would be hopelessly late. By that time the union would be committed to striking. It was on Prior's advice that the Prime Minister moved swiftly, to insist that this meeting be held immediately—on Wednesday—and that the government should give more money to the NCB.[26]

The February 1981 surrender was not to be the last word on pit closures. By the time of the 1983 election the policy had been irrevocably put into operation without strike action ensuing, largely because of the miners' own balloted wishes not to make it a strike issue.[27]

One of the most important public sector disputes of the first Thatcher administration took place in 1981 when the Civil Service unions went on strike over pay. Civil servants, a privileged group under successive governments, had gained above-average pay rises, index-linked pensions, job security denied to those in the private sector—and other parts of the public sector—as well as increasing manpower levels. Not surprisingly, they regarded the approach of the Thatcher government as anathema and followed a 19 per cent pay claim in January 1981 with strike action which was to last until the end of July. The impact of the strike delayed the receipt of tax revenues, disrupted car registrations, delayed court administration procedures, affected air traffic control and reduced the effectiveness of customs checks. The government, however, refused to increase its 7 per cent offer—arguably a not ungenerous offer to a group of workers having no difficulty being recruited at existing rates—and eventually the unions backed down and settled for an extra 0.5 per cent only.

This success in winning the dispute was despite the attempts of Lord Soames, the minister responsible for the Civil Service, whose earlier attempts to foist a compromise deal had been rejected by Mrs Thatcher and the Cabinet. Indeed, the final 7.5 per cent settlement which was agreed at the end of July had been rejected only a week earlier by the unions. The twenty strong Civil Service union executive voted unanimously against acceptance. The government had clearly demonstrated that it was prepared to resist industrial action where necessary without such action, as under previous governments, being a prelude to capitulation. In this respect its handling of the Civil Service strikers was skilful, given the complete absence of any convincing arguments on the union's side. One casualty of the dispute in the long run was Lord Soames himself, who was dismissed in September 1981, partly as a result of his lack of stomach for sticking out the strikes.

Strikes were being seen to be unsuccessful, given the government's response and the predicted Winter of Discontent had failed to materialise. In January 1982 the miners voted to reject Arthur Scargill's strike call over pay, but two other public sector disputes were unavoidable in that year. In the Health Service the familiar call for strike action over 'low pay' led to a long dispute, and the railways were severely disrupted by strike action. In the railways dispute the issue of flexible rostering led ASLEF members to strike in January 1982, but a stop-gap 3 per cent pay increase temporarily settled the issue. It turned out, however, that Sir Peter Parker, BR's chairman had not abandoned flexible rostering—the jargonised term for efficient manning levels and working practices—as Ray Buckton of ASLEF had thought. Indeed, at the time of the February agreement Sir Peter had stated that 'if we can now get moving and modernise working practices, I think we have a pretty good chance of convincing the government on all the significant things we put into railway policy last year'.[28] On the other hand, Ray Buckton's view was that 'Aslef's very firm policy is against any elimination of the guaranteed eight-hour day, and we shall be pursuing that policy right the way through the negotiations',[29] which seemed to make further conflict inevitable.

In the summer of 1982 the flexible rostering issue duly emerged again. This time Sir Peter Parker was not prepared to give way nor was the government prepared to sanction any surrender. The BR management kept open the rail network to encourage strike breaking and threatened strikers with dismissal. The response showed that ASLEF could not command the total support of its members, and 8 per cent of trains ran even during a total stoppage, prompting Clifford Rose, BR's board member responsible for personnel, to declare that the response had been 'modestly encouraging, giving us a clear indication that the drivers are very concerned about the strike'.[30] When BR management finally decided to close down the rail network, strikers were threatened with dismissal, Sir Peter Parker declaring that 'It would be inconceivable that we could keep on those people who have brought this industry to this catastrophic pass. We have to try to avoid making predictions, but we should be prepared for a long hard siege'.[31] Mrs Thatcher took a similarly tough line, informing the Commons that:

There is no future for the railways unless working practices agreed in 1919 are updated. The problem can be quickly over now if the ASLEF workers will return to work and accept flexible rostering in accordance with the BR offer...we cannot make progress unless we have flexible rostering, but the question has been considered for a long time, and a few months earlier this year, after considering it, Lord McCarthy said that unless progress was made on this question the outlook was bleak and unpromising. The external limit this year is £900m and last year it was £930m and the operating grant this year, included in that is £800. Those investment projects, in which the British taxpayer is investing, cannot give a return, unless we improve present practices.[32]

The hard line was soon to pay off and the strike collapsed on 18 July when the TUC supported the introduction of flexible rostering, causing a furious Ray Buckton to express his bitterness against his colleagues. Mr Buckton became engaged in a public slanging match with NUR leader Sid Weighell, whose own union had been forced to abandon its strike over pay in June 1982 because of lack of support from the membership. Criticising Mr Weighell, Mr Buckton declared that 'the public utterances of the general secretary of the NUR have been contrary to every principle of trade unionism. He has, by his actions, assisted the BR board at every stage'.[33] Thus the collapse of two rail strikes, the acceptance of flexible rostering and the TUC's failure to support ASLEF had all justified the government's approach to the dispute and its backing for BR's ultimately tough line. Subsequently, in March 1983, BR could announce the commencement of driver-only trains and the running, after previous union refusal, of the £150 million Bedford to St Pancras commuter line, where modern trains had stood idle in sidings for more than a year.

The Health Service dispute which dragged on for eight months in 1982 was competently handled from the government's point of view, even if the spectacular victory over the rail unions was not to be repeated. The Health Service unions, however, mindful of their unpopularity in the Winter of Discontent, 1978–79, when their strike action seemed to be designed to maximise patient distress,[34] in 1982 kept disruption to patient care to a minimum. It can be argued that this change of mood by the unions reflected the wide change of public mood which the Thatcher government had sought to express.

Nevertheless, there were several crises caused by strike action and a twenty-four hour stoppage in June severely reduced hospital services with non-emergency patients no longer being admitted for treatment. In August it was reported that:

A children's hospital specialising in open-heart surgery and spine operations was selected as the target for angry health-workers in their attempt to force the government into meeting their pay claim. The Royal Liverpool Children's Hospital, Liverpool, was left without even emergency cover as the bulk of the 150 catering staff, porters, cleaners and store workers went on a mass walk-out. Hospital officials were given less than 24 hours' warning of the action, taken despite pleas by union leaders to the workforce to provide cover for emergencies.[35]

Similarly, a TUC sponsored 'day of action' in support of the Health Service ancillary workers caused widespread disruption and a mass rally of health unions in Hyde Park pledged continuation of the battle for higher pay. As a result, a series of selected and highly publicised regional stoppages ensued, all backed by the TUC. However, the Social Services Secretary, Norman Fowler, refused to give way, and in December the NHS unions accepted the 6 per cent for ancillary workers and 7.5 per cent for nurses that had been on offer since June 1982. Rodney Bickerstaffe, the NUPE General Secretary, confessed to being 'bitterly disappointed ', adding that 'Health workers have been a dedicated and exploited group of workers for a very long time. The dedication will continue but so will the exploitation'.[36] *The Times* was thus able to observe accurately that 'this clear defeat for the consistent attempts by the health unions to improve the June offer to somewhere nearer their original 12 per cent claim leaves the Prime Minister with no obvious threat on the pay front'.[37]

Even more significant for the government was the reaction of the miners to two strike calls from Arthur Scargill's leadership during the last six months of the Thatcher administration. These major defeats for the union leadership marked the success of the government's policy of appealing above the heads of the union leaders to trade union members in the hope of avoiding industrial action. The issue concerned, ironically, pit closures which had forced the government's hand in February 1981. But in October 1982 an overall majority of two to one was recorded against strike action linking job loss and pay, thus enabling the NCB to initiate the closure of three chronic-loss-making pits, Snowdon in Kent, Kinneil in Scotland and Britannia in Wales. Despite a national campaign of rallies, at which Mr Scargill's oratorial powers were skilfully deployed, enthusiasm for strike action was very weak, which in the Midlands and north-east a four to one vote against industrial action demonstrated.

In March 1983 a repeat of the October ballot brought a further severe rebuff for Mr Scargill. NCB plans to close loss making pits was again the issue and the miners at the threatened Tynmawr Lewis Merthyr's colliery had already begun strike action. But the miners themselves in the national ballot preferred the views of Mr Siddall, the NCB chairman who appealed against strike action by arguing that a strike would endanger not protect jobs. The government had effectively reversed the trend of their decision of two years before. *The Times* was not slow to point out that:

Exactly two years ago a strike in South Wales against an investment plan implying an increased rate of pit closures produced such a surge of sympathy among miners throughout the country that the government suddenly made the most ignominious retreat of its career and offered large subsidies to reprieve most of the loss-making pits. Today the South Wales miners are again on strike over the closure of a colliery and union leaders up and down the country are calling their men out in support. But this time there is no case for another government retreat. The miners' case is less good, their belief in it is not yet proven, and their tactical position is significantly weaker than it was two years ago.[38]

Thus the miners' decision not to strike in March 1983 had enabled the Thatcher government to achieve what had eluded the Heath government, an administration free from the severe disruption a miners' strike can cause. Moreover, the Thatcher government could claim that the model the miners had set—the rejection by union members of their leaders' strike call—was applicable to the rest of industry and gave added legitimacy to legislative reform on secret strike ballots. This point was also illuminated in April 1983 when BL Cowley workers voted five to one to end the 'washing time' dispute, which had led to considerable lost production over a month.

The final major public sector dispute of the Thatcher administration was the 1983 water-workers strike. The disruption caused by the strike was not as extensive as had been feared but nevertheless the dispute was referred to the arbitration of a committee headed by Dr Tom Johnson, the principal of Heriot-Watt University whose generous recommendations favoured the unions rather than the National Water Council. The government had discreetly kept out of the negotiations and was embarrassed by the management's apparently needless surrender. Water-workers were neither low paid nor exploited, and there was no difficulty recruiting them at their existing wages. The case for the 10.4 per cent agreed deal was, therefore, less than convincing. However, the National Water Council was acting within its financial limits, and there was nothing ministers could have done short of exhortation to the NWC to stand firm. The lessons learned from the dispute— such as the advisability of using troops as strike breakers and the advisability of avoiding unnecessary arbitration machinery—were applicable in other contexts, even though the government had found itself hamstrung by the employers' lack of willingness to win the dispute. One backbench MP put it that there 'was an obvious justification for using troops in the water workers strike. After Heath, ministers were reluctant to be seen in the front line of disputes, which were to be left to the employers'.[39] If the outcome of the water-workers strike was regrettable, the blame lay not with the government but with the employers.

The handling of public sector disputes as a whole in the period between 1979 and 1983 had been conducted with realism and determination from a government standpoint. Unnecessary disputes caused by incomes policy stipulations had been avoided and having decided to stand firm against strike action the government had had the political will to see it through. This resolution had been shown with the steel strike, Civil Service strike, ASLEF strike and Health Service disputes, which in turn had discouraged action by other unions. The government had given the impression that it was not worthwhile for strike action to take place, because such action would not succeed. Only the 1981 climbdown to the miners and the 1983 water settlement could count as political defeats, and the latter was reversed by the miners' decisions in 1982 and 1983 not to strike to save loss-making pits. In short, the government handled public sector dispute with greater acumen than its predecessors of both Labour and Conservative persuasions. As a result, strikes were down in number and 'winters of discontent' studiously avoided. Moreover, trade union power was less visible and arguably less decisive.

DECLINE IN UNION MILITANCY

The overall decline in trade union power and militancy is one of the most remarkable and unexpected results of the first Thatcher administration. Over a decade of growing trade union power had been fundamentally reversed. The crisis of 1974 which produced the 'who rules? government or unions?' election in February seemed light-years away in 1983. The ungovernability of Britain at the hands of trade union power had faded into past experience rather than current policy determination. The agonising that Conservatives subjected themselves to in the late 1970s over whether they could 'work with' the unions proved to have been in vain. The corporatist model, whereby 'working with' the unions occupied many hours of ministerial time in tripartite or NEDC talks, was jettisoned in favour of a solely government-determined economic policy. Thus, as Patrick Jenkin recalled, 'the ending of beer and sandwiches was a major factor in changing attitudes, especially on the shop floor. There were no norms and no pay limits, and the Treasury simply said what we could afford'.[40] One CBI official similarly thought that 'you can afford to pay different rates of pay to people with a future and not to those in decline. What the government did was to change attitudes of a great many people in a great way. It was a major change away from collectivism and the belief that the money is always there'.[41] To those who had always opposed the rigidities of incomes policy, partly because they brought extra industrial strife, the Thatcher government's record between 1979 and 1983 brought empirical confirmation of the accuracy of their assessment.[42]

This is not to argue that the government was pro-union or successfully appeased union power. On the contrary the Thatcher government was the most determinedly anti-union since the second World War—or rather, it was anti the abuses of trade union power. The Thatcher government's assessment of the role of trade unions and the need to remove their excessive and damaging power reflected the general public mood, including that of individual trade union members. During the 1983 election campaign it was normal practice rather than tactlessly provocative for Mrs Thatcher to attack the 'death wish' mentality of striking car workers. Nor were the ritual threats of trade union opposition to government policies effective in influencing, let alone reversing, government policies. In October 1980 Len Murray left a meeting at 10 Downing Street[43] bemoaning that 'we're in two different worlds'.[44]

Similarly, NEDC meetings, stripped of the cosy tripartite corporatism which so often previously had ignored economic realities, were occasions of battle or no consensus. In August 1981 TUC leaders bitterly criticised Geoffrey Howe, whose paper presented to the meeting rejected the TUC's reflationary proposals. Unable to influence government policy, Len Murray stated that talks with the government were 'arid lectures on Adam Smith and the need to reduce pay settlements . . . in my thirty years at the TUC this is the worst government I have known'.[45] Determined to reject trade union solutions to Britain's economic problems, the government was equally as critical of the TUC.

John Hoskyns, once he had resigned from the No. 10 policy unit, launched a strong political attack on the unions in two articles in *The Times* in September 1982, by which time the reduction in trade union militancy was self-evident. Hoskyns argued:

Today, union prestige and authority have declined beyond recognition. They are more disliked, less feared, less respected. The rift between members and leaders grows, as does that between unions in the public and private sectors. Union leaders no longer claim to speak for 'the working people of this country' because the public no longer pays attention...

There is no sign that union leaders have learned anything about economic or business reality in the past ten years. Their pronouncements still betray a frightening ignorance. When the Chancellor spoke last July of the need for a near-zero increase in the next pay round, Mr David Basnett, Secretary of the GMWU, immediately promised that public utility workers would lead the drive to breach any figure the government might suggest.

It was as if Sir Michael Edwardes had publicly pledged that BL cars would always cost more than their competitors. Mr Basnett seemed not to understand that he was talking about the price of labour, at a time of recession. The long-run futility of most union actions becomes obvious once the ancient mythology is stripped away.

All that remains is the picture of a 'worker army' taught to fight against itself. Its actions are as futile as those of a football team striking for its fair share of goals or a man picketing his back garden because his vegetables won't grow.[46]

Moreover, in his second article Hoskyns openly speculated that 'perhaps we have now reached the point where we should dare to consider, quite seriously, the removal of all the immunities surviving from the Trades Disputes Act of 1906'.[47] Such a suggestion could not have been publicly forthcoming from any official or minister of any previous post-war government. In jettisoning the corporatist respect for trade union power, the Thatcher government had rendered that power less usable and consequently less politically as well as economically practicable.

If one single example demonstrated the new impotence of union power under Mrs Thatcher it was the attempt by Alex Kitson of the TGWU to break the back of the Thatcher government. Advocating a petrol tanker drivers' strike following the failure of the 1981 BL strike, Kitson made his political intentions clear, declaring that 'If it goes on long enough, Mrs Thatcher will either be forced economically to make a U-turn or she may go back to the country. And I can bring her down if she wants to do what Heath did in 1974'.[48] The threat completely failed to materialise as the tanker drivers rejected strike calls. Indeed, strike calls went mostly unheeded during 1979–83, demonstrating the lack of union militancy and a new sense of realism by the mass of moderate union members. 1980's strike figures were the lowest since 1941, despite the lengthy steel-strike stoppage. Working days lost to industry fell to less than half the annual average of the previous decade. In 1981 the number of strikes fell yet again, 1,280 compared to 1,330 in 1980, and the number of working days lost was also down. During the 1983 general election campaign, the low number of strikes was a marked feature of Conservative party political broadcasts, in marked contrast to the abject record presented to the electorate in 1974. Critics of the Thatcher government's economic policies, such as Peter Riddell, do their cause little good by refusing to give credit to the government for this not inconsiderble success.[49]

Declining union militancy was also accompanied by declining union membership. In 1979 the Conservatives had gained power when union membership was at a record high level following the legislation of the 1974–79 Labour government extending union powers. In 1979 52 per cent of the working population was unionised. By 1982 a fundamental reversal of this trend was reflected in the TUC's own statistics. As Table 4 shows, union membership was in sharp decline.

Table 4: *TUC membership: the falling numbers (in thousands)*

Union	1979	1982
Transport and General Workers Union	2,086	1,503
Engineering Workers	1,218	1,001
General and Municipal	967	825
Nalgo	753	784
Public Employees (NUPE)	692	702
Scientific and Technical (ASTMS)	491	410
Shopworkers (USDAW)	470	417
Electricians and plumbers (EETPU)	420	380
Construction workers (UCATT)	348	261
Mineworkers (NUM)	289	245
Teachers (NUT)	249	222
Civil and Public Servants Association	224	199
Postal Workers (UCW)	203	198
White collar engineering (TASS)	201	172
Railway (NUR)	180	150
Bank workers (BIFU)	132	152
Boilerworkers	139	115
Society of Civil and Public Servants	109	96
Iron and Steel Workers (ISTC)	104	95
Seamen (NUS)	47	25
(All figures to the nearest thousand)		

Source: *The Official Report, 1983*

One experienced industrial correspondent, Paul Routledge, commented on the figures that 'we are probably witnessing the start of [the trade union movement's] long-term decline through a mixture of economic, political and social factors'.[50]

For Conservatives such factors as declining union membership, declining union militancy, declining strike levels and declining TUC influence on government policy represented a major victory in a long-fought war with union power. The Thatcher government had successfully challenged not only union power but many of the basic assumptions about British government and its alleged dependence on that power. The Thatcher government had attempted the 'politically impossible' and had succeeded far beyond the expectation that even the most ardent opponents of union power had predicted. Barnes and Reid, in their authoritative study of government relations with the unions 1964–79 had concluded that:

> It could be, therefore, that the relationship between governments and the trade union movement in the eighties will continue much as in the past. The economic consequences of attempting to control inflation in the face of trade union power and collective bargaining are not, however, attractive, and there are other reasons related to the nature of the trade union movement why at some point government may find the situation unacceptable.
>
> It is true that the trade union movement is not the only pressure group whose activities cause inflation, or the only pressure group to compel governments to change or abandon policies. It has, however, special characteristics which distinguish it from others. It is a 'mass' group—it claims to speak for millions and to have a continuing mandate which overrides that of the political parties. It exerts its pressures on governments in full view of the public, and often by means which cause serious public inconvenience and hardship. One of the two governing parties is openly dependent on it. The use of industrial power for political purposes, discredited for forty years, is no longer discredited and unions are prepared to employ this power. The traditional view the union movement has taken of itself as being 'outside the law' and of being committed to transforming the system in which it operates has persisted in spite of the effective industrial and political power it now exercises within that system.[51]

Such an assessment was not incorrect when it appeared in 1980, but by 1983 virtually every aspect of it had undergone radical change, reversing the seemingly irreversible growth of union power. The Thatcher government, by abandoning the corporatism on which unions thrived for political legitimacy and by appealing to union members over the heads of union leaders had effected fundamental changes that not only Conservatives but also the general public believed in.

7 Contemporary Conservatism and Industry Policy

One evening in the autumn of 1952 Churchill sent for me and said, 'I am very worried about my poor friend Daladier losing his seat in the French Chamber. You really must attend to the matter'. I asked what this could possibly have to do with me, and he explained, 'His district exports glace cherries, which you have brutally stopped coming into this country'. It was not entirely in the light of this touching story that I repented, but by slow degrees the restrictions were relaxed and we began to work actively to bring about a freer system of trade and payments, and thus give to our exporter wider opportunities. I was the last to use such import controls and must testify to their efficiency.

R.A. Butler, 1971[1]

CONFLICT WITH THE CBI

The Thatcher government took office with the welcome backing of private industry, and the 1979 Conservative manifesto had pointedly stated that 'Profits are the foundation of a free enterprise economy. In Britain profits are still dangerously low'.[2] A return to higher profit levels and the removal of restrictions on entrepreneurship were widely anticipated after the profits squeeze and state controls under Labour. However, despite these expectations, conflict between the CBI and the Thatcher government was a marked and continuous feature of the years from 1979 to 1983. The rival Institute of Directors was a staunch supporter of the government, as were individual businessmen and firms, but the attention focused more often than not on the CBI, the traditional representative of manufacturing industry opinion, which opposed government policy on a number of issues—interest rates, the level of the pound, reflationary packages and the employers National Insurance surcharge. One senior CBI official recalled that:

the role of government as the CBI saw it was to create the environment to earn our livings more effectively—to earn what the politicians had promised. We were in support of the government's *aims*. Where we disagreed and were disappointed was when the government was trying to control the money supply with excessively high interest rates. It was an appallingly difficult time for industry, particularly when it contributed to the pound being so high.[3]

Although conflict between the CBI and Conservative governments was not a new phenomenon[4] it is arguable that the conflict with the Thatcher government was more public and pronounced than before. In May 1980, with interest rates and the pound higher, the CBI President, Sir John Greenborough, attacked the government for the 'crippling' level of interest rates and also appealed for an easing of the 'enormous pressures' on the private sector caused by the NI surcharge. The monthly CBI surveys during 1980 took an almost permanently pessimistic view of the economy, often tinged with criticism of the government's deflationary policies. In July 1980 James Cleminson, the CBI's Economic Committee Chairman, declared that the economic outlook was 'as gloomy a picture [as] is possible for anyone to paint'.[5] The government in turn was critical of industry, and Mrs Thatcher attacked 'patchy' management that had 'found it convenient to be regulated by government and saved by subsidies'.[6] However, one Cabinet minister commented that 'it was a nightmare for business—they were so exposed. Oil was bound to nullify their exports, and we couldn't have rigged the exchange rate as it's a free market, thank God. If we'd have left it in the ground as Michael Edwardes said the opposition would have said get it out and translate it into pensions'.[7]

Relations between the CBI and Industry Secretary Sir Keith Joseph were also somewhat strained. One CBI official recalled that 'Keith is a fundamentalist—he's an anarchist really. He didn't believe that anything the government could do would help. Handing out government money was anathema to him. At our first meeting he asked why we even needed a Department of Industry. His officials just stared and sat there glassy-eyed'.[8] Another CBI official thought that 'Keith Joseph couldn't really stand the outside world. He once came to a luncheon and refused all food but a boiled egg. But he sent that back as it was too runny'.[9] Joseph's successor, Patrick Jenkin, was slightly, but not significantly, more conducive to CBI lobbying. One senior CBI official recalled that 'Patrick Jenkin wasn't terribly effective in Cabinet as he didn't want to be accused of being a wet'.[10] The CBI was therefore never able to find a ministerial champion in Cabinet or Whitehall.

From October 1980 onwards CBI criticisms became even sharper with the appointment of the Ford Chairman and Managing Director, Sir Terence Beckett, as the new Director-General. Beckett, an energetic and shrewd man made an immediate impact, and November 1980 produced an outline 'master plan' which warned that if present policies continued, the position of manufacturing industry would be 'really parlous'. But a much more serious conflict soon followed. Barely six weeks into his new job, Beckett attacked the government with a ferocity usually reserved only for TUC opponents, calling for—in a phrase that became his hallmark—a 'bare knuckle fight' with the government. Addressing the CBI conference, Beckett told a generally approving audience that:

You had better face the brittle fact that the Conservative party is a rather narrow alliance. How many of them in Parliament have actually run a business? This matters. They don't all understand you. You think they do, but they don't, not all of them. They are even suspicious of you—many of you—what is worse they don't take you seriously. I would not advocate what I am going to say were the cause not noble—we have got to take the gloves off and have a bare knuckle fight because we have got to have an effective and prosperous industry. The alternative isn't the end of the world. It is just inexorable and miserable decline into shabby gentility if we were lucky, or more probably Bennery.[11]

Moreover, the CBI conference passed a motion criticising Conservative policies on the interest rate, the exchange rate, energy policy and public spending. As *The Guardian* rightly observed, 'not since the Heath administration introduced the interventionist Industry Act in 1972 has the gulf between industry and the Conservative government been so wide'.[12] Nor did the CBI's annual budget representation to the Chancellor augur better relations, requesting for the first time a positive foreign exchange policy to reduce the level of the pound. However, one Treasury official recalled that the 'CBI were not terribly impressive on the pound because they had no explanation of what to do. You must remember that the CBI is a confederation. They can only unite on a broad brush approach, so that the pound and NIS were things they were enthusiastic about'.[13] One backbench wet explained that 'the CBI made a great cockup with the bare knuckled fight and then went into their bunker to fight skirmishes. There was a good link between the wets and the CBI, and we got together with Terry Beckett and kept them briefed. But the CBI was between the wets on social programmes and the dries on economic policies'.[14] One junior minister whose department had close contacts with the CBI recalled that 'the CBI's survey of business intentions has established a validity. But the CBI is too dominated by manufacturing, not services, the boys from engineering, whose living is based in yesterday's world. They had access to the PM and Chancellor and they were good naggers'.[15]

The 1981 budget, the most significant in the government's anti-inflationary strategy, was strongly attacked by CBI president Raymond Pennock who called it a 'kick in the teeth at the worst and a brush off at the best'. He accused the government of failing to provide industry with the means to win the fight against recession. 'What was needed was a bold boost for industry. What we got will give industry little opportunity to improve economic performance of this country, which we so desperately need'.[16]

Yet the CBI's criticisms should not be taken as conclusive proof of private sector condemnation. The increasingly influential Institute of Directors, according to its Director General, Walter Goldsmith, 'stands four square behind the Prime Minister [who] ... deserves better from industry than the caterwauling which went up from some of our leaders after the budget'.[17] One economic adviser recalled that the 'CBI were loathed more than the Bank of England. But Walter Goldsmith would be welcome and Geoffrey Howe would see him. He wasn't in the first line of importance but he became more important from 1981–82'.[18] A Cabinet minister also noted that 'we did listen to the CBI, but we didn't see them as the sole authentic voice of UK industry. They are an amalgam of views and they had become a rather corporatist body. NIS was not that crucial and I didn't feel it was worth going to the stake over'.[19] Similarly, City opinion and the commercial, as opposed to the manufacturing, sector of the economy was inclined to support the government's approach. One senior Treasury knight accurately assessed the position as being split between those for and against the government in that 'the Secretariat headed by Terence Beckett was in favour of a most competitive exchange rate but small businessmen made it clear that there was to be no criticism of the government. The predominant analysis of such members was that the government had rescued them from a fate worse than death'.[20] The CBI's stance was undeterred. In September 1981 the CBI advocated a £6 billion reflation in its policy document *Agenda for Recovery* in the apparent hope that this could be achieved without refuelling inflation. Many businessmen were also reported as seriously considering contributions to the SDP, fearing an 'anti-business Labour administration following disillusion with Tory policies'.[21]

The 1981 CBI conference was predictably critical of the government. A 'modest' £1.5 billion reflation was urged, even if it meant increasing the PSBR with 'some selective profitable investment in the public sector, where it can be justified by rigid criteria'.[22] The CBI's outlook for 1982, as contained in its monthly trends, was extremely gloomy, emphasising the gap between the organisation and the government. For example, Industry Secretary Patrick Jenkin optimistically told the Commons that the latest figures suggested that productivity in manufacturing industry was 9 to 10 per cent higher in the third quarter of 1981 than at the end of 1980. Partly because of this remarkable achievement, unit labour-cost rises in the United Kingdom were among the lowest of our competitors. The figures certainly lent support to Mr Jenkin's argument that what had happened under the pressure of the recession was that firms, right across industry, had become more efficient in order to survive. The unspoken corollary of Mr Jenkin's assessment was that before the recession many firms had had inefficient managements and were consequently lacking in competitiveness.

CBI policy, however, was to press, like the TUC, for reflation of some kind. A £3 billion boost was requested for the 1982 budget in the CBI's submission *A Winning Budget*, which specified a 15 per cent cut in business rates, financed by central government grant, which it calculated would save industry £850 million a year; it also requested a reduction in interest rates and a £250-million increase in spending of public capital projects, building up to £1,000 million in 1983–84. The document stated:

The priority for this budget must be to reduce the disproportionate burden on the business sector. Business has made major adjustments at great cost—all in line with government policy. We now call on government to reduce the costs which it imposes on business, improve competitiveness and redress the imbalance of pressure in the economy which has borne less heavily on government and consumption and much more heavily on production and investment.[23]

Immediately following the budget, the CBI launched a major concerted attack on 'crazy' interest-rate levels, then in May 1982 it saw 'no evidence of any noticeable recovery in activity'[24] and in June proclaimed that the fledgling export drive was faltering. In August the CBI's *Economic Situation Report* showed a consensus on the stagnant nature of the economy, declaring that 'production appears to be flat, in all regions and in some cases may even be falling, while the pattern of orders erratic'.[25] Government ministers' claims of economic recovery were thus politically easy to undermine. Indeed, one minister frustratedly attacked the CBI following a 'summit' meeting between Sir Terence Beckett and Labour's Shadow Chancellor, Peter Shore.

Mr John Wakeham, Minister of State at the Treasury, said that although it was not wrong for Sir Terence Beckett to have talks with Mr Peter Shore it may have been unwise for two reasons: it gave the impression to some that the CBI had sympathy with 'nonsensical' Labour policies, and second, the CBI had among its members nearly all the big companies and corporations, including the nationalised industries, which were the cause of Britain's uncompetitiveness. The CBI, Mr Wakeman said, is the main representative body of manufacturing industry, whose competitiveness fell between 1977 and 1981 by 76 per cent. But the Confederation had not pointed out that the manufacturing sector is much less important than in the past, accounting for only 25 per cent of the gross national product compared with 60 per cent for the service industries. If the CBI had been reporting on overall prospects it would have highlighted the fact that capital investment in the manufacturing, distribution and service industries rose by 5 per cent in the first quarter of 1982 to return to the record level of 1980.[26]

Sir Geoffrey Howe also attacked the CBI's pessimistic views of the economic prospects, resolutely declaring that he would not change his policies and criticising the CBI who should 'not allow gloom to feed upon itself'.[27] Furthermore, Sir Geoffrey could point to the fall in the pound, which the CBI had advocated, plus reductions in the NI surcharge worth £600 million to industry. According to one CBI official, the NIS was 'most important, and there was resentment because it's a tax on jobs and exports but imports don't suffer. We did a lot with backbenchers and got key businessmen to lobby their MPs about it, and in the end the reductions in NIS were not small'.[28]

By the end of 1982, and as election speculation grew during 1983, the CBI's attacks on the government decreased, although the policy differences remained as pronounced. Sir Terence Beckett noted that 'a rather artificial storm' had now blown over and that the CBI did not have 'substantial' differences with the government.[29] At the 1982 CBI conference the stridency of criticism was less evident, and the government's success at reducing inflation so effectively earned respect and praise. The conference even voted two to one against a resolution urging the government to 'adopt an exchange-rate policy that will encourage manufacturing industry'. Moreover, *The Times* Business Forum's survey of business opinion found widespread support for the government, which was also reflected in the national opinion polls.

Although the CBI's budget proposals called for a £3 billion reflation, involving the abolition of the NI surcharge and lower business rates, in March 1983 the monthly trends showed Britain's recession to be ending with 'anecdotal reports from CBI regions confirming that a widespread recovery in demand and output could be underway'.[30] In April the CBI's survey showed that business confidence was at its highest for seven years with orders, output and exports improving. For the first time since 1979 the CBI's verdict on the economy corresponded to that of ministers, which was just as well during the general election campaign. On 10 June, as Mrs Thatcher's landslide became clear, the CBI duly welcomed the victory, adding the familiar ritual plea for lower interest rates.

Despite the accord between government and CBI in mid 1983, the Thatcher government had had a difficult relationship with the employers organisation during the preceding four years. The level of conflict had been deep and mistrust had been more evident than co-operation. Manufacturing industry did, and still does, have special needs and requirements which require government sympathy. Yet the verdict on the conflict shows the government to have been the more justified in its policy priorities. To be sure, the pound fell from roughly $2.50 to $1.50, aiding manufacturing exports as the CBI had hoped. Also the NI surcharge, a real tax on jobs, was a legitimate CBI grievance. But the reflationary package urged by the CBI would have had disastrous consequences on inflation, and taxation and may have driven interest rates still higher. Similarly, the recession improved productivity and efficiency by making management more competitive and efficient. Moreover, the government exercised responsibility for the whole economy, and the CBI representing manufacturing industry, which continued to decline in comparison to service industry, could not legitimately hope for its own pressure-group interests to be given priority. The conflict between the Thatcher government and the CBI demonstrated the changing nature of the economy as much as Mrs Thatcher's policital monetarism demonstrated the changing nature of contemporary Conservatism.

NATIONALISED INDUSTRIES

The Conservatives inherited a wretched situation in relation to Britain's nationalised industry jungle following the long-term decline of nationalised industries fossilised by subsidy into perpetual inefficient loss-makers. As one Cabinet minister recalled, 'we had to unravel the nationalised Morrisonian structure, but the nationalised industries can't be treated en masse—each one is unique. The management we inherited was

a difficulty'.[31] Richard Pryke, in his authoritative study of
Britain's nationalised sector, has also analysed management
failures in that 'the most clear-cut examples of bad management
have been in planning and capital expenditure'.[32] Another
Cabinet minister thought that 'the laws of economics had been
retarded for the nationalised industries, and politicians had
found it easier to have them losing money than slimmed down
with a better balance sheet'.[33] Sir Keith Joseph, the first
Industry Secretary of the 1979–83 period, recalled that 'it was a
mammoth inheritance from previous governments. I had a
whole mews of Augean stables. Bankruptcy was
constitutionally impossible with steel because of the Act in force
which said BSC should supply the nation's steel requirements. I
used to talk of unbankruptable industries. We had to simulate
bankruptcy'.[34] As we argued in Chapter 2, the emphasis of the
Thatcher government was on a more market-orientated
economy but with the intention of denationalising the
profitable parts of state industries only. Thus the 1983
Conservative manifesto had stated:

A company which has to satisfy its customers and compete to survive
is more likely to be efficient, alert to innovation and genuinely
accountable to the public. That is why we have transferred to private
ownership, in whole or in part, Cable and Wireless, Associated British
Ports, British Aerospace, Britoil, British Rail Hotels, Amersham
International and the National Freight Corporation. Many of their
shares have been bought by their own employees and managers, which
is the truest public ownership of all.

We shall continue our programme to expose state-owned firms to
real competition. In telecommunications, we have licensed a new
independent network, Mercury, and have decided to license two
mobile telephone networks. We have allowed competition in
commercial postal services. Already standards of service are
beginning to improve. Investment is rising. And better job
opportunites are being opened up.[35]

The problems of the nationalised sector however, were more
acute than the incoming government had realised, and the
amount of public money involved in loss-making capacity was
far greater than had been feared.

One of the most chronic loss-makers was British Steel, whose workers, as was discussed in Chapter 6, went on strike over pay for two months in early 1980. The position of BSC, perilous before the strike, was even more precarious after it. As Adrian Hamilton put it in *The Observer*:

The steel strike is coming unsteadily to a close. The steel crisis is still gathering pace. Over the next 12 months the British Steel Corporation has been charged with returning to the black in what, even before the strike, were highly unpromising conditions ... The tragedy that is the British steel industry is only now beginning to dawn on the public conscience. Within a space of five years British Steel, once the highest hope of UK public sector investment, will have lost over one and a half billion pounds, closed down capital plant on a scale equivalent to the Concorde programme and made redundant over 100,000 employees, or half its workforce. Few would now argue that nationalisation of the industry had worked. Whilst the private sector has managed to survive by concentrating on high-value products and cheaper steel-making processes based on scrap metal, British Steel has put its all in a series of integrated modern coastal plants built just as the market has nose dived.[36]

In May 1980 the government's hope of returning BSC to financial stability was epitomised by the controversial appointment—at £1.8 million 'transfer fee' from Lazard Freres—of American businessmen Ian MacGregor as BSC's new Chairman. Sir Keith Joseph strongly defended his decision, and Mrs Thatcher was 'ebullient' about the appointment.[37] Mr MacGregor was a more forceful man than his predecessor, Sir Charles Villiers, and the new Chairman made it plain on taking office that tackling the industry's serious overmanning would be one of his priorities. A series of cutbacks and closures of loss-making plants duly followed. At Consett and Bilston the workforce was reduced by 4,150 by September 1980.[38] Nevertheless, the government sanctioned a further £400 million of taxpayer's money as an interim measure to keep BSC afloat while Mr MacGregor completed his assessment of BSC's future finances and structure.

Consequently, in December 1980 MacGregor's corporate plan was unveiled. A further 20,000 jobs were to be shed, steelmaking capacity reduced, profitability aimed at for 1982–83 and liquidation envisaged for the failure to meet these aims. When the plan was announced, BSC was losing £2 million per day and the elimination of this haemorrhage of public money was the central aim of the MacGregor plan. Although the ISTC voted against the plan, the workforce as a whole voted to accept it with a 78 per cent majority of vote, and in February 1981 Keith Joseph announced a £6.6 billion rescue package as a backcloth to the MacGregor plan. Such a huge sum of money, representing almost half the total figure for the 1981–82 PSBR of £13 billion, was a massive and arguably irresponsible use of taxpayer's money. As one commentator put it, 'Keith Joseph as Industry Secretary behaved very differently from what he was expected to behave beforehand'.[39] Patrick Jenkin, Sir Keith's successor as Industry Secretary, recalled that 'with steel there was and always will be the strategic defence argument about maintaining British production'.[40] This defence of the government's policy is less than fully convincing. As one senior Treasury official put it, 'steel is so plentiful anyway and even if war breaks out we shall not be at war long enough for it to make any difference'.[41]

However, the government was determined to give the MacGregor plan its chance, and the gradual contraction of the industry began. Corby in Northamptonshire was closed, 750 redundancies announced at Port Talbot and Llanwern and 9,000 jobs were shed at Scunthorpe. Yet BSC's financial problems continued. In October 1981 a £250 million loss was announced following 1980's £668 million record deficit. In December 1981 the loss was cut to £196 million and BSC sought a further £80 million on its external financing limit. In February 1982 it was back for more, only this time it requested a further £100 million. In the revised corporate plan Mr MacGregor made it clear that BSC's break-even targets were extremely volatile, particularly given the possibilities of European steel being shut out of the American market.

The break-even plans which Mr MacGregor trumpeted optimistically in May 1982 because of 'dramatic progress at all levels' were soon to prove abortive. In July a £338 million loss was declared, £20 million higher than that forecast by Mr MacGregor, and a further round of redundancies swiftly followed, involving 1,675 jobs in Sheffield and the west of Scotland and 1,300 jobs at Brierly Hill. By December 1982 the extent of the crisis surfaced again with a further 5,000 redundancies, a continuing pay freeze and an extra £150 million subsidy from the Industry Secretary, Patrick Jenkin. In the Commons Mrs Thatcher rightly linked the perilous financial position to the thirteen-week strike in 1980. She noted:

With regard to falling steel demand in this country which he represents as greater than elsewhere we had a thirteen-week steel strike in which many people who had loyally purchased steel from the British Steel Corporation had to buy from overseas, and at the same time a condition was put on their purchase that they should continue to purchase some steel from overseas.

Many of them said that in future they wished to buy their stocks from two different origins and not rely on the British Steel Corporation again. Undoubtedly, the steel strike cut the demand for steel. Those who went on strike were warned about it at the time.[42]

No wonder Mrs Thatcher was to comment during the 1983 election campaign that she was not responsible for workers who strike themselves out of jobs.

As the election approached it was clear that breaking even in 1982–83 was to be an impossibility. In April 1983 BSC's losses still amounted to £6 million per week and the government's break-even date postponed to March 1985. A new corporate plan was again approved, involving £665 million of new investment of public money, though Mr Jenkin did warn that 'I recognise that the steel ·market remains difficult and that the future of any particular plant or works will continue to depend on the way in which markets for its products develop and on the costs and efficiency of their operation'.[43]

The 1983 Conservative manifesto did not mention the revised corporate plan or the colossal sums of taxpayer's money injected into BSC. It merely stated that it was the aim to make 'substantial parts of British Steel' into private sector companies.[44] Such a laudable aim—as had been Mr MacGregor's corporate plans—did not tackle the immediate problem of vast wastage of public money. The BSC problem was thus deferred rather than solved.

Another nationalised industry headache concerned the ailing British Rail. The flexible rostering dispute of 1982 has already been discussed in Chapter 6 and may be regarded as typical of the industry's deep-seated troubles. Much of British Rail was seriously overmanned with poor service to the customer a common complaint. In 1981 the government was granting BR £110 million merely to subsidise uncommercial and rural services, and BR's loans and grants limit for 1982–83 was £950 million. But following the 1982 strikes the financial outlook became more perilous. A 15,000, or 8 per cent cut in the workforce was proposed, and James Urquhart, BR's board member for operations and productivity, stated that the strikes had cost £240 million, so BR's finances were 'in tatters' with the industry 'fighting for its life'.[45]

Following the publication of the Serpill Report, which rejected Sir Peter Parker's electrification plan in favour of sweeping economies, the government considered the splitting-up of BR into semi-autonomous bodies, but the possibility of unpopular line closures affecting marginal constituencies—a familiar political chestnut—pushed any decision into the future as the 1983 election approached. (A far cheaper and more customer-effective way of overcoming this political objection would be to replace local line closures with subsidised 'socially justifiable' bus services in the affected, largely rural, areas.) According to one observer, 'David Howell's reception of Serpill was mild and weak'.[46] The opportunity for a radical change had passed by. However, in Sir Peter Parker's 1983 BR Board Annual Report it was disclosed that BR's finances could have broken even but for the 1982 strikes. 'As it was, the strikes cost us £170 million and the group result was a loss, after interest, of £174 million',[47] the report stated. BR's position was thus much better than BSC's and the possibility of breaking even in future years ought to revive Conservative plans to radically restructure industry through operational devolution or privatisation. As one Treasury adviser put it, 'We should have got flexible rostering earlier—Parker had two goes at it—and there's no problem selling BR assets, but not as a railway'.[48]

British Shipbuilders similarly faced a grim future, which had been made worse by a world recession and Third World shipyards' competitiveness and efficient working practices. In 1981 the annual report of the General Council of British Shipbuilding noted that overmanning and lack of orders indicated a difficult future. In December 1981 a £25 million deficit was announced by BS, an improvement on the £110 million deficit of 1979, but there was some optimism on breaking even by 1984–85. However, as with many nationalised concerns the optimism was misplaced.

In 1982 a half-year loss of £28 million, £18 million above the government's £10 million limit, was followed by catastrophic news that losses for 1982–83 were expected to reach £100 million. Sir Robert Atkinson, British Shipbuilder's Chairman, sought a further £200 million of public aid as the best way to save the industry. 8,500 further redundancies were proposed on top of the decline in the workforce from 87,000 to 63,000 since 1977. The prospect was for continued massive subsidisation of a chronic loss-making industry, and there were few grounds for agreeing with the Minister of State for Industry, Norman Lamont, who told the Commons that 'we shall bear in mind our commitment to the industry and the importance we attach to a viable UK shipbuilding industry with a long term future'.[49]

The problems of the coal industry also became more acute during 1979–83 (the miners' reluctance to strike to 'save' jobs has been considered in Chapter 6). In April 1980 the government, in keeping with its overall nationalised industries policy, set the NCB a profit target of breaking even by 1983–84. Optimistically, John Moore, the Junior Energy Minister, declared:

The task will be demanding but I am confident that the industry can achieve it ... Although operating grants will still be paid where special circumstances warrant them, as a general rule the declining total of grants to the board will take the form of an explicit deficit grant. This is an important change. Our purpose is to reflect the reality of the situation and to enable the NCB's progress in moving towards the agreed target to be clearly seen ... We are convinced that future general revenue support to the NCB must be explicit and taper off year by year under a plan fixed in advance.[50]

These expectations proved abortive. Against the background of the recession the NCB was producing more coal than the market needed and at such a high price that it was cheaper to import coal from Australia. Overmanning and the existence of loss-making pits was a deeply entrenched weakness and despite the progress on closing specific loss-making pits in 1982–83, a radical transformation of the NCB's finances was not forthcoming. Even the NCB's own plan to close sixty pits was timed for 1990 and a confidential government study in September 1982 envisaged public expenditure running at hundreds of millions of pounds for the rest of the 1980s.[51]

The government's response was to appoint Ian MacGregor as Norman Siddall's successor as NCB Chairman, in the teeth of considerable political opposition in March 1983, in the hope that pit closures and efficient financial restructuring could be speeded up. Indeed, the all-party Commons Select Committee on Energy, headed by Conservative Ian Lloyd, had criticised the Coal Board and the Energy Department for deferring harsh decisions. The MPs' report stated, rightly, that:

Our fear is that the current review procedure could provide the board with a pretext for avoiding or at least deferring, some of the harsh decisions about the industry's capacity which we believe to be inescapable.

We certainly remain sceptical as to whether further subsidies would increase domestic coal sales significantly in the short run and given the very much lower production cost of both deep-mined and open-cast coal in many parts of the world it is far from clear how far the prospects for overseas sales might be improved.[52]

The seriousness of the NCB's position and the unduly optimistic calculations of the government in 1980 were put into further stark perspective in May 1983 when Mr Siddall reported a £100 million loss, demand falling by 7 million tonnes, and record coal stockpiles. The government's laudable attempt to produce profitability had proved unattainable, and the argument for a more radical solution to such a use of public money has grown as a result.

British Leyland—now renamed simply BL—had been an industrial relations jungle and public expenditure nightmare since the mid 1970s. Poor product ranges had been the root cause of BL's problems, which other evils such as overmanning and poor industrial relations had exacerbated.[53] However, during 1979–83 there were signs of improvement at BL, and the 1983 Conservative manifesto envisaged the sale to the private sector of 'substantial parts ... of BL'.[54] Two new models, the Metro and Maestro, remedied many appalling design faults in the 1970s BL range and proved popular with the public. Strikes, while periodic, were less well supported on the shop floor, where the management's threat to sack strikers plus the increasingly clear intention of the government not to prop up BL indefinitely had their effect.

To be sure, a £990 million government handout to BL in January 1981 followed a £181.5 million loss in the first half of 1980, but thereafter a new mood of realism was apparent, and Mr Tebbit declared that the government would not carry on supporting BL if its performance did not improve. For example, in November 1981 the BL Chairman, Sir Michael Edwardes, threatened liquidation if strikes crippled the company's production. Reductions in overmanning were successfully implemented—by 2,000 at Longbridge, once the home of union militancy—and productivity increased. So when Sir Austin Birde succeeded Sir Michael Edwardes in December 1982, he was able to consider an eventual future of total private ownership. Although BL's financial position was still precarious and the prospects of breaking even were elusive until the mid to late 1980s, there was some optimism that BL would not remain a perpetual drain on public spending. BL's future, however, depended on customers not governments, a fact the first Thatcher government showed it recognised in contrast to its Labour predecessor. The attitude of one backbench dry was less favourable to the government's record, noting that 'a number of us were critical of BL's appetite and even how there's still a long way to go. The government should have dismembered BL'.[55]

British Airways proved another nationalised industry worry for the government. The ultimate intention was, again, transfer to the private sector, but in the absence of a bankruptcy policy this was postponed as BA's problems proved severe. In November 1980 BA made its first loss—£2 million—which was followed by a big increase to £145 million loss in August 1981. Sir John King, the Chairman, promptly announced 9,000 redundancies to cure overmanning and a re-examination of flight routes. In April 1982 Sir John announced a radical restructuring plan aimed at profitability in 1983–84, but this hope proved unrealistic as could have been easily predicted. Thus Sir John was pleading for the government to wipe out

BA's £1 billion of debts in October 1982, and consequently privatisation plans receded even further. The workforce, trimmed from 56,000 in 1980 to 41,000 in 1982, was purged yet again in January 1983 by 2,000, on target for 1983–84. However, in February 1983 Sir John ruled out full privatisation of BA before the end of the decade and noted that the government bore the prime responsibility for ridding BA of its £1 billion debt. The BA problem had become long-term and, arguably, perpetual.

The same could also be said of the Meriden Motor Cycle Co-operative, beloved of Tony Benn, the Industrial Secretary 1974–75. In September 1980 Sir Keith Joseph provided a £9 million lifeline to the Company, but by 1983 government patience had rightly run out and liquidation duly ensued, as indeed it should have done in the early 1970s. The history of Meriden was a sorry story of public spending waste without the slightest commercial justification, given the design deficiencies of the Meriden motorbikes. Other examples of lame duck rescues at the taxpayer's expense were the £200 million bailout of ICL in March 1981 and the writing off of the National Film Finance Corporation's £13 million debts in March 1980, both of which were quite incompatible with the government's expressed intention of encouraging markets rather than extensive state subsidisation of the large lame ducks, which may be regarded as crowding out private sector potentialities. As one MP put it during the 1981 budget, 'If we had not allowed so much money to be siphoned off into British Leyland, steel and coal, more money would be available to create jobs in the new growth areas of industry, and the budget could have more to ease the lot of small businesses. That is our central problem'.[56]

However, these disappointments may be offset partially by the denationalisation or privatisation policy of the 1979–83 Thatcher government. The achievements were not inconsiderable, and the 1983 Conservative manifesto could therefore boast that the government had transferred to private ownership, in whole or in part, Cable and Wireless, Associated British Ports, British Aerospace, Britoil, British Rail Hotels, Amersham International and the National Freight Corporation. In addition, it had licensed a new independent telecommunications network, Mercury, as well as two mobile telephone networks, and allowed competition in commercial postal services.[57] Moreover, the government's splitting of the Post Office in its determination to end its monopoly powers augured well for future private capital injection. As one junior industry minister put it, 'breaking British Telecom's monopoly was one of our biggest decisions. It galvanised the pace of privatisation'.[58] Privatisation policy, while successfully implementing the government's intentions to strengthen and encourage the private wealth-creating sector of the economy, may still be regarded as peripheral to the overall struggle with the nationalised industries between 1979 and 1983. One commentator noted that 'I would have privatised more with more public services going into the market and simultaneous announcements of reductions in taxation'.[59] The greatest problems were not those of privatising existing profitable, or near profitable, public sector assets but were with the chronic loss-making nationalised sector, where the only realistic outlook was perpetual financing at the taxpayer's expense. It is in this area that a more radical alternative needed to be found.

THE RADICAL ALTERNATIVES

Conservatives have always been wary about industrial strategies, partly because they are associated with Labour governments and centralised state planning. However, while the industrial strategy of the first Thatcher government—transforming nationalised industries to profitability before privatisation—was a move in the right direction, it may be argued that it was doomed to failure in a number of cases. Profitability was remote for many nationalised industries which were perpetual and chronic loss-makers, industrial fossils artificially preserved from a previous age. As Pryke has argued hitherto, 'public ownership removes the threat of bankruptcy and provides access to government funds for investment'.[60] The radical alternative the government would have been wise to consider was liquidation. Allowing firms to go bankrupt has never been properly understood by politicians of all parties susceptible to constituency pressures to 'save' jobs, Department of Industry vested interests and special pleading for 'temporary' industrial capital aid. However, when a firm goes into liquidation its physical assets are not destroyed but revalued downwards. This enables purchasers to be found and new uses to be found for land and plant involved. Indeed, this process reached record levels under the Thatcher government as bankruptcies increased during the recession on a scale unknown before. But as ministers rightly pointed out, the formation of new business also reached new record levels, many of which had taken over businesses previously bankrupt. This process was a daily happening and economic fact of life in Britain between 1979 and 1983. Yet a different attitude emerges if bankruptcy is suggested for a public sector industry, based usually on the 'political' objection outlined above. However, as John Burton has correctly argued, the alleged political impracticality of implementing a bankruptcy policy has been exaggerated. Burton argues convincingly that:

One apparent barrier to this course of action is the belief in some political quarters that it is impossible to sell the ownership rights in loss-making state enterprises because no one would want (or perhaps be foolish enough) to buy them. When Secretary of State for Industry, Sir Keith Joseph told the 1980 gathering of the Mont Pelerin Society that this was the reason for not seeking to privatise BSC.

This notion is incorrect. It is not true that all loss-making enterprises have a zero or negative value, and thus cannot be sold at a positive price. The price an entrepreneur is willing to pay for a loss-making enterprise is determined not by its current performance but by his estimate of what the assets would be worth after reorganisation. One possibility would be for him to sell off the physical assets of the enterprise to others. Alternatively, having acquired the ownership rights, he may wish to keep the enterprise (or parts of it) as a going concern with a view to undertaking internal reorganisation—of the product line, marketing strategy, management team, manning arrangements, and so on. Whatever his precise strategy, the argument is that loss-making enterprises can be sold at a positive price provided someone perceives the potential of profit after reorganisation or asset disposal.[61]

The liquidation alternative therefore has much to commend it. First, it maximises economic change and creates new investment opportunities and employment prospects. Second, it prevents the fossilisation of industries that have outlived their economic usefulness and which cannot even satisfy customers, despite indefinite government subsidy. Third, and most crucially for the Thatcher government liquidation of chronic nationalised industry loss-makers and lame ducks would reduce public spending, even allowing for the initial costs. In Chapter 5 it was argued that the cuts across the board harmed good and legitimate areas of public spending traditionally approved and advocated by Conservatives. These cuts could have been avoided by a liquidation policy to reduce the colossal levels of industrial fossilisation in order to free money for reductions in the PSBR, tax cuts, better public spending allocation, or a combination of all three.

The most common objection to this policy is that it would increase unemployment and social security spending. To a limited extent this would happen. But these disadvantages would be outweighed by extra jobs created or saved both elsewhere in the public sector or in the private sector. Indeed, this philosophy was central to the excellent work of Ken Baker, whose sponsoring of information technology which the private sector can adapt was an example of successful relations between government and entrepreneurs. All public spending is a matter of choice. The same money spent on nationalised industry fossilisation cannot be spent on information technology or micro-chip innovation. Moreover, many nationalised industry jobs are artificial in any case and represent overmanning, as was shown by the redundancy programmes of nearly all the existing nationalised industries during between 1979 and 1983. It would also be the case that profitable parts of bankrupt nationalised concerns would be bought up privately to continue in business with the potential for job expansion. The point is of great significance in promoting economic devolution and self-reliance. Thus Pryke has argued that:

the fact that nationalised undertakings are so large and are in public ownership converts what would otherwise be a collection of local difficulties and divisions into a national problem about which pressure groups and trade unions become concerned and politicians adopt policies. Corner shops have been quietly closing for years but if retailing had been nationalised there would have been a great outcry some years ago when it became known that the Shops Board had a ten-year plan to close many of its uneconomic local outlets... If the Coal Board did not exist and the railways had not been nationalised the problems of closing down loss-making pits and withdrawing unprofitable rail services would be less formidable.[62]

However, the greatest benefits of the radical alternative would be in reducing public spending. This would enable the government to reduce interest rates—the CBI's greatest complaint against the Thatcher government—and so increase investment. Thus new private sector investment, previously crowded out by the nationalised sector, would be able to take root. As John Burton has convincingly argued, the level of nationalised industry job subsidy is a positive burden which restricts the private sector.[63] A liquidisation policy for the public sector lame ducks would be politically controversial, but its advantages in terms of reducing public spending and encouraging the private sector would be both beneficial to economic change and compatible with Conservative philosophy.

Radical alternatives are not confined to the public sector, however. Indeed, the Thatcher government's provision of help to the small business sector was imaginative and praiseworthy. The scheme to encourage unemployed workers to set up their own businesses with £1,000 of their own plus £40 a week from the government was a radical and creative measure. The 1983 Conservative manifesto could proudly proclaim:

We have reduced the burdens on small firms, especially in employment legislation and planning, and cut many of the taxes they pay, particularly Corporation Tax. Our Loan Guarantee Scheme has already backed extra lending of over £300m to about 10,000 small firms. The new Business Expansion Scheme, a major extension of the Business Start-up Scheme, will encourage outside investment in small companies by special tax reliefs. The construction of new premises for small businesses has more than doubled.

To help the engineering industry and the areas most dependent on it, we have introduced and now extended a very successful scheme of grants (SEFIS) to smaller firms, which help them to buy new machinery.

Thanks to these policies and over one hundred other important measures, the climate for new and smaller businesses in the UK has been transformed and is now as favourable as anywhere in the world.[64]

Such schemes could be greatly expanded by the transfer of resources from the loss-making nationalised sector, as previously suggested. The old Department of Industry propping up lame ducks should become a new Department of Science and Technology, geared to assisting the private sector in infant stages of development. As Professor Richard Stapleton has argued, there is still great scope for reducing barriers to entrepreneurship by changes in the taxation system. As Stapleton has put it:

> One of the main problems that remains is the bias against investment in new and expanding firms. Basically, if I remortgage my house and risk £50,000 to start up a new firm, the Inland Revenue does not allow the loss of the capital against income tax. But if I make a profit, the Inland Revenue will take its share. Thus government can win but not lose, whereas enterprise takes all the losses and only half the gains.
>
> This tax treatment contrasts with the position of established companies making profits. They can invest in plant and machinery and receive a 100 per cent capital allowance. Here the Inland Revenue pays half the investment and gets a half-share in the gains. Even worse is the tax position of new sole traders who are often taxed on the revenue (not the profits) they generate and have to prove every expense to the Inland Revenue before they can be repaid the tax. A bigger disincentive for people to become self-employed could not be imagined.[65]

Similarly, another economist, Christopher Hawkins, has persuasively advocated that double taxation discourages entrepeneurship because of taxation on interest 'which is needed to repay the real value of what was borrowed, i.e. the tax payments that are made to compensate for capital evasion. Yet these in no sense represent income. They represent getting back what we have lent—in real terms'.[66] This damaging classification of payments made to cover capital evasion as interest has mitigated against entrepreneurial talent and investment because of tax disincentives. Reforms of the tax system, no less radical than reforms of the nationalised industry fossilisation programme, are long overdue. Contemporary Conservatism should not be afraid of them. Edward Heath's comment during the 'Quiet Revolution' phase of the 1970–74 Conservative government that 'you cannot create a healthy and prosperous economy just by going on pouring money into firms which can't make ends meet'[67] was as relevant in 1983 as it had been in 1971.

8 Contemporary Conservatism and the 1983 General Election

Afterwards, the campaign of 'Firm but Fair' met with complaints both that it was too 'hard' and, more usually, too 'soft'. Conservative backbenchers had gone through much since June 1970, and perhaps nothing was more embarrassing than the U-turn over incomes policy, as the nagging voice of Mr Powell frequently pointed out. And to what end? A senior backbencher argued after the election: Decisions in politics are always difficult but it helps if you derive them from a philosophy of a set or principles. Many of us feel that we made too many concessions here. It is not so bad if you can compromise your principles and can justify it by success. But we lost the election as well.

D.E. Butler and D. Kavanagh, 1974

ELECTION DECISION

The years from 1979 to 1983 confirmed the trend of increasing electoral volatility which had been evident in the 1970's. Mrs Thatcher's forty-three-seat overall majority in May 1979 would obviously be slightly eroded by by-election defeats, which it duly was, but unlike her predecessor, Jim Callaghan, the opportunity to decide the timing of the next election was never in doubt. What was in doubt for most of the period 1979–83 was that the Conservatives would be re-elected. At the end of 1980, Labour dominated the opinion polls, and twelve months later the SDP was similarly well placed; by-election defeats were spectacular and the added threat of the Liberal/SDP Alliance was, for a while, an unknown factor for potentially large electoral change. Moreover, as the electoral prospects of re-election seemed remote in 1980 and 1981, the Prime Minister was vulnerable to the attacks of the wets, who argued that reflation would help the economy and win voters. This argument was only finally discredited with the 1983 general election result itself.

After nearly a year in office, the portents were not too bad for the Conservatives. Teddy Taylor won Southend East against what he considered to be a below-the-belt campaign by the Liberals in March 1980, and in the following month an opinion poll in *The Observer* showed Mrs Thatcher's popularity increasing and also running far ahead of that of any Conservative rival.[2] Then, for the next two years, government popularity plummeted and re-election doubts predominated. In May 1980 Labour's local election successes gave them power in almost 75 per cent of the big cities amid 436 Conservative losses and 509 Labour gains. In November Michael Foot replaced Jim Callaghan as Labour leader and the party began to split apart as the Left's march seemed unstoppable. However, even this welcome development to the Conservatives only produced a bandwagon effect for the newly formed SDP and then the SDP/Liberal Alliance. An opinion poll in February 1981 actually showed the main support for a new centre grouping would come from Conservative rather than Labour voters,[3] rekindling fears of the periodic Liberal revivals during Conservative administrations.

In the May 1981 local elections, Labour gains returned it to power in fifteen of the counties it lost in 1977, and Ken Livingstone become the GLC's Labour leader. But the events of the summer of 1981 brought about the open speculation of a challenge to Mrs Thatcher's leadership. The government's political monetarists found themselves beleaguered. As David Blake has put it:

For Mrs Thatcher, the low point came in July 1981. In the early weeks of that month, Britain's inner cities were scarred by riots, giving new arguments to those wanting to ease up in the fight against inflation and try harder to cut unemployment.

The economic recovery which Sir Geoffrey Howe had started to discern that spring showed no signs of materialising. And at a Cabinet meeting the Prime Minister and Chancellor found themselves virtually isolated as their colleagues refused pressure for another round of spending cuts.

That meeting was the low point for Mrs Thatcher and it was the high point for her Conservative critics. They thought that they had won the battle. By September 14 three of the leading wets in the Cabinet—Sir Ian Gilmour, Lord Soames and Mr Mark Carlisle—had been dismissed and Lord Thorneycroft, who described himself as 'rising damp', had been removed as Chairman of the Conservative party.[4]

Despite the purge of the wets, the electoral prospects were still alarming. The Alliance was recording remarkable successes in local Council by-elections,[5] and in November Shirley Williams won Crosby from the Conservatives, overturning a 19,272 majority. In March 1982, with unemployment now over three million—and assumed by many politicians and commentators to be the key electoral barometer—Roy Jenkins won Hillhead from the Conservatives to establish the full 'gang of four' in Parliament.

The Falklands War, which began with the Argentine invasion in April 1982, is thought to have ended the government's unpopularity. However, crucial though Mrs Thatcher's handling of the Falklands campaign was to public opinion, there were signs of an upturn in Conservative support *before* the crisis broke. Wapshott and Brock correctly noted that the rise in popularity had begun some time earlier. Thus in MORI polls the Conservative rating had been a steady 27 per cent from September to December the previous year; it had risen to 29 per cent in January, 30 per cent in February and 34 per cent in March. The same applied to her personal rating: satisfaction with Thatcher had fallen to 25 per cent, the lowest point in a long decline since the General Election, in December 1981. It had climbed back to 36 per cent by March; after the Falklands campaign it was standing at 59 per cent. The little-noticed recovery in popularity before April may help explain why the 'Falklands factor' did not wear off as fast as pundits predicted that it might.[6]

At any rate, the Falklands War had greatly assisted the Conservatives' re-election chances, irrespective of the improving underlying trend. One junior minister recalled that 'I remember the lobby correspondent Bob Carvel coming up to me at the '81 party conference saying that the next election was beyond recall for the Tories, who would be submerged on a scale worse than in 1945. Nine months later the same Bob Carvel said the Tories would be in power for goodness knows how long'[7] The build-up to the 1983 election effectively began at the end of 1982, by which time the option of a quick 'Falklands election' had been, wisely, rejected.

The Conservatives' position was enhanced by the continuing self-destructive turmoil in the Labour party and the Alliance's inability to recapture the electoral momentum of a year before. Indeed, during the Falklands campaign the Conservatives had gained Merton, Mitcham and Morden from the SDP's defector from Labour Bruce Douglas-Mann. In October 1982 the *Observer*/NOP poll put the Conservatives ahead with 45 per cent, Labour with 32 per cent and the Alliance trailing badly with 21 per cent.[8] The Alliance came third in the Northfield by-election in October, which Labour narrowly won, and thereafter Alliance fortunes were not to recover until the Bermondsey by-election in February. The loser on that occasion was Labour, and the Conservatives' opinion-poll lead remained intact.

During 1983 election speculation was therefore, bound to grow. Mrs Thatcher in a New Year broadcast stated that the government was 'bubbling with ideas' for a second term,[9] which confirmed the role of Sir Geoffrey Howe as overlord of policy groups providing raw material for the election manifesto. In January the PPSs told the Prime Minister in a private meeting to consider holding an early poll in June rather than October 1983. Mrs Thatcher herself dropped a hint by saying:

There comes a time when uncertainty can tell and it can affect a current government's performance. At such times one has to consider what is the best date for an election. Sometimes you find people thinking, well, there is an election coming up, I wonder what view will be taken after the election, when you are doing big international negotiations; that is the kind of uncertainty I'm thinking of.[10]

Not all Conservative opinion favoured the early poll. John Biffen was known to be a sceptic, and Edward Heath—arguably scoring an own goal—warned that the government should not underestimate the difficulty of winning the next election with unemployment so high. The campaign, he told a London Broadcasting Company audience, could swing to unemployment and it would take a comparatively small movement to change the political balance. One junior minister, ridiculing this argument, recalled that 'Whatever happened to unemployment there would still be 84 per cent or so of people employed with the government having achieved something akin to price stability. Heath said no Tory government had been elected with three million unemployed, but the evidence of the 1930s pointed in the opposite direction. People have turned to the Conservatives where times have been difficult'.[11] Nevertheless, the Conservatives' advantageous electoral position was proving stable, and privately many Conservatives were pleased that Labour held Darlington in March with the SDP coming third, not least because this ensured Mr Foot's tenure as Labour leader. A *Sunday Times* leader summed up the Foot factor in British politics:

There is a simple case for saying that Michael Foot should voluntarily surrender the leadership of the Labour party. This case is not malignantly inspired. It has nothing to do with the evil capitalist press. In fact, it is probably against the interests of the capitalist press. If the press was so nefarious and political as the Foot camp says it is, it would not be publishing stories saying that he was about to be overturned, or citing the numerous Labour MPs who say he should be. It would be trying, on the contrary, to keep him safely in place, as the Tories' favourite Labour leader.[12]

Cecil Parkinson, the Conservative party Chairman, commenting on the Darlington result, jibed that 'Mr Foot has been saved for the Tory party. I confess we were very worried about Mr Foot. He has recently been something of an endangered species, and we need him at the General Election to remind the nation of just how unacceptable Labour policies are.'[13]

Following the 1983 budget, which was politically shrewd in reducing taxation and thus encouraging the Conservative performance in the local government elections, the election speculation became a fever dominating most political considerations. Mrs Thatcher bided her time, informing the House of Commons that she and not the press would decide the date of the general election and that she could not rule out any options. Among backbench Conservative MPs *The Times* noted 'the ardour for a June election remains undimmed'.[14] Finally, on 9 May Mrs Thatcher decided that polling would take place on 9 June, a decision endorsed by the Conservative party in Parliament and the professionals at Central Office. The election decision for most Prime Ministers is an election dilemma. Moreover, it is a decision with a long history of failure. Mrs Thatcher's decision was less of a dilemma for any Prime Minister since Anthony Eden in 1955, and the prospects of failure at the outset of campaigning looked to be less that those at any election in the twentieth century.

THE CAMPAIGN AND ECONOMIC ISSUES

That the 1983 general election campaign was *not* particularly dominated by economic issues was ironic in a number of ways. First the new political monetarist approach to office in 1979 had been largely economic, and it was in the areas of the economy and trade union law that radical action was promised. Second the economy had dominated the life of the Thatcher government with the exception of the 1982 Falklands campaign. Third the Tory wets' attack on government policies had centred on the electoral implications of high unemployment as much as the economic and social consequences. Thus one left-wing Conservative MP recalled that 'I hardly mentioned economic policy in my campaign speeches. The Tory party behaved as it should not on unemployment. I take the Harold Macmillan line. We didn't get the rhetoric right about the human tragedy of unemployment'.[15] Both the Opposition parties hoped and expected that economic issues would come to their aid during the 1983 campaign.

In fact, the 1983 campaign was not dominated by any one issue, as previous elections had been by the government's economic record. Defence, the unilateralist case, Labour's internal troubles, council house sales, the threat to leave the EEC, the Falklands and the government's overall 'resolute approach' were all key issues at various stages until polling day. The economic issues appeared periodically as vital but were by no means the only major concern to the voters. Nevertheless, in the context of this book, they deserve further attention. The Labour party made the Conservatives' record on unemployment and Labour's reflationary panacea the centrepiece of its manifesto, *The New Hope for Britain*. It declared:

The present hideous level of unemployment is not an accident. It is the direct result of the policies of this government. The Tories have cut public investment and services, and increased taxes, taking spending power out of the economy and destroying jobs in both public and private sectors alike. They have forced up interest rates and kept the pound too high—a combination that has crippled British industry, and helped lose us markets at home and abroad.

Our approach is different. We will expand the economy by providing a strong and measured increase in spending. Spending money creates jobs. More spent on railway electrification means jobs, not only in construction, but also in the industries that supply the equipment—as well as faster and better trains. If we increase pensions and child benefits, it means more spending power for the elderly and for parents, more bought in shops, more orders for goods, and more jobs in the factories. More spending means that the economy will begin to expand: and growth will provide the new wealth for higher wages and better living standards, the right climate for industry to invest, and more resources for the public services.

Our central aim will be to reduce unemployment to below a million within five years of taking office. We recognise the enormous scale of this task. When we set this as our target, unemployment was 2.8 million, according to the official figures. On this basis, it is now at least 3.2. million. Our target will thus be all the more difficult to achieve. It remains, however, the central objective of our economic policy.

To achieve it we will need five years of economic growth, with a Labour government carrying through all of the industrial, financial and economic policies outlined here. But we will also work with other governments—especially socialist governments—to bring about a co-ordinated expansion of our economies.

Economic expansion will make it possible to end the waste of mass unemployment. But it will also reduce the human costs of unemployment—the poverty, the broken homes, the increase in illness and suicides. And it will provide the resources we need to increase social spending, as we must, at least in line with the growth of the economy.[16]

But the age of such undiluted Keynesianism had long since gone, not only for the policy-makers but in its electoral appeal. Labour had failed to learn one of the lessons of the 1979 election—that unemployment could not be made a central issue in a campaign in the way it had been in the immediate post-war era.[17] Moreover, as Lord Thorneycroft later observed, 'the three million unemployed and the Falklands can't just be put into balance on either side. The electorate doesn't look on unemployment as it used to. It is not associated with the abject poverty of the Jarrow marchers'.[18] Alan Walters has also ventured that:

I suspect that the political corner was turned in the latter part of 1981, and certainly by the first quarter of 1982. Although I am not qualified to chart and explain this political process, I did observe that most political pundits were quite convinced that a government presiding over three million unemployed, would never be re-elected. Food for thought here, a little humble pie, perhaps.[19]

Similarly one backbench dry argued that 'the wets throughout '79–83 totally misread public opinion and the way it was moving. They had no conception of the mood of public realism'.[20]

The Alliance, like labour, found that the unemployment issue would not necessarily win them votes. The joint manifesto offered by the Liberals and SDP entitled *A Joint Programme for Government* advocated a £3 billion reflation to reduce unemployment with an old-style incomes policy to prevent inflation. There is no evidence to suggest that this Keynesian solution was any more electorally appealing than Labour's, and when the Alliance's support duly increased it was because of Labour's self-destructive extremism rather than because of the Alliance's policies. Those few observers who defied conventional thinking in 1981 and considered the Alliance vulnerable on its economic policy were to be proved right in the end.[21] Thus, as an alternative to the Conservatives' successful record in reducing inflation, in 1983 the Alliance offered (as well as a public sector incomes policy):

New arrangements to discourage excessive pay settlements in the private sector. Pay settlements in the private sector will be negotiated with no direct interference in settlements made by small and medium-sized businesses. We intend to set up a Pay and Prices Commission to monitor pay settlements in large companies, with powers to restrict price increases caused by wage settlements which exceed the agreed range. At the same time, we shall legislate to introduce a Counter Inflation Tax, giving the government the power to impose the tax if it becomes necessary. The tax will be levied by the Inland Revenue on companies paying above the pay range. It will be open to successful companies where productivity increases have been high to pay above the agreed range if they do so through the distribution of shares which are not immediately marketable.[22]

It is extremely difficult to believe that even Alliance leaders thought such a policy would be electorally attractive.

At the end of the first week of the campaign when the Labour and Alliance manifesto launches had made the economic issues the central concerns, the polls showed a 4 per cent swing to the Conservatives, and the government, far from being apologetic on the unemployment figures, vigorously attacked the reflationary alternatives as offering no real solution. For example, Mrs Thatcher told ITN's *News at Ten* that Labour's manifesto 'would change the whole basis of our society. It looks to me as if they are virtually saying: "Well, if you don't do what we want, or if industry doesn't do what we want, or the banks don't do what we want, well we shall take them over, or take powers to regulate them'.[23] Similarly, a Conservative television election broadcast informed the viewers to a photographic background of Attlee, Wilson and Callaghan that every previous Labour government had put up unemployment

The Conservative manifesto pledged curbs on union rights to call strikes without secret ballots, the abolition of the GLC and English Metropolitan Counties and stressed the government's success in reducing inflation; its title, *The Challenge of Our Times*, embodied the 'resolute approach' to both the Falklands and the economy. Arguably, it caught the public mood more than its Labour and Alliance rivals simply because it promised so much less in the way of instant panaceas. Labour's desperation on the failure of its economic package was apparent on 19 May when Denis Healey accused the government of lying over the unemployment figures, a charge which led to counter accusations from Norman Tebbit. Not surprisingly, *The Sunday Times* declared on 22 May that 'the jobless issue isn't working for Foot'[24] as poll evidence showed a growing Conservative lead. Moreover, the Conservatives claimed that Labour defence cuts would cost 400,000 jobs in 271 constituencies, a theme that tied in well with the constant attacks on Labour's unilateralist, or allegedly unilateralist, policy. One Cabinet minister recalled that 'Labour became more left wing, thinking that Mrs Thatcher hadn't fudged so why should we fudge'.[25] The electorate, however, had outgrown the attractions of socialist panaceas.

The cost of Labour's reflationary proposals also turned the unemployment fire away from the Conservatives. One estimate was a £30 billion cost per year, or a doubling of the 30p standard rate of income tax. But Labour's own blundering came to the Conservatives' aid. On television Michael Foot said Labour would not increase National Insurance charges, despite party pledges to abolish the upper ceiling of £220 a week on earnings-related contributions. Asked, 'Do you now give a pledge that National Insurance charges will not go up under Labour's programme?' Mr Foot replied:

Yes, we are certainly not proposing any such increase. Indeed, we want to in some respects reduce such payments in order to be able to ensure we carry through the expansion. Nobody could ever say that no insurance charges should ever be increased, of course not. It depends on some other factors as well, but we have set out very clearly, in our budget, our approach to the matter as the best way of doing it.[26]

In fact, that budget—a statement issued by Mr Peter Shore, the Shadow Chancellor, on 10 March—as well as the manifesto, had both pledged the abolition of the upper ceiling of £220 a week on earnings-related National Insurance contributions.

Similarly, Labour's programme was equally vulnerable to Conservative claims that six large firms—Beecham's, GEC, Glaxo, Plessey, Barratt and Taylor Woodrow—would be nationalised and that a future Labour government would take control of people's savings in pensions and insurance funds for investment in British industry. According to Mrs Thatcher, 'Under a Labour government there is virtually nowhere you could put your savings where they would be safe from the state. They want your money for state socialism and they mean to get it. Put your savings in the bank and they will nationalise it. Put your savings in a pension fund or a life assurance company and the Labour government would force them to invest the money in their own socialist schemes'.[27] Such Conservative attacks deflected Labour and Alliance criticism of the relatively disappointing Conservative record on taxation. Moreover, taxation was an issue as far as the electorate feared that it would rise more under Labour than under the Conservatives, who had, at least, cut income tax. One backbench MP recalled that 'In '79–83 we didn't reduce taxation because we rightly refused to print money. But during the campaign I didn't find many people attacking us for failing to reduce the burden of tax. Even on direct tax, it wasn't an election issue'.[28] Leon Brittan's view was that 'the public was wiser than the economists and commentators on taxes. People saw the National Insurance increases as increasing services and with the basic and higher rates of income tax down the electorate didn't share the black picture of taxes as a percentage of GDP'.[29] The Conservatives' alleged vulnerability on taxation was consequently never a major election issue.

At the end of May the polls were still showing a comfortable Conservative lead, but Labour's vote was beginning to haemorrhage and the Alliance vote to increase largely because of Labour's poor campaign performance, particularly on such issues as defence, housing and the EEC. The Alliance campaign, following the Ettrick Bridge summit, stressed David Steel rather than Prime Minister designate Roy Jenkins, and Mr Steel's skilful and televisual campaigning had an immediate effect. With a week to polling, a Conservative victory seemed assured, and the main question was who would come second. Even leaked government documents and a scandal over an ex-National Front candidate had not eclipsed Labour's turmoil. On 29 May the *Sunday Times* observed that at 'Tory Central Office, party workers could hardly believe their luck. Despite her confidence in the final result, Mrs Thatcher had warned them to expect a "rough patch" in the middle of the campaign. Without Labour's difficulties to distract attention, last week could easily have been not just rough, but disastrous'.[30] Labour's misery seemed to be summed up by their inability to make headway on the unemployment issue and their vulnerability to their own internal quarrels. Michael Foot appearing on the same platform as Militant Tendency supporter Pat Wall and lecturing him on Labour's MPs 'undertaking…an obligation to uphold the constitution of the

Labour party'[31] seemed to sum up the party's plight. (Moreover, Pat Wall contrived to lose Bradford North, a safe Labour seat, to the Conservatives.)

The issue of inflation and the government record in reducing it received its expected boost when the Williamsburg economic summit of Western leaders, to which Mrs Thatcher had flown, produced an agreed pledge to work for lower inflation and interest rates. The communique read like a Conservative Central Office document, stating that the recession was caused by a 'decade of cumulative inflation'.[32] It contained a commitment jointly to pursue monetary and budgetary policies that would both lower unemployment and generate higher productivity. One Cabinet minister recalled that 'our success on inflation was part of what led people to believe we were a competent government. In '74 we had lost the identity with our own supporters, but '83 by common consent the campaign went very well. We didn't step on any banana skins, and our opponents produced a whole box-full for themselves'.[33] A week before polling, the unemployment figures showed a 100,000 fall, adding further credibility to the Conservatives' claim that the economic recovery was real not illusory. Labour's best hope of denting the Conservative vote—alleging the abolition of the NHS—was played with full vigour. But it was the Alliance that seemed to prove more successful in worrying the Conservatives, by appealing to voters not on the economic issues but in order to prevent a 'landslide' majority. Reg Prentice, however, recalled that 'the only difficulty I had with the campaign was the way we treated the SDP. There was the long-term fear of the SDP, but it was clear they were taking more votes from Labour than us. I feel that on balance the Alliance helped us; the real divide is between Labour and extremist socialism on the one hand and everyone else on the other'.[34]

Labour's final own goal—in a series of many—was the attack on the government's Falklands record by Mr Healey and Mr Kinnock. One Conservative Cabinet minister recalled that 'We made the decision *not* to raise the Falklands. It was undesirable to do so. It was Labour who raised it'.[35] The economic issue had moved into the background and the issue that seemed to dominate the final days of the campaign was the Labour party itself, which proved an electoral asset to both the Conservatives and the Alliance. Tactical voting rather than unemployment was a greater threat to the Conservatives as the campaign ended. Mrs Thatcher hoped for 'as big a majority as I can possibly get' and confessed that 'When I am out on a campaign trail, yes, I am exhilarated by it. Nevertheless, it seems to be quite a long campaign, because my mind cannot help addressing itself to the longer-term problems, and yet I have to discipline myself and say, no, you must not count your chickens'.[36] The contrast between Mrs Thatcher on the eve of victory and the shambling, incompetent campaign of Edward Heath in February 1974 could not have been lost on many Conservative supporters. One Cabinet minister, a veteran of many election campaigns since the 1950s, thought that 'of all the elections we've fought, it was the most professional and expert campaign, even though our opponents not only kicked the ball into their own goal but did so from the other end of the field. The public knew that the Labour party could not win'.[37]

Indeed, the role of the economic issues in the 1983 campaign related directly to two distinct Conservative styles and economic approaches. Between 1964 and 1974 the Conservatives lost four out of five elections, the last two on a distinctly leftish, Keynesian platform. The one victory—in 1970—had been on an avowedly more right-wing economic platform, the 'Quiet Revolution' philosophy that was overthrown by Mr Heath's interventionist, reflationary dash for growth. In both 1979 and 1983 Conservative campaign successes had focused on lower inflation, less public spending and greater private sector rather than public sector growth. These election facts are not a coincidence. The Conservatives' natural supporters are middle-class people and the entrepreneurial and managerial communities. They, above all, resented the high levels of inflation that destroyed savings and the high levels of taxation required to finance the ever growing public sector. The Thatcher government brought down inflation to its lowest level in fourteen years and had shown determination, if not outright success, in reducing the burden of the public sector. The low inflation rate had greatly assisted the 1983 campaign carrying with it middle-class, prosperous Conservatives. Unlike in 1974, when many voted Liberal in protest, in 1983 they stayed loyal to the Conservatives.

If the inflation success was a key ingredient of victory, it follows that reflationary policies—had they been forthcoming in 1981, for example,—would by generating inflation have lost the Conservatives many middle-class votes. The electorate's dislike of inflation also should not be underestimated. Many low-income people who had suffered from rising prices and costs welcomed the low inflation rate and comparative price stability evident in 1983. It is, indeed, astonishing to consider Lord Kaldor's view of inflation in the light of its electoral unpopularity. Kaldor argues that 'continued inflation causes an erosion of the wealth of the *rentier* class, which directly or indirectly owns the National Debt, in favour of the state—which means the community as a whole. Whether this process is regarded as good or bad is a prima facie political question which does not admit a single "right" answer'.[38] Kaldor's economics, which have always been vulnerable to strong critical analysis, would not have been an appetising option had they been put before the 1983 electorate. The Thatcher government's insistence on making inflation control the central tenet of its 'political-monetarist' strategy had, therefore, considerable electoral ramifications. Reflation, as suggested by the wets, would have undermined these gains.

Equally as important to contemporary Conservatism as to the economy as a whole was the government's reaction to unemployment. This account has argued in Chapter 4 that the Thatcher government was not essentially responsible for the rise in unemployment since 1979. Nor during the 1983 campaign did Conservatives display guilt at over three million unemployed. Yet the reaction flew in the face of the accepted post-war Conservative wisdom—that high unemployment must be reflated away to prevent electoral defeat. The level of unemployment did not lead to the defeat of the Thatcher government; nor as an issue did it work against the Conservatives during the campaign. The cost of Labour's reflation and the electorate's scepticism that Labour could actually reduce unemployment were arguably more crucial issues which mitigated in the Conservatives' favour. Indeed, opinion polls found that even among the 14 per cent of the population that were unemployed, there was no consensus in blaming the government. The 86 per cent employed, at previous elections, had already shown that the issue was rapidly losing its political priority appeal. In 1983 this trend was confirmed. Even if there had been a reflation to reduce unemployment, there is little ground for believing that the Conservatives would have benefited electorally. The more likely scenario would have been like that in February 1974, when a colossal reflation was followed by a Conservative defeat. As one backbench MP put it, 'normally it's factors beyond the PM's control that can lead to defeat, but in '83 the factors beyond control helped us—Foot as leader and the Falklands. The media failed to take into account how the party could use the Falklands factor on the economic issues'.[39]

The 1983 campaign laid the ghosts of 1945. The orthodox wisdom of that era, which formed the wets' own electoral strategy, had decreed that the Conservatives would lose office if unemployment was too high, or full employment relegated in importance. The 1983 election landslide has utterly invalidated this hypothesis in contemporary British politics. Contemporary Conservatism, as a result, has changed as well. The new emphasis of lowering inflation and encouraging home ownership by the sale of council houses to their tenants is in keeping with the wishes of the modern, affluent, mass electorate. The wets' reflationary strategy had failed to take this into account by assuming that the electorate, and the working-class electorate in particular, was still conditioned by the experiences of the 1930s. In this sense it is Mrs Thatcher who represents the oldest of Conservative traditions—the willingness to change—by accurately assessing the electorate's own requirements and priorities. It is the wets who, in refusing to change to this new reality, were out of line. Their brand of Conservatism had long since outlived its economic justification as successive reflations brought only higher inflation and economic decline. In 1983 it showed it had outlived its electoral usefulness as well. One Cabinet minister, referring to unemployment, commented that 'time and again during the campaign people told me that there had been overmanning before and that Britain had been riding for a fall. They wanted us to stick to our policy'.[40] Although non-economic issues played a large part in the 1983 Conservative victory, the economic issues helped the Conservatives not their opponents.

Indeed, the economic issues were reinforced by the great non-economic success—the Falklands. Patrick Jenkin recalled that 'there was a shift from the Falklands factor to the Thatcher factor. I went round north-east Lancashire ten days before polling and our tails were really up. It was no coincidence that we were the first government to be re-elected with inflation falling'.[41] Thus, as David Blake rightly put it:

> The government's success in selling its economic policy was part of a much wider triumph in persuading the people that it represented a new idea of what Britain stood for. At its core was 'the resolute approach' and at the core of that as a credible doctrine was the Falklands War. What began as one of biggest British humiliations of the present century turned into a triumph; and with that came governmental confidence that as long as they were determined in what they were doing they would carry the day. The attitude permeated through economic management, trade union relations and institutions like the Civil Service.[42]

Had the Thatcher government not stuck to its economic policies, a different outcome may have been forthcoming.

VERDICT

The Conservatives won the 1983 general election with an overall majority of 144, 101 more than the overall 1979 majority. Mrs Thatcher became only the second Conservative Prime Minister ever to be re-elected after a full term, and her margin in seats and votes was the largest won by any party since 1935. The majority of 144 was only two less than that achieved in Attlee's 1945 landslide, which more than anything else, forced the Conservatives to adopt for thirty years the Keynesian middle way. In 1983 the Conservatives won 397 seats, Labour 209, the Liberals 17, the SDP only 6, with 21 others making the total of 650.

In percentage terms, which is less significant in a first-past-the-post plurality system than many commentators make out, the Conservatives won 42.4 per cent, Labour 27.6 per cent and the Alliance 25.4 per cent of the total votes cast. As Butler and Waller rightly say, 'the Conservatives could only win this huge victory on so small a vote because the Opposition was divided'.[43] However, the British electoral system is the same for all parties and to divide and split the Opposition is a skill in itself which, as the Conservatives showed, they profitably used. The power of Conservative attacks on Labour's internal turmoil and self-doubts undoubtedly helped to increase the Alliance vote, as many traditionally loyal Labour voters, who could never bring themselves to vote Conservative, switched in protest to the Alliance. This electoral phenomenon was created as much by the Conservatives' aggressive campaign as by Labour's policy shambles and the Alliance's moderate, all-things-to-all-men appeal. For this reason, in many northern seats in particular, the Conservatives came through the middle to win because Labour voters had voted Alliance in protest. The Conservative vote of 42.4 per cent, compared to 43.9 per cent, in 1979 held up very well, especially as the Alliance played on the fear of a large, unwieldy majority in the final week of polling. Nevertheless, the percentages are unimportant in Britain as opposed to, say, in proportional representation Italy. The constituency battles were effectively won by the Conservatives either beating Labour in key marginals, with the Alliance third, or winning some Labour safe seats by splitting—or helping to split—the anti-Conservative vote. It simply will not do for any allegedly dispassionate analysis to agree with Roy Jenkins that the election result was a 'total distortion of the desire of the voters'.[44]

For Michael Foot and the Labour party the result brought despair and acrimony. Mr Foot put it that 'It was a deeply reactionary and offensive campaign fought by our opponents. That makes all the more scandalous and unforgivable the treachery of those who helped to enable the Tories to win the election—defectors from our own ranks. The Liberals are entitled to their case, but those who are seeking to inflict injury on us at all times are an entirely different story'.[45] However, Labour's campaign had proved vulnerable to the Conservatives wider appeal on such issues as home ownership and stable prices. The floating voters had deserted Labour and a score of defeated candidates acknowledged that the desire for home ownership, which the Conservatives had stressed, had lost Labour votes. Sir Keith Joseph recalled that 'we didn't adopt the council-house sale policy for electoral reasons. It was part of the coherence of the general stance to increase people's choice. It would have electorally blunted us if Labour had agreed with our policy'.[46]

Tony Benn, who lost his seat, bitterly spoke of the brass knockers on front doors which spelt new Conservative attitudes. Thus, as one Cabinet minister put it, 'the sale of council houses was such a major issue. I went to forty-three key marginal seats and you could see people in their gardens or painting and decorating or having home improvements. In London the swing to us was greater because we had sold council houses'.[47] *The Sunday Times* rightly noted:

Labour is now the party of declining Britain, Thursday's poll results show. Overall, Labour did badly, losing a fifth of the votes which it won in 1979. But in relatively prosperous Britain—southern, home-owning, white Britain outside the cities—it performed catastrophically. Forced back into its heartlands by a continuation of trends apparent now for several general elections, its prospects of forming another majority government in Britain are now remote.[48]

Moreover, the Conservatives' success in winning a number of previously safe Labour seats and their good performance in other Labour areas had vastly reduced Labour's once impregnable heartlands. Seats that were marginal in 1979 were safe Conservative seats in 1983. But the names of some of the constituencies won by the Conservatives demonstrated Labour's demise: Bradford North, all the Nottingham seats, Newcastle-upon-Tyne Central, Hyndburn (better known as Accrington), Halifax, Sherwood, York, and Glanford and Scunthorpe. The Conservatives even won Barrow-and-Furness, where Robert Waller, in his shrewd and authoritative constituency study, had observed that 'the tide seems to be flowing Labour's way in this industrial backwater, and Albert Booth should be able to absorb the impact of Ulverston quite comfortably'.[49] The Conservative majority in Barrow and Furness in June 1983 was 4,577. The argument that the Conservatives could never win seats in the northern Labour heartland because Mrs Thatcher's Conservatism was, in Ian Gilmour's phrase, a retreat to 'behind the privet hedge', had to be reassessed. The Conservative vote held up well in Labour areas; it was Labour's vote that was vulnerable.

In the South of England the Alliance had replaced Labour as the Conservative's main challenge. But apart from the fall of Yeovil to the Liberals the Conservatives' vote proved solid. As Butler and Waller noted, '273 of 397 Conservative MP's now have as their principal opponent an Alliance candidate'.[50] But the same analysts also observed that:

The Alliance found that it had to contend with the so-called 'plateau effect'—its share increased least in those seats in which it had already obtained a strong second place. This was exemplified in the Liberals' disappointments in Richmond and Barnes, in Chelmsford and in Cornwall North. One explanation is that in the best Liberal hopes, the Labour vote had already been squeezed as much as practicable in previous general elections. Defections by Labour supporters may well have assisted the Liberals in their strong performances in seats such as Yeovil, Montgomery, Cheltenham, Torbay and Edinburgh West. In Montgomery and Gordon the Conservatives lost their seats despite an increase in their share of the vote; an apparent triumph for 'tactical voting' by squeezed Labour voters.[51]

Tactical voting had emerged as a greater threat to the Conservatives than the unemployment figures, or for that matter any other single issue.

Once the voters' wishes had been made known, Mrs Thatcher reshuffled her ministerial team. Nigel Lawson, a loyal monetarist, became Chancellor, Leon Brittan went to the Home Office, Geoffrey Howe fulfilled a long ambition by becoming Foreign Secretary and Party Chairman Cecil Parkinson took charge of a remerged Department of Trade and Industry. William Whitelaw accepted a hereditary peerage, and Francis Pym, the wets' most formidable Cabinet exponent, was sacked as Foreign Secretary. Mr Pym had made injudicious remarks during the election campaign about not really wanting a landslide majority, but his long opposition to Mrs Thatcher's transformation of contemporary Conservatism away from the old guard paternalists was well known. Such a dismissal showed her strength; after all, a majority of 144 had again made the Conservative party the natural party of government, a mantle it had lost in the 1964–79 period. One Cabinet minister commented that 'Mrs Thatcher had established her authority—like a presidential De Gaulle figure—and that was a big advantage in the election'.[52] In only nine years the policies and electoral performance of Ted Heath's party had been transformed. The party of Keynesian consensus and interventionism had become the party of political monetarism; but the party of 1974's abject and wretched electoral defeats had become the party of a 144 majority.

PART III

Concluding Thoughts

9 Margaret Thatcher's Conservatism

There is another aspect of the way in which incomes policy is now operated to which I must draw attention. We now put so much emphasis on the control of incomes that we have too little regard for the essential role of government, which is the control of money supply and management of demand. Greater attention to this role and less to the outward detailed control would have achieved more for the economy. It would mean, of course, that the government had to exercise itself some of the disciplines on expenditure it is so anxious to impose on others. It would mean that expenditure in the vast public sector would not have to be greater than the amount which could be financed out of taxation plus genuine saving. For a number of years some expenditure has been financed by what amounts to printing the money. There is nothing laissez-faire or old-fashioned about the views I have expressed. It is a modern view of the role the government should play now, arising from the mistakes of the past, the results of which we are experiencing today.

Margaret Thatcher, 1968[1]

SOURCES OF ECONOMIC POLICY FORMATION

The main feature of the first Thatcher administration was the Prime Minister's near total dominance over economic policy formation. The initial strategy, the refusal to change course, the Cabinet purges of the wets, the reliance on the key personnel were all at the behest of Mrs Thatcher's own initiative and reflected her personal political strategy. As Lord Thorneycroft recalled, 'the basic policy was Margaret Thatcher. She knew what she wanted to do before she got into office and there was a respect for someone who had a goal and absolute confidence. People in the country who didn't understand monetarism respected her'.[2]

One Cabinet minister similarly put it that:

I think the central personality was Mrs Thatcher, who had got hold of certain propositions and had a dogged Chancellor with a loyal belief who thought that he'd get the boot if he didn't do what he was told. Policy was made by a group of politicians who had the bit between their teeth so that Cabinet was a rubber stamp for what had been worked out before in E committee.[3]

Reg Prentice recalled, 'I'm a great fan of hers, warts and all. I only attended two or three Cabinet committees which she chaired, and she was more like Wilson than Callaghan as a chairman—leading from the front'.[4] This prime ministerial dominance of the economic policy process was not new in British politics.

Ted Heath had exemplified prime ministerial power in the speed and execution of the 1972-74 U-turns,[5] and Jim Callaghan's handling of the 1976 IMF crisis deployed prime ministerial power at the expense of Cabinet colleagues.[6] Margaret Thatcher continued this trend. She herself was the prime source of economic policy formation. The key personnel would suggest and advise but the overall strategy was never removed from No. 10's control. Indeed, it was centralised at No. 10 and imposed on other more traditional policy sources—the Treasury and Civil Service, the Cabinet, the CBI and the trade unions. One Treasury official recalled that 'although the details were left to Geoffrey Howe, Mrs Thatcher's particular interest was monetary, economic policy and key expenditure issues'.[7] Another Treasury adviser observed that 'a number of people were involved in policy formation before the '79 election, and they came to the Treasury to put the framework into play. The Prime Minister was determined to stick with the framework'.[8] One junior minister suggested that 'she changed the nature of Cabinet government. Little was done in Cabinet—it was done in the 'E' committee and in ad hoc groups. But I don't think she listened too much to people like Hoskyns or Mount'.[9] 'She's not one for large committees, and special advisers are a legitimate part of government, which she, like all Prime Ministers, was entitled to' commented one Cabinet dry.[10] The old guard Conservatives were particularly excluded from the policy formation process. As one of them, MP Julian Critchley, has acidly put it:

It would be hard to exaggerate the effect of Margaret upon the Conservative party. The old Tory party was a coalition of the classes. It was led up by the upper, sustained by the middle and kept in office by the votes of the Tory working-man. The party's grandees, however, took care to recruit to the ranks the more intelligent of what Ralf Dahrendorf has called the 'acquiescent middle-class.'

Today, Mrs Thatcher is the spokeswoman of the 'new' middle class, the Rotarians of Grantham who, dissatisfied with much that they see, welcome the Prime Minister's call for radical change, and who comprise a modern version of the Victorian middle-class. It was revealing that Sir John Nott, in his valedictory, should have described both Mrs Thatcher and himself as 'nineteenth-century Liberals.'

Thus, of the two, Norman Tebbit stands closer to a state of nature. The Conservative party seems no longer concerned to advance the precepts of 'One Nation'; we are all now expected, on pain of promotion, to give fulsome support for the market economy as if we had all been schooled in Manchester.[11]

Thus excluded from policy preparation, the wets have had to sink into acquiesence or to dissent in the wilderness.

This facet of prime ministerial control over policy has been particularly demonstrated in Cabinet. The left-wing rebels have leaked and also criticised in code for public discussion. They have much support still in the Conservative party as a whole, but in the policy process their influence has been minimal. The Cabinet committee system, perfected by successive Prime Ministers to expressly avoid the full Cabinet, has made the wets' impact negligible. Though the full Cabinet pressure for a U-turn in 1980 and 1981 was extensive, the levers of policy control remained, unaltered, in the Prime Minister's hands. Only a year after taking office, Adam Raphael noted:

Her lack of a natural Cabinet majority has forced the Prime Minister to seek other methods of control. Her power to rig Cabinet agendas and fix the composition of Cabinet committees is considerable. She has slimmed the number of committees and restricted their membership. She has also taken to convening small ad hoc groups of ministers, to reach a consensus in advance of important Cabinet decisions. She has learnt painfully that she has little to gain from all-out rows. This reluctance to accept collective decisions is not a habit that endears her to colleagues.[12]

One Cabinet minister also recalled that 'every PM has a group of people to talk about a particular subject either informally or more formally in Cabinet committee'.[13]

Moreover, as successive Cabinet reshuffles replaced wets with enthusiastic supporters of the government's existing policies, the Cabinet's role as a dissident forum declined. The bilaterals between the Treasury and spending ministers continue, as before, to generate conflict but details not overall strategy are the elements of dispute. St John Stevas, Soames, Carlisle, Pym, Gilmour have been sacked, Carrington resigned and Prior was moved to the political Siberia of Northern Ireland. The 1983 Cabinet of Lawson, Tebbit, Fowler and Brittan does not present the difficulties of perpetual dissent that the initial 1979 Cabinet provided. The key-personnel approach in the Civil Service, with the No. 10 policy advisors, has been extended to the Cabinet level. 'The Falklands brought her the support of the voters but she had beaten the Tory establishment the year before', one admirer said.[14] A Cabinet minister who was sacked by Mrs Thatcher recalled that:

The Treasury team just got solid support from Mrs Thatcher for the cut-everything approach. There was a belief that you had to have a MTFS—set it and stick to it and keep bringing down the PSBR. There was a bitter argument in 1981 over whether the PSBR should be £10 billion or £12 billion—I don't think it made a blind bit of difference. The Treasury got the full backing of No. 10 throughout and they felt that if they didn't cut, cut and cut again they wouldn't get the backing.[15]

Outside the Cabinet other power sources in the Conservative party have backed Mrs Thatcher's policy approach. The majority of backbenchers supported her economic strategy, particularly those with painful memories of the Heath era of U-turns. The party in the country—as it is expected to do—has given its loyalty, and after the 1983 election triumph, its unrestrained admiration. The CBI, during the build-up to the 1983 election started to warm to Mrs Thatcher's economic policies but for the most part of 1979–83 its strong opposition did not represent any restriction on policy formation. The 'bare knuckled fight' approach did not produce the changes the CBI sought, and even when the pound fell sharply this was because of external factors rather than at the CBI's behest. The CBI's budget submissions to Geoffrey Howe were politely but firmly repudiated as policy suggestions. The hated NIS, while cut, has not been abolished and still burdens industry. The CBI was essentially forced to react to government policies rather than to shape them.

The same can be said, with even more certainty though, about the trade unions' influence. The abandonment of the corporatist model of intended government-union close cooperation was more important than the 1980 and 1982 Employment Acts in reducing trade union power. The unions' legitimacy under previous governments had depended on the way that the corporatist model had exalted their political status and enhanced their policy input. Social contracts and tripartite talks had brought the unions into economic policy-making, as had the blatant exercise of union industrial power. Thus the Thatcher government, in removing trade union policy input, removed the trade union veto on policies considered 'politically impossible'. Between 1979 and 1983 the unions returned to their traditional role of defending what they considered to be their members' interests, instead of acting as an arm of the government machine. It was cash limits, public spending cuts and the absence of the Keynesian incomes policy approach which broke the unions' power, not the legislative reforms of 1980 and 1982, however justifiable they may also have been. The Thatcher government was the first since the Second World War to remove the unions' position at the policy strategy 'top table', and in doing so rendered as obsolete many myths about trade union power being invincible.

The Treasury's role as *primus inter pares* among Whitehall departments was preserved under the Thatcher government, and Treasury policy reflected the wishes of the political masters. Bilateral negotiations between the Chief Secretary and spending ministers achieved much headline attention, which seemed to suggest that the Treasury, as an institutional power source, was supportive of the Thatcher economic line. In fact, the Treasury as an institutional policy source was downgraded from the start. After a year in office, one experienced lobby correspondent reflected that 'When Mrs Thatcher arrived at Downing Street a year ago, many predicted she would become as much a prisoner of the Whitehall machine as the man she had ousted, Edward Heath. But after a year in office there is absolutely no sign of that'.[16] The 'inside' Treasury appraisal of policy options did not restrict the government's freedom of movement. The Treasury orthodoxy, exemplified by Permanent Secretary Sir Douglas Wass, was Keynesian, in favour of incomes policy, devaluation and consensus and opposed to monetarism, either political or technically economic. One special adviser recalled that 'Douglas Wass was not a policy initiator, but I don't go along with the view that he obstructed. He and the Treasury did everything to co-operate. They got on with it'.[17] Only with the appointment of Peter Middleton—who supported the government's approach—as Sir Douglas' successor in March 1983 could the Prime Minister be said to have more than a reluctant obedience from the Treasury. The old Treasury establishment mentality, like that of the old guard Conservatism, was put on the retreat as the Thatcher years developed. In the policy-creation process the Treasury was more acquiesent than innovative. According to one Treasury adviser, 'the role of the Treasury as Douglas Wass had developed it was a managerial one of the right people coming in to bat in the right order. There weren't negative pressures from the Treasury. Officials did what ministers wanted. In the '81 'budget, for example, I don't recall a dispute between the officials and minsters'.[18] Another Treasury official recalled that 'Douglas Wass didn't sabotage from within. The policy was in place when the government came to office, and Douglas' role was to co-ordinate official advice'.[19]

Given that policy formation and co-ordination was essentially prime ministerial, who made the policy inputs that could count? The answer lies in the key-personnel style of government—the reliance on a small group of loyal and expert people with access to information and to 10 Downing Street. The Wilson Kitchen Cabinet of the 1964–70 period, so exquisitely described by Dick Crossman, is the nearest to a previous model of policy advice. But it is not a direct analogy. Mrs Thatcher's key personnel were given official power and institutional control in a way that Wilson's Kitchen Cabinet was not.

First, a loyal core of Cabinet supporters could influence

policy formation. Sir Geoffrey Howe as Chancellor was crucial
to the determination of policy detail and budgetary planning.
One economic adviser recalled that 'Geoffrey Howe made
policy more than any other person except Mrs Thatcher. He
started as a newcomer in 1975 but by 1979 he had picked it up
and was convinced and committed to the new economic
approach. There was no doubt in my mind that he knew where
he was going'.[20] John Biffen recalled that 'Geoffrey Howe's not
an obviously charismatic man, but he wasn't to be pushed
around. He's the tortoise not the hare'.[21] Sir Keith Joseph's
influence was generally thought to have been more symbolic
than specific, yet his support in Cabinet and Cabinet
committees was quite consistently loyal. Willie Whitelaw was a
trusted adviser on general political matters and during the
Falklands, but was not central to the economic policy machine,
except as the Chairman of the Star Chamber. John Nott proved
a talented advocate of political monetarism and a key figure on
the Cabinet committees. His retirement was the key personnel's
only loss at the Cabinet level.

Norman Tebbit, although only promoted to the Cabinet in
September 1981, was quickly established as one of Mrs
Thatcher's most closely respected advisers. One assessment of
his influence surmised that:

Few gain access to the innermost sanctum, the sitting-room in the flat
above Downing Street. One is Norman Tebbit, the Employment
Secretary, probably the man she most admires in her Cabinet.
'Basically she thinks that everyone is useless except Norman', says a
backbencher who knows her well. Tebbit shares her gut right-wing
instincts; like her he comes from a lower middle-class background and
has got where he is through hard work and determination. He
identifies entirely with her cause and he believes that if she has a fault
it is that she is not sufficiently ruthless. He could be heard complaining
some time ago that she should have sacked more people, earlier. She
tells him almost everything, and he never ever leaks it, to anyone.[22]

Nigel Lawson and Leon Brittan were also late recruits to the
Cabinet; their Treasury portfolios were central to the control of
Treasury policy. Lawson, not surprisingly, became Chancellor
in June 1983 as he had established a reputation for intellectual
toughness in defence of government's economic policies. One

Treasury official recalled that 'Lawson was a key figure from the start as Financial Secretary. He had a lot of influence on Geoffrey [Howe]'.[23] Norman Fowler and Patrick Jenkin, while more peripheral to the grand strategy, were essential to the implementation of its detail. Their promotion within the Cabinet pecking order duly ensued.

Ian Gow, the Prime Minister's PPS 1979–83, was part of the key-personnel team but not in the direct policy-creation sense. Gow, acting as the PM's eyes and ears at Westminster, would report the mood of the party among the backbench MPs. He cultivated the niceties on behalf of Mrs Thatcher that MPs appreciate. One commentator noted that Gow's job at the Commons 'is to scurry around all day, four days a week collecting information and exuding goodwill'.[24] This function should not be overlooked in the overall assessment; Ted Heath's abrupt and rude style of leadership antagonised MPs, and Mrs Thatcher, who had become leader because of backbench opinion, was determined not to repeat his mistake.

Within the bowels of the economic policy machine, Mrs Thatcher's key personnel have used the power invested in them by prime ministerial fiat. John Hoskyns, until 1982 the No. 10 policy unit head, was a Thatcherite hard-liner, impatient with the obstructionism and defeatism of the Civil Service and scornful of trade union power privileges. Hoskyns' advice usually sided with the tough option; for example, his advocacy of swiftly reducing through the cash-limit system the 1981 public sector pay bill. According to one Conservative official, Hoskyns 'although stimulating as a companion was rather taken with things like government structures and techniques. He wanted the PM and others to go further with special advisers'.[25] Sir Keith Joseph recalled that 'I have a very high regard for John Hoskyns, who has a powerful analytical mind and I respect his sequential analysis. I share with him a sense of astonishment that the establishment—the parties, the city, the academic world and the Civil Service—concealed from themselves the deepening economic plight of the '60s and '70s'.[26] Hoskyns himself has argued strongly, and with some justification, in favour of widening the pool of executive talent available to government. As he put it in his lecture to the Institute of Fiscal Studies:

we need to replace a large number of senior civil servants with politically appointed officials on contracts, at proper market rates, so that experienced top-quality people would be available. They might number between ten and twenty per department. Some of them would fill senior positions in the department. Others might work as policy advisers to the Cabinet minister concerned. There is no reason why, in some cases, the Permanent Secretary should not be an outsider, with a career official as Second Permanent Secretary, responsible for the day-to-day running of the department.[27]

Alan Walters, who became the No. 10 Economic Adviser, was another powerful figure with direct access to the Prime Minister and hence to the policy source. Walters, with Hoskyns, were the most eloquent advocates of a deflationary 1981 budget, believing Sir Geoffrey's initial calculations to be somewhat generous. Terry Burns, the Thatcher appointee as the Economic Adviser to the Treasury also favoured the full rigours of the political-monetarist strategy. Burns defended government policy against the criticisms that monetary policy had been too tight and was a constant advocate of public spending restraints. Another outside adviser brought in to aid the Chancellor at the Treasury was Adam Ridley, who was utterly committed to the intellectual rightness of the government's economic policy. One backbench wet bemoaned that 'four or five people at No. 10 made policy, and power emanated from Mrs Thatcher. She just did what she wanted'.[28]

In short, the major sources of economic policy formation between 1979 and 1983 were a number of officials—the key personnel—who were empowered, because of their loyalty and ability, to devise the details of an economic strategy, the broad outline of which was controlled by the Prime Minister. Such a system of policy creation may be described as prime ministerial simply because other major institutional power sources were effectively neutralised. The Cabinet, the Treasury establishment, the CBI and the unions were on the outside looking in. In April 1980 one commentator noted that 'During discussions on the second round of public expenditure cuts last autumn, it was clear that the Prime Minister, despite the support of her economic ministers, did not have a majority. "She just rammed them home without taking a vote", said one participant'.[29] During the next three years, as the majority of wets was purged, even the problem of ramming home policy without a vote was overcome. Mrs Thatcher and the key personnel never relinquished their control over the economic policy machine.

THE THATCHER STYLE OF GOVERNMENT

Mrs Thatcher's high-profile style of government, involving the continuous leading of opinion from the front, embodied her philosophy of change and a new radical Conservatism. As has been argued, Mrs Thatcher was not averse to the exercise of Prime Ministerial power right up to its legitimate constitutional limits. The government was a crusade as much as an administration both before and after the Falklands campaign. Economic policy and the changes sought thereby were thus often presented in a framework of dragging a reluctant Britain kicking and screaming into the latter two decades of the twentieth century. Mrs Thatcher's Conservatism was the new Conservative radicalism of the political-monetarist strategy.

John Biffen recalled that 'it was a government of fabian monetarists. Mrs Thatcher is highly political, she's not a theologian or ideologue. We maintained levels of social spending to counter the recession, but it was the most Conservative government since the war. You'd got a government of the radical right and eventually a Cabinet of the PM's making. The 1945 Labour government started from a congenial situation, but Mrs Thatcher had to change a great deal and had a great economic impact. It was a fascinating period of economic and political ramifications'.[30] Nevertheless, the changes brought about by Mrs Thatcher's style and tone have had far-reaching consequences. Not only within her own party but in the outside establishment the radicalism of the political-monetarist approach has disrupted and antagonised. Peter Riddell has correctly put it that 'For those outside the Conservative tribe Thatcherism has appeared to be a bogey. The biggest shock has been for the centrist establishment—the world of senior civil servants, lawyers, top bankers, university lecturers and pundits. These have recoiled from the style as well as the content of Thatcherism, from its deliberate rejection of the consensus cherished by so many of them. Their doubts have been reinforced by Mrs Thatcher's own evident dislike for the institutions in which many of them work—the Foreign Office, the BBC and the Bank of England'.[31]

Thus two years after coming to power the Prime Minister, questioned about her beliefs and philosophy, declared:

What's irritated me about the whole direction of politics in the last thirty years is that it's always been towards the collectivist society. People have forgotten about the personal society. And they say: do I count, do I matter? To which the short answer is, Yes. And therefore, it isn't that I set out on economic policies; it's that I set out really to change the approach, and changing the economics is the means of changing that approach. If you change the approach you really are after the heart and soul of the nation. Economics are the method; the object is to change the heart and soul.[32]

A similarly radical set of convictions could have been found in no other Prime Minister since Attlee. Moreover, few Prime Ministers have been as emphatic as to what they are against and are striving to avoid. As Mrs Thatcher put it:

There are some people who are deeply hostile to everything I believe in because they don't want to work a free enterprise system. They want to destroy it. They are out to create anarchy and chaos because they don't want recovery under this system. They want a closed, tight, controlled system run by government, where everyone will have to depend on government for their housing, their jobs, everything.

There's nothing I can do about them, except to try and show them for what they are. But the vast majority of people don't want that. . . But, if I give up, we will lose. If I give that up I just think we will lose all that faith in the future. We'd lose the justification. I hope that doesn't sound too . . . arrogant.[33]

For Mrs Thatcher the fear that defeat would be a defeat for her ideals—not only for herself—was a genuine aspect of her style of government. Her fear of accelerating state socialism was a driving and motivating force in her determination to carry through her policies.

Towards the end of her first term Mrs Thatcher's conviction politics had not been trimmed by office. Her sense of the clear alternatives facing Britain was matched only by her clear assessment of long-term economic decline and how to reverse it. In a revealing interview with Hugo Young she stated that:

> The Labour party were creating two nations by trying to get so many people into public sector jobs that they could say 'You vote for us, your job's at stake. Vote for us in those council houses, we'll keep your rents down', Oh, yes. Look at Glasgow.
>
> I am much nearer to creating one nation than Labour will ever be. Socialism is two nations. The privileged rulers, and everyone else. And it always gets to that. What I am desperately trying to do is create one nation, with everyone being a man of property, or having the opportunity to be a man of property.
>
> ...I would like us to become the savers' party. Good Lord, my grandmother, who was the wife of a railway guard, had saved £600 when she died in 1935. That generation did. My father earned 14 shillings as a manager of someone else's grocery shop, of which 12 shillings went to digs, one shilling went to saving and one was for spending. How they saved. And my goodness, government after government plundered their savings by what they called reflation. £100 in 1935 is worth only £8.70 now.[34]

The Thatcher style of government and its ultimate objectives were truly revealed in such statements. The fundamental opposition to Labour party privilege based on the public sector; the bankruptcy of reflation as an economic panacea; and the encouragement of thrift and savings—Victorian values as she has since, rather unwisely, called them. Moreover, Mrs Thatcher's crusading style was not mere rhetoric. The marshalling of facts and statistics, the historical parallels and the avoidance of complicated jargon were all features of a Thatcher speech or television appearance. Her parliamentary performances were also impressive, and one Cabinet minister recalled that 'she used PM's question time not as a ritual to be borne but as a launching pad for a whole series of views and propaganda. She used question time better than anyone'.[35] Her relations with the general public were also good despite the usual political protests attendant upon any visit to a factory or area of high unemployment. The Thatcher style, unlike that of Ted Heath, Alec Douglas Home, Harold Macmillan or Anthony Eden, was unashamedly populist. Lord Thorneycroft recalled that 'the nature of the party membership has changed.

There's more entrepreneurs in the party who've made their own way from nothing, and it's not an aristocratic party in the way it once was. In fact, it's a more national party and those are the roots from which Margaret Thatcher draws her support'.[36]

Significantly, Mrs Thatcher told a luncheon guest in early 1983 that 'the battle of ideas. . .we must win the battle of ideas';[37] this exemplified her commitment to convince the electorate not merely to please them. This aspect of the Thatcher first term was given its full emphasis during the 1983 election, when a number of speeches returned to themes rather than just the selectively presented facts that are the stuff of election campaigns. The stress on the 'resolute approach' both to the Falklands and the economy was more effective than lists of statistics in winning the voters' hearts and minds. In her battles with the wets, with the Civil Service and with the Opposition parties, Mrs Thatcher displayed a determination that some call stubbornness and an intellectual grasp that others call dogmatism. One backbench MP on the left of the party recalled that 'the bunker mentality grew over the period. She won't relax and she's still fighting her corner within the parliamentary party. I'm disappointed with the way she's handled power. The number of people who believed in M3 was about ten to thirteen, a very small number'.[38] The Thatcher style of government could never have been based on consensus and compromise. The Thatcher government forced the economic policy priorities into a new mould and the Conservative party in a new philosophical direction. Not surprisingly, the Thatcher style of government proved controversial, challenging and abrasive.

FINAL ASSESSMENT

Mrs Thatcher's most far-reaching change has arguably been the change in the nature of contemporary Conservatism. In nine years as leader, party policy and the party image have been completely transformed. The party's electoral prospects were revitalised. The Conservative party's role as the natural party of government was restored. Conservatives have been reinvigorated by their electoral success and the march of Wilsonian Labourism—and, for that matter, Bennite socialism—have been halted. The changes within the Conservative party have been equally far-reaching. Mrs Thatcher's defiant ideological style has replaced the pragmatism of the 1945–75 era; the socialist ratchet effect, even allowing for the ambiguity of its nature, has been reversed. The Conservative old guard of aristocracy and breeding have been replaced by a meritocratic and assertive middle class, reflecting the political and economic aims of reducing the state's power and role. Thus, as one Cabinet minister observed, 'the party is more Thatcherite with more people from the maintained school sector in the parliamentary party and Cabinet—there's only Lord Hailsham as an old Etonian in the Cabinet now. The new right in British politics has replaced the Macmillan consensus as much as the new Republicanism in America has replaced the old East Coast Establishment'.[39] Similarly, Leon Brittan recalled that 'the Conservative party was behind the Thatcher approach. The question was, would we stick to it?—unlike Mr Heath and Selsdon man. What Mrs Thatcher offered wasn't very different from Selsdon man. There's nothing like an idea whose time has come'.[40]

After nine years of Mrs Thatcher's leadership and four as Prime Minister, contemporary Conservatism has arguably been remoulded in such a fundamental way as to make a return to the Keynesian middle-way consensus impossible. Attitudes had been changed to major political problems. One Cabinet minister recalled that '1979–83 was a period of nervousness, of laying foundations. Attitudes have been changed so radically. Everyone accepts privatisation now. Suddenly privatisation was mainstream in British politics'.[41] The battle between dries and wets, to be sure, is likely to continue and will remain as bitter. But the scale and extent of the Thatcher revolution in Conservative thinking will make any attempted reversal to the Heath policies virtually impossible. The wets' argument that the Thatcherites have temporary control on the Conservative party only and that 'true Conservatism' will reassert itself is wide of the target. Mrs Thatcher's personal position following the 1983 election is impregnable. Moreover, Mrs Thatcher's policies have become synonymous with Conservatism to the electorate as a whole, to whom the coded speeches on Disraeli and One Nation mean very little. Mrs Thatcher's economic policies are now irrevocably linked with the Conservatives' wider 'resolute approach' and patriotic stance. Patrick Jenkin rightly observed that 'those who had seen Mrs Thatcher as a prissy schoolmaam now saw her as a leader of great character and people saw what she was trying to do in relation to the economy. There was a Thatcher effect, not just a Falklands effect'.[42]

Irrespective of the 1983 election victory, how does the record of the first Thatcher government stand up? The record on inflation has been exemplary, especially as the pressures to reflate were considerable in 1981 following the inner city rioting. However, as one Treasury official recalled, 'I never felt we were about to change policy in a major way. There were some bad times when everyone outside the Treasury seemed to see things differently, but by autumn of '81 the signs were that things had turned with a substantial breakthrough on inflation'.[43] One backbencher's comment was typical: '1979-83 did everything we set out to do. It kept faith with inflation control'.[44] The inflation rate was reduced, furthermore, without the headlong dash down the blind alley of incomes policy 'norms', 'comparability commissions', 'special cases', 'sanctions against employers', 'price commissions', 'guiding lights', 'wage freezes', 'dividend control', 'rent freezes', 'relativity reports', and so on. The comparison with the Heath government, which pursued the incomes policy route and lost control of inflation, is a striking testimony to the success of the Thatcher policy. Thus one Cabinet minister noted that the 'absence of incomes policy was crucial. We were determined not to be trapped by a target so that the unions could all rally round the flag as under Heath'.[45] The unemployment record, contrary to popular belief, is not one of which the Thatcher government could feel ashamed. As was argued in Chapter 4, there are many different types of unemployment with as many diverse causes and simply blaming the government is to misunderstand and to simplify complex and often long-term problems. The government was right to resist the clamour to 'do something' as the figures rose, while at the same time attempting to alleviate social hardship with palliative schemes. The alternative approaches suggested in Chapter 4—the 'Social dividend' two registers system, ending of the Wages Councils, and an expansion of the 'Walters plan' are all compatible with the government's belief that ultimately it is customers, in Britain and overseas, who create real jobs.

Similarly, the government was right to resist the 'growth target' mentality that engulfed the Heath government and has remained fashionable among left-of-centre economists such as Michael Nevin, who has advocated:

The principal goal of economic policy should be, quite simply, economic growth. The government could almost forget about all the other targets; because high employment, low inflation, and a strong trading position, will all flow naturally from a growth economy, as they have in West Germany and Japan.

Economic policy should be targeted towards the attainment of a steady growth rate of at least five per cent a year in real terms. Anything lower would be insufficient to make significant inroads into unemployment. In order to achieve this growth rate, the aggregate level of investment must be increased, and its quality improved. The instruments of economic policy should be designed to achieve this.[46]

Such targeting of economic policy is dangerously naive. One can no more achieve real growth by setting a 'growth target' and 'investing' in the public sector than one can achieve higher real employment by subsidising over-manning and restrictive practices. The realism of the Thatcher government, in contrast to such remedies, was highly laudable.

On the trade union front also the Thatcher government deserves credit. The abandonment of the corporatist policy-making model was long overdue and the legal reforms of the 1980 and 1982 Employment Acts were a beneficial reversal of the legislative trends of the 1974–79 Labour government. Trade union power, the abuses of which had paralysed the body politic in the mid 1970's, was reduced to its appropriate and legitimate level in a pluralist society. Moreover, the winds of change among the union membership, whereby the leaders' militancy would be rejected, were fanned by the Thatcher government. The revolution in attitudes among union members, and the workforce generally, was an achievement made more laudable by the scepticism of received wisdom which prevailed in May 1979.

The Thatcher government was less successful, however, in reducing public spending. As was argued in Chapters 5 and 7, the astronomical costs of industrial subsidisation greatly burdened the taxpayer and led to beneficial areas of public spending being subject to cuts. The 'bleeding stump' tactic was never conquered by the government and should come high on the agenda for the second term in relation to the continuing crisis of financing high levels of public expenditure. The across-the-board public spending cuts were a poor alternative to a reassessment of what public spending should be aiming to do. One Treasury adviser recalled that:

quantum cuts are very difficult. The politics of expenditure control meant that in some of the hassles some ministers didn't take their colleagues seriously. The Foreign Office thinks it is a sacred cow and defence was totally outrageous from the start. Some ministers felt that the policy wouldn't work and the sacrifices weren't worthwhile. We could have done more with the nationalised industries.[47]

For Conservatives the public sector has never been sacrosanct or a sacred cow to be spared slaughter; neither has it been an area of neglect. Conservatives have argued, rightly, that defence, education and an efficient safety net National Health Service are all legitimate areas of state provision. The same must not be argued for chronic loss-making nationalised industries or industrial fossilisation under a regional policy disguise. The politics and economics of Meriden, De Lorean, and BSC must be finite. This area of public expenditure should have been—and still remains—the prime candidate for spending cuts that are justified in the wider strategy of lowering inflation, reducing interest rates, cutting taxes and releasing investment for the private sector.

However, it must be pointed out in the government's defence, that without its tough approach to public expenditure, accompanied by the severity of the international recession, public spending would have been even higher in aggregate terms. One only has to look at the Labour and Alliance reflationary prescriptions to realise that any other government would preside over another augmentation of public spending on the familiarly damaging pattern of the 1960s and 1970s.

The final assessment of the first Thatcher government is, overall, an encouraging and good one. The economic changes initiated reflected economic reality, and the achievements on inflation and trade union power were, arguably, outstanding. Much promise for the future was also evident in Ken Baker's success as Junior Minister for Information Technology, and such a crucial area of entrepreneurial innovation certainly merits a Cabinet portfolio for an independent Department of Technology and Science. Further diligence and detailed scrutiny and improving the methods by which the political machinery can beneficially affect the real economy is still required, but the first Thatcher government took a number of constructive steps in the right direction. On the purely political side, the transformation of the Conservative party in 1974—both in policy and electoral performance—to the party of the 144 majority in 1983 has been little short of a revolution. This political dimension has meant that the Thatcher era, and the Thatcher phenomenon which propels it, will be the dominant feature of British political life for some time to come.

Notes

Unless otherwise stated, the place of publication of the following references is London.

1. THE GOVERNMENT'S OBJECTIVES

1. Lord Home Of Hersel, *The Way the Wind Blows: An Autobiography* (Fontana, 1978).
2. Interview, Lord Thorneycroft.
3. For a comprehensive analysis of the Heath government and its place in modern Conservatism, *see* M. Holmes, *Political Pressure and Economy Policy: British Government 1970–74* (Butterworth, 1982). *See also* R. Behrens, *The Conservative Party from Heath to Thatcher* (Saxon House, 1981) for a discussion of the contrasting leadership policy priorities and leadership styles.
4. For an analysis of the 1979 campaign and economic issues, *see* M. Holmes, *The Labour Government 1974–79: Political Aims and Economic Reality* (Macmillan, 1985), Ch. 9.
5. *See* N. Wapshott and G. Brock, *Thatcher* (Futura, 1983) for a description of the personal animosity.
6. Interview, Cabinet minister.
7. For a further discussion of this theme, *see* Holmes, *op. cit.* (1982), Ch. 9. An opposite view is provided by Ian Gilmour's *Inside Right: A Study of Conservatism* (Quartet, 1977).
8. *See* Ian Gilmour, *Britain Can Work* (Martin Robertson, 1983), p. 100.
9. *See* Holmes, *op. cit.* (1985), Ch. 2. for further discussion of the failures of incomes policy, O.S.C. *see* S. Brittan and P. Lilley, *The Delusion of Incomes Policy* (Temple Smith, 1977).
10. For an overall view of the Thatcher government and the unions, *see* M. Holmes, 'Trade Unions and Governments in *Developments in British Politics,* H. Drucker, ed. (Macmillan, 1983), Ch. 10.
11. Interview, former Conservative Cabinet minister.
12. *See* R. Bacon and W. Eltis, *Britain's Economic Problem: Too Few Producers* (Macmillan, 1977).

13. *See* Holmes, *op. cit.* (1985), Ch. 10.
14. Sir Walter Salomon, *Fair Warning* (Churchill Press, 1983), London p. 18.
15. Interview, Sir Keith Joseph.
16. *See* Holmes, *op. cit.* (1985), Ch. 5.
17. It was widely anticipated, correctly, that Hugh Clegg, Professor of Industrial Relations at Warwick University, would advocate generous pay increases based on 'comparability'.
18. For a full discussion of the Labour government's policy 1974–9, *see* Holmes, *op. cit.* (1985).
19. P. Minford, *Unemployment: Cause and Cure* (Martin Robertson, 1983).
20. Interview, economic adviser.
21. *The Observer*, 6/5/79.
22. Interview, former Conservative Cabinet minister.
23. Interview, Lord Thorneycroft.
24. Interview, junior minister.
25. *See* Holmes, *op. cit.* (1982), Ch. 8, for a full description of the Heath style of leadership.
26. Wapshott and Brock, *op. cit.*, pp. 189–90.
27. *The Guardian*, 14/5/79.
28. Such predictions by CBI Director-General John Methven reflected the view that the government may be forced into an incomes policy and that the unions, following the Winter of Discontent, would be liable to repeat such action.
29. *The Observer*, 17/6/79.
30. Wapshott and Brock, *op. cit.*, p. 190.
31. *The Guardian*, 13/6/79.
32. Wapshott and Brock, *op. cit.*, p.190.
33. *The Guardian*, 13/6/79.
34. *Ibid.*
35. *The Guardian*, 14/6/79.

2. POLICY FORMATION

1. R.H.S. Crossman, *Diaries of a Cabinet Minister, 1964–70* (Hamish Hamilton and Jonathan Cape, 1977).
2. Interview, Conservative party official.
3. Hugo Young, *The Sunday Times*, 27/4/80.
4. Peter Paterson, *The Sunday Times*, 27/4/80.
5. Max Beloff and Gillian Peele, *The Government of the U.K.: Political Authority in a Changing Society* (*Weidenfeld and Nicolson* 1980), p. 75.
6. Quoted in Wapshott and Brock, *op. cit.*, p. 199.
7. Interview, John Biffen.
8. Interview, senior Cabinet minister.
9. Interview, economic adviser.
10. *The Observer*, 7/10/79.
11. Interview, Reg Prentice.

12. For a comprehensive overview of the Thatcher government and the Civil Service, *see* Gillian Peele in Drucker, ed., *op. cit.*, Ch. 4.
13. *See* L. Chapman, *Your Disobedient Servant* (Penguin Books, 1979).
14. Interview, senior Treasury knight.
15. Interview, Cabinet minister.
16. *The Guardian*, 20/7/79.
17. Raising education standards was the central feature of Conservative education policy.
18. Interview, Conservative MP
19. Interview, Patrick Jenkin.
20. *The Guardian*, 24/7/79.
21. Sir Leo Pliatsky, *Getting and Spending* (Blackwell: Oxford, 1982), p. 176.
22. For a full account, *see* Holmes, *op. cit.*(1983).
23. *See* Holmes, *op. cit.* (1982 and 1985) for comprehensive accounts.
24. Interview, John Biffen.
25. Interview, senior Treasury knight.
26. Reported in *The Guardian,* 23/8/79.
27. *The Observer*, 2/9/79.
28. Interview, Leon Brittan.
29. Christopher Hawkins, *Britain's Economic Future* (Wheatsheaf Books: Brighton, 1983), p. 87.
30. *See* Holmes, *op. cit.* (1982) for a full account.
31. *The Guardian*, 19/9/79.
32. *See* Holmes, *op. cit.* (1985), Ch. 3.
33. *The Guardian*, 18/7/79.
34. W. Grant, *The Political Economy of Industrial Policy* (Butterworths, 1982), p. 110.
35. Interview, Sir Keith Joseph.
36. *The Guardian*, 23/10/79.
37. *See* W. Grant, *op. cit.*, pp. 92–5.
38. *The Daily Telegraph*, 12/12/79.
39. *See* Holmes, *op. cit.* (1985), Ch. 3 for a full description of British Leyland's tribulations.
40. John Burton, *The Job Support Machine* (Centre for Policy Studies, 1979), pp. 62–3.
41. *The Guardian*, 21/7/79.
42. *See* Holmes, *op. cit.* (1982) Ch. 3.

3. CONTEMPORARY CONSERVATISM AND INFLATION

1. Lord Robbins, *Political Economy: Past and Present* (Macmillan, 1976).
2. Conservative manifesto, 1979.
3. Conservative manifesto, 1970. *See also* Holmes, *op. cit.* (1982), Ch. 1.
4. Sir W. Salomon, *op. cit.*, p. 9.

5. Interview, Cabinet minister.
6. Conservative manifesto, 1983.
7. Peter Riddell, *The Thatcher Government,* (Martin Robertson, 1983), p. 7.
8. Interview, Lord Thorneycroft.
9. *The Guardian,* 4/3/80.
10. *The Sunday Times,* 23/3/80.
11. I. Gilmour, *op. cit.,* p. 145.
12. Sir A. Walters, *Challenging Complacency: A First-Hand Look at the Government's Experience* (The Fraser Institute, 1983), p. 9.
13. Interview, senior Treasury knight.
14. *Ibid.*
15. Interview, economic adviser.
16. *The Guardian,* 27/3/80.
17. CEPG—Economic Policy Review (Gower: Aldershot, 1980).
18. *Ibid.*
19. For further analysis of this argument, *see* this chapter, pp. 69–74.
20. *The Guardian,* 25/9/80.
21. Interview, Treasury adviser.
22. David Gowland, *Controlling the Money Supply* (Croom Helm: Beckenham, 1982), p. 126.
23. Interview, Treasury official.
24. Interview, senior Treasury knight.
25. *The Guardian,* 10/10/80.
26. *The Guardian,* 25/11/80.
27. *The Sunday Times,* 7/12/80.
28. Interview, economic adviser.
29. Interview, Treasury official.
30. Interview, junior minister.
31. Wapshott and Brock, *op. cit.,* p. 201.
32. Interview, Sir Keith Joseph.
33. Interview, junior minister.
34. Interview, Treasury adviser.
35. Peter Browning, *Economic Images* (Longman, 1983), p. 124.
36. In June 1981 Prof. Niehans outlined his thesis at a seminar at the LSE.
37. *See* this chapter, pp. 69–74, for further discussion.
38. Interview, Lord Harris of High Cross.
39. Interview, Leon Brittan.
40. Walters, *op. cit.,* p. 10.
41. *The Guardian,* 12/3/81.
42. Interview, senior Treasury knight.
43. *The Sunday Times,* 29/3/81.
44. Samuel Brittan, *The Role and Limits of Government: Essays in Political Economy* (Temple Smith, 1983), pp 243–4.
45. Interview, Treasury official.
46. Interview, Treasury official.
47. Interview, Treasury minister.
48. Interview, senior Treasury knight.
49. Interview, junior minister.

50. Interview, Jim Prior.
51. *The Times*, 15/9/81.
52. *See* this chapter, pp. 74–83.
53. *See* Holmes (1985), *op. cit.*, Ch. 5.
54. *The Times*, 17/10/81.
55. *The Times*, 10/3/82.
56. The Prime Minister's popularity also revived and it is arguable that public admiration of resolution in the Falklands was transferred to admiration for economic resolution also.
57. *The Times*, 22/1/83.
58. *The Times*, 16/3/83.
59. *The Times*, 16/3/83.
60. Interview, Treasury official.
61. Interview, Lord Thorneycroft.
62. Interview, Cabinet minister.
63. Interview, Treasury minister.
64. *The Guardian*, 21/5/80.
65. *See* Holmes, *op. cit.* (1985), Ch. 7.
66. *The Guardian*, 12/11/80.
67. *The Guardian*, 17/11/80.
68. Interview, junior minister.
69. *The Times*, 20/8/81.
70. *The Times*, 16/9/81.
71. *The Times*, 18/12/81.
72. *See also* Holmes, *op. cit.* (1983) for a further account.
73. Interview, Cabinet wet.
74. *The Guardian*, 30/6/80.
75. Riddell, *op. cit.*, p. 45.
76. Interviewed on *Panorama*, 6/10/80.
77. *The Guardian*, 6/11/80.
78. Interview, Cyril Townsend.
79. *The Guardian*, 31/10/80.
80. Interview, backbench MP.
81. Wapshott and Brock, *op. cit.*, p. 204.
82. Interview, Cyril Townsend.
83. Interview, Cabinet minister.
84. Interview, Cabinet minister.
85. Interview, Michael Brown.
86. Interview, Conservative MP.
87. Interview, Conservative MP.
88. *The Guardian*, 2/7/81.
89. *The Guardian*, 4/7/81.
90. Interview, Conservative MP.
91. Interview, junior minister.
92. Interview, Reg Prentice.
93. Interview, Leon Brittan.
94. *The Times*, 14/10/81.
95. Interview, Sir Keith Joseph.

96. *The Times,* 15/10/81.
97. Interview, former Conservative minister.
98. Interview, Conservative MP.
99. Interview, Cabinet minister.
100. Interview, Patrick Jenkin.
101. Interview, senior Cabinet minister.
102. Sir L. Pliatsky, *op. cit.,* p. 206.
103. Interview, Patrick Jenkin.
104. *The Times,* 26/1/82.
105. Interview, Cyril Townsend.
106. *The Times,* 8/10/82.
107. Interview, Conservative MP.
108. Interview, Michael Brown.
109. Interview, Conservative MP.

4. CONTEMPORARY CONSERVATISM AND UNEMPLOYMENT

1. James Callaghan, speech to the Labour party conference, 1976.
2. *See* Holmes, *op, cit.,* 1982, Ch. 3–5.
3. I. Gilmour, *op. cit.,* p. 11.
4. *The Guardian,* 15/2/80.
5. *The Guardian,* 26/5/80.
6. Sir W. Salomon, *op. cit.,* p. 39.
7. *The Guardian,* 24/7/80.
8. *The Sunday Times,* 30/11/80.
9. *The Guardian,* 2/6/81.
10. Interview, Sir Keith Joseph.
11. *The Times,* 11/8/81.
12. Interview, Lord Thorneycroft.
13. Interview, Treasury official.
14. Interview, senior Treasury knight.
15. S. Brittan, *op. cit.,* pp. 249–50.
16. *See* this chapter, pp. 94–104.
17. White Paper, *A New Training Initiation: A Programme for Action* (HMSO, 1981).
18. Interview, Cabinet minister.
19. *The Times,* 26/1/82.
20. Interview, Cabinet minister.
21. Interview, Patrick Jenkin.
22. Interview, Leon Brittan.
23. *The Times,* 28/7/82.
24. *The Times,* 28/7/82.
25. *The Times,* 26/8/82.

26. *Coping with Unemployment* (Economist Intelligence Unit, 1982). It may not be unreasonably assumed that the true figure was much higher than 8 per cent.
27. *The Times,* 14/4/83.
28. Conservative manifesto, 1983.
29. For a good account of the different types of unemployment, *see* Robert Miller and John B. Wood, 'What Price Unemployment?' (IEA), *Hobart Paper 92,* 1982.
30. Miller and Wood, *op. cit.,* p. 58.
31. Ian Gilmour, an advocate of reflation, also believes the myth that 'Hitler's New Deal...succeeded in dealing with unemployment'. (*Britain Can Work, op. cit.,* p. 78). Even with the artificial massaging of figures, the restrictions on female employment, conscription, and a massive increase in bureaucrats, it is quite untrue that Hitler solved unemployment. He simply redefined the unemployed, or employed them in non-productive ways. Contrary to much contemporary belief, the Nazi economy functioned very badly and was hopelessly underprepared for war in 1939.
32. Interview, Cabinet minister.
33. *The Times,* 12/3/83.
34. *The Guardian,* 16/1/81.
35. Patrick Minford, *Unemployment: Cause and Cure* (Martin Robertson, 1983), p. 82.
36. S. Brittan, *op. cit.,* p. 175.
37. Treasury Press Notice 173/79, 16/11/79.
38. S. Brittan, *op. cit.,* p. 245.
39. Gilmour, *op. cit.,* p. 148.
40. Miller and J.B. Wood, *op. cit.,* pp. 38–9.
41. Minford, *op. cit.,* pp. 62–3.
42. *Ibid.,* p. 7.
43. Miller and J.B. Wood, *op. cit.,* pp. 66–7.
44. Samuel Brittan, *The Economic Consequences of Democracy* (Temple Smith, 1977), p. 130.
45. It would still be an offence to work full-time and claim Unemployment Benefit or to earn above a pre-set income and claim benefit.
46. A.L. Ilersic, *The Economics of Avoidance/Evasion* (IEA, 1979).
47. Interview, Arthur Seldon.
48. A. Heertje *et al., The Black Economy* (Pan, 1980), p. 114.
49. *The Times,* 20/10/81.
50. *See* Holmes, *op. cit.,* 1985.
51. Gilmour, *op. cit.,* pp. 167–8.
52. *See* S. Brittan, *The Financial Times,* 6/10/83, for an excellent discussion of this theme.

5. CONTEMPORARY CONSERVATISM AND PUBLIC SPENDING

1. Samuel Brittan, *Steering the Economy* (Pelican, 1970).
2. Interview, John Biffen.
3. *See* Holmes, *op. cit.* (1985), Ch. 5, for a full analysis of Public Spending Cuts and the IMF crisis.
4. Pliatsky, *op. cit.*, pp. 184–5.
5. Interview, Conservative MP.
6. *The Times*, 22/8/80.
7. Interview, Cabinet minister.
8. *The Guardian*, 4/11/80.
9. *The Guardian*, 9/4/81.
10.. Interview, Conservative party official.
11. *The Times*, 11/5/82.
12. *The Times*, 11/11/82.
13. *The Times*, 6/10/82.
14. For a full discussion of the politics of 'bleeding stump' tactics, *see* C. Hood and M. Wright, *Big Government in Hard Times* (Martin Robertson,) 1981).
15. Hood and Wright, *op. cit.*, pp. 208–9.
16. *See*, for example 'More Jobs for Bureaucrats but Nurses Must Go', *Oxford Mail* 14/10/83.
17. Interview, Cabinet minister.
18. Interview, Cabinet minister.
19. *The Times*, 4/10/82.
20. Excluding the independent University of Buckingham.
21. *The Guardian*, 11/5/81.
22. Norman Barry 'The Political Economy of Higher Education: An "Austrian" Analysis', *Economic Journal*, July 1983.
23. *The Times*, 12/2/82.
24. The Hillingdon Borough ski-slope springs instantly to mind.
25. Sheffield City Council even employed a Peace Officer, presumably to defend the Nuclear Free Zone.
26. *The Guardian*, 21/9/83.
27. *The Guardian*, 16/4/80.
28. *The Guardian*, 20/6/80.
29. N. Bosanquet, *After the New Right* (Heinemann, 1983), p. 200.
30. *The Guardian*, 29/8/80.
31. *The Guardian*, 17/12/80.
32. *The Times*, 16/2/82.
33. Interview, Cabinet minister.
34. Conservative manifesto 1983.
35. Interview, Cabinet minister.
36. *See* Peele in Drucker, *op. cit.*, Ch. 4.
37. *The Times*, 2/9/82.
38. Interview, Cabinet minister.

39. Hood and Wright, *op. cit.*, p. 203.
40. *See*, for example, *The Times* report, 23/10/82, of the comments of Justice Heilbron on the waste of public money on granting legal aid to divorced wives pursuing maintenance claims against husbands living on Social Security.
41. Interview, Sir Keith Joseph.
42. Interview, economic adviser.
43. Interview, senior Cabinet minister.
44. David Howell, *Political Quarterly*, October 1983.
45. *Ibid.*
46. *See* T. Stonier, *The Wealth of Information* (Methuen, 1983) for a stimulating discussion of this theme.
47. Interview, Ken Baker.
48. *See*, for example, *The Times*, 12/5/83, Mrs Thatcher interviewed by Julian Haviland.
49. Interview, Lord Harris of High Cross.
50. For an excellent account of the economic value of the arts to tourism, *see* Bernard D. Nossiter, *Britain: A Future that Works* (Deutsch, 1978).
51. John Burton, 'Picking Losers ... ?', *Hobart Paper 99*, p. 71.
52. Interview, Cyril Townsend.
53. Burton, 'Picking Losers?' *op. cit.*, p. 44.
54. Michael Nevin, *The Age of Illusions: The Political Economy of Britain 1968–82* (Gollancz, 1983), pp. 154–5.
55. Conservative manifesto, 1983.
56. Interview, senior CBI official.

6. CONTEMPORARY CONSERVATISM AND TRADE UNION POWER.

1. *See* Holmes, *op. cit.*, (1982), Ch. 2 for a full account.
2. *The Guardian*, 18/2/80.
3. Interview, Conservative MP.
4. Interview, Reg Prentice.
5. *The Guardian*, 1/9/80.
6. *The Guardian*, 9/10/80.
7. 1980 Employment Act, section 18.
8. *Trade Union Immunities*, Cmnd 8128, 1981.
9. *The Guardian*, 1/7/81.
10. *The Times*, 25/11/81.
11. *The Times*, 13/4/82.
12. *The Times*, 8/9/82.
13. Interview, senior CBI official.
14. *The Times*, 12/1/83.
15. *The Times*, 17/2/83.
16. Conservative manifesto, 1983.
17. Interview, Leon Brittan.

18. Interview, Cabinet minister.
19. For a further discussion of these facts *see* Holmes, *op. cit.* (1983).
20. *The Guardian*, 15/1/80.
21. Interview, Reg Prentice.
22. *The Sunday Times*, 22/2/81.
23. Interview, Treasury adviser.
24. Interview, Cabinet minister.
25. *Daily Express*, 19/2/81.
26. John Fryer and Michael Jones, 'What Really Made the Lady Turn', *The Sunday Times*, 22/2/81.
27. *See* this chapter, pp. 145–146.
28. *The Times*, 19/2/82.
29. *Ibid.*
30. *The Times*, 6/7/82.
31. *The Times*, 15/7/82.
32. *The Times*, 16/7/82.
33. *The Times*, 19/7/82.
34. *See* Holmes, *op. cit*, (1985), Ch. 8.
35. *The Daily Telegraph*, 11/8/82.
36. *The Times*, 16/12/82.
37. *The Times*, 16/12/82.
38. *The Times*, 2/3/83.
39. Interview, backbench Conservative MP.
40. Interview, Patrick Jenkin.
41. Interview, senior CBI official.
42. *See* Holmes, *op. cit.*, (1983) for a further discussion of this point.
43. The meeting was indeed only the second since the May 1979 election result.
44. *The Guardian*, 15/10/80.
45. *The Guardian*, 4/9/80.
46. *The Times*,1/9/82.
47. *The Times*, 2/9/82.
48. *The Sunday Times*, 8/11/81.
49. *See* Riddell, *op. cit.*, pp. 186–91.
50. *The Official Report*, 1983.
51. *The Times*, 2/9/83.
52. D. Barnes and E. Reid, *Governments and Trade Unions: The British Experience 1964–79* (Heinemann, 1980), p. 227.

7. CONTEMPORARY CONSERVATISM AND INDUSTRY POLICY

1. R.A. Butler, *The Art of the Possible* (Hamish Hamilton, 1971).
2. Conservative manifesto, 1979.
3. Interview, senior CBI official.
4. *See* Holmes, *op. cit.* (1982), Ch. 3.

5. *The Guardian*, 30/7/80.
6. *The Guardian*, 22/4/80.
7. Interview, Sir Keith Joseph.
8. Interview, senior CBI official.
9. Interview, CBI adviser.
10. Interview, senior CBI official.
11. *The Guardian*, 12/11/80.
12. *The Guardian*, 11/11/80.
13. Interview, Treasury adviser.
14. Interview, Conservative MP.
15. Interview, junior minister.
16. *The Guardian*, 12/3/81.
17. *The Guardian*, 25/3/81.
18. Interview, economy adviser.
19. Interview, Cabinet minister.
20. Interview, senior Treasury knight.
21. *The Observer*, 15/11/81.
22. *The Times*, 4/11/81.
23. *The Times*, 11/2/82.
24. *The Times*, 6/5/82.
25. *The Times*, 31/8/82.
26. *The Times*, 20/8/82.
27. *The Times*, 4/8/82.
28. Interview, CBI official.
29. *The Times*, 24/9/82.
30. *The Times*, 28/3/83.
31. Interview, Cabinet minister.
32. R. Pryke, *The Nationalised Industries: Policies and Performance Since 1968* (Martin Robertson, 1981), p. 246.
33. Interview, John Biffen.
34. Interview, Sir Keith Joseph.
35. Conservative manifesto, 1979.
36. *The Observer*, 6/4/80.
37. *The Guardian*, 3/5/80.
38. Between Sept. 1979 and Dec. 1980 40,000 jobs were cut in BSC.
39. Interview, Lord Harris of High Cross.
40. Interview, Patrick Jenkin.
41. Interview, senior Treasury knight.
42. *The Times*, 30/11/82.
43. *The Times*, 20/5/83.
44. Conservative manifesto, 1983.
45. *The Times*, 5/8/82.
46. Interview, Arthur Seldon.
47. *The Times*, 12/5/83.
48. Interview, Treasury adviser.
49. *The Times*, 19/4/83.
50. *The Guardian*, 19/4/80.
51. *The Times*, 1/9/82, carried the details.

52. *The Daily Telegraph*, 23/12/82.
53. *See* Holmes, *op. cit.* (1985), Ch. 3.
54. Conservative manifesto, 1983.
55. Interview, Conservative MP.
56. Hansard, 21/3/81, Col. 1063.
57. Conservative manifesto, 1983.
58. Interview, Junior Industry Minister.
59. Interview, Arthur Seldon.
60. Pryke, *op. cit.*, p. 257.
61. Burton, 'Picking Losers?', *op. cit.*, pp. 41–2.
62. Pryke, *op. cit.*, p. 265.
63. Burton, *The Jobs Support Machine*, *op. cit.*
64. Conservative manifesto, 1983.
65. Richard Stapleton in 'Could Do Better', *IEA Occasional Paper*, no. 62, p. 89.
66. Hawkins, *op cit.*, p. 19.
67. Quoted in Holmes, *op. cit.*, (1982), p. 42.

8. CONTEMPORARY CONSERVATISM AND THE 1983 GENERAL ELECTION

1. D.E. Butler and D. Kavanagh. *The General Election of 1974* (Macmillan, 1974).
2. *The Observer*, 27/4/80.
3. *The Sunday Times*, 1/2/81.
4. *The Times*, 11/6/83.
5. Winning two out of every three by December 1981.
6. Wapshott and Brock, *op. cit.*, p. 251.
7. Interview, junior minister.
8. *The Observer*, 24/10/82.
9. *The Daily Telegraph*, 31/12/82.
10. *The Times*, 22/1/83.
11. Interview, junior minister.
12. *The Sunday Times*, 27/2/83.
13. *The Observer*, 27/3/83.
14. *The Times*, 15/4/83.
15. Interview, Cyril Townsend.
16. Labour manifesto, 1983.
17. *See* Holmes, *op. cit.*, (1985) Ch. 9. for a further discussion of this point.
18. Interview, Lord Thorneycroft.
19. Walters, *op. cit.*, p. 11.
20. Interview, Conservative MP.
21. Significantly, at the 1983 SDP conference in September Dr David Owen, the new SDP leader, jettisoned the party's commitment to a private-sector, bureaucratically-imposed incomes policy.
22. Liberal/SDP manifesto, 1983.

23. *The Times*, 17/5/83.
23. *The Sunday Times*, 22/5/83.
25. Interview, Cabinet minister.
26. *The Times*, 1/6/83,.
27. *The Times*, 24/5/83.
28. Interview, Michael Brown.
29. Interview, Leon Brittan.
30. *The Sunday Times*, 29/5/83.
31. *The Times*, 30/5/83.
32. *The Times*, 31/5/83.
33. Interview, Cabinet minister.
34. Interview, Reg Prentice.
35. Interview, Cabinet minister.
36. *The Times*, 8/6/83.
37. Interview, Cabinet minister.
38. Lord Kaldor, *The Scourge of Monetarism*, (Oxford University Press: Oxford, 1982), p. 100.
39. Interview, Michael Brown.
40. Interview, Cabinet minister.
41. Interview, Patrick Jenkin.
42. *The Times*, 11/6/83.
43. D.E. Butler and R. Waller, 'Survey of the voting' in '*The Times Guide to the House of Commons*' (June 1983), p. 253.
44. *The Times*, 11/6/83.
45. *The Times*, 11/6/83.
46. Interview, Sir Keith Joseph.
47. Interview, Cabinet minister.
48. *The Sunday Times*, 12/6/83.
49. Robert Waller, *The Almanac of British Politics*, (Croom Helm and St Martin's Beckenham: 1983), p. 251.
50. Butler and Waller, *op. cit.*, p. 257.
51. *Ibid.*
52. Interview, John Biffen.

9. MARGARET THATCHER'S CONSERVATISM

1. Margaret Thatcher, speech at Conservative party conference, 1968.
2. Interview, Lord Thorneycroft.
3. Interview, Cabinet minister.
4. Interview, Reg Prentice.
5. *See* Holmes, *op. cit.* (1982).
6. *See* Holmes, *op. cit.* (1985).
7. Interview, Treasury adviser.
8. Interview, Treasury official.
9. Interview, junior minister.
10. Interview, Cabinet minister.

11. *The Observer,* 9/1/83.
12. *The Observer,* 27/4/80.
13. Interview, Cabinet minister.
14. Quoted in Simon Hoggart, 'All the Prime Minister's Men, Observer Review, 9/1/83.
15. Interview, Cabinet minister.
16. *The Observer,* 27/4/80.
17. Interview, economic adviser.
18. Interview, Treasury adviser.
19. Interview, Treasury official.
20. Interview, economic adviser.
21. Interview, John Biffen.
22. *The Observer,* 9/1/83.
23. Interview, Treasury official.
24. *The Observer,* 9/1/83.
25. Interview, Conservative party official.
26. Interview, Sir Keith Joseph.
27. Sir J. Hoskyns speech, 12/10/82, London, Institute of Fiscal Studies.
28. Interview, Conservative MP.
29. *The Observer,* 27/4/80.
30. Interview, John Biffen.
31. Riddell, *op. cit.,* p. 17.
32. *The Sunday Times,* 3/5/81.
33. *The Sunday Times,* 3/8/80.
34. *The Sunday Times,* 27/2/83.
35. Interview, Cabinet minister.
36. Interview, Lord Thorneycroft.
37. Quoted in Wapshott and Brock, *op. cit.,* p. 230.
38. Interview, Cyril Townsend.
39. Interview, John Biffen.
40. Interview, Leon Brittan.
41. Interview, Cabinet minister.
42. Interview, Patrick Jenkin.
43. Interview, Treasury official.
44. Interview, Michael Brown.
45. Interview, Cabinet minister.
46. Nevin, *op. cit.,* p. 167.
47. Interview, Treasury adviser.

Select Bibliography

R. Bacon and W. Eltis, *Britain's Economic Problem: Too Few Producers*, Macmillan, 1977.

D. Barnes and E. Reid, *Governments and Trade Unions: The British Experience 1964–79*, Heinemann, 1980.

Norman Barry, *The Political Economy of Higher Education: An "Austrian" Analysis*, Economic Journal, July 1983.

R. Behrens, *The Conservative Party from Heath to Thatcher*, Saxon House, 1981.

Max Beloff and Gillian Peele, *The Government of the U.K.: Political authority in a Changing Society*, Weidenfeld and Nicolson, 1980.

N. Bosanquet, *After the New Right*, Heinemann, 1983.

Samuel Brittan, *The Economic Consequences of Democracy*, Temple Smith, 1977.

Samuel Brittan, *The Role and Limits of Government: Essays in Political Economy*—Temple Smith, 1983.

S. Brittan and P. Lilley, *The Delusion of Incomes Policy*, Temple Smith, 1977.

Peter Browning, *Economic Images*, Longman, 1983. John Burton, *The Job Support Machine*, Centre for the Policy Studies, 1979.

John Burton, *Picking Losers . . . ?*, Hobart Paper, IEA, 1983.

D.E. Butler and K. Kavanagh, *The General Election of 1983*, Macmillan, 1984.

D.E. Butler and R. Waller, *Survey of the Voting in The Times Guide to the House of Commons, June 1983*.

L. Chapman, *Your Disobedient Servant*, Penguin Books, 1979.

Ian Gilmour, *Inside Right: A Study of Conservatism*, Quartet, 1977.

Ian Gilmour, *Britain Can Work*, Martin Robertson, 1983.

David Gowland, *Controlling the Money Supply*, Croom Helm, 1982.

W. Grant, *The Political Economy of Industrial Policy*, Butterworths, 1982.

Christopher Hawkins, *Britain's Economic Future*, Wheatsheaf Books, 1983.

A. Heertje et al, *The Black Economy*, Pan, 1980.

M. Holmes, *Political Pressure & economic policy: British government 1970–4*, Butterworth, 1982.

M. Holmes, 'Trade Unions and Governments' in *Developments in British Politics*, H. Drucker et al, Macmillan 1983 ch. 10.

M. Holmes, *The Labour Government 1974–9: Political Aims and Economic Reality*, Macmillan, 1985.

C. Hood and M. Wright, *Big Government in Hard Times*, Martin Robertson, 1981.

David Howell, *Political Quarterly*, October 1983.

A.L. Ilersic, *The Economics of Avoidance/Evasion*, IEA, 1979.

Lord Kaldor, *The Scourge of Monetarism*, Oxford U.P., 1982.

Robert Miller and John B. Wood, *What Price Unemployment*, IEA, Hobart Paper 92, 1982.

Patrick Minford, *Unemployment: Cause and Cure*, Martin Robertson, 1983.

Michael Nevin, *The Age of Illusions: The political economy of Britain 1968–82*, Gollancz, 1983.

Sir Leo Pliatsky, *Getting and Spending*, Blackwell, 1982.

R. Pryke, *The Nationalised industries: Policies and Performance since 1968*, Martin Robertson, 1981.

Peter Riddell, *The Thatcher Government*, Martin Robertson, 1983.

Sir Walter Salomon, *Fair Warning*, Churchill Press, 1983.

T. Stonier, *The Wealth of Information*, Methuen, 1983.

Robert Waller, *The Almanac of British Politics*, Croom Helm/St. Martin's, 1983.

N. Wapshott and G. Brock, *Thatcher*, Futura, 1983.

Index

Printed in Great Britain
by Amazon

34176812R00139